IMAGES
of America

OAKHAM

IMAGES
of America

OAKHAM

The Oakham Historical Association

ARCADIA
PUBLISHING

ISBN 978-0-7385-6405-0

Published by Arcadia Publishing
Charleston, South Carolina

Printed in the United States of America

Library of Congress Catalog Card Number: 2008940194

For all general information contact Arcadia Publishing at:
Telephone 843-853-2070
Fax 843-853-0044
E-mail sales@arcadiapublishing.com
For customer service and orders:
Toll-Free 1-888-313-2665

Visit us on the Internet at www.arcadiapublishing.com

Contents

Oakham

Business Notices.

Allen G..Farmer
Bemis J. C..Propt "Spring House," Cold Brook
Collier A. I..Shoe Maker
Frirbank J. C..Manufr of Cordage, Elizabethport, N. J. Res Oakham Centre
Hall A. P..Farmer
Mathews E. G..Manufr of Agricultural Tools for F. F. Holbrook & Co, No 10 South Market st, Boston
Morse J. M..Table Maker, Oakham
Nurss B..Farmer, Oakham
Parker D. M..Manufr of Lumber, Plough Handles, Cheese Boxes, also of "Scott's Patent Milking Stool," Cold Brook
Russell O..Clergyman, Oakham
Stearns A. C..Agt for B. P. Clark, Dealer in Dry Goods, Groceries, Boots, Shoes and all goods kept in a Country Store. A Specialty made of Flour, Cold Brook
Winslow Z. L..Farmer
Ware A. B..Boot Maker and Farmer

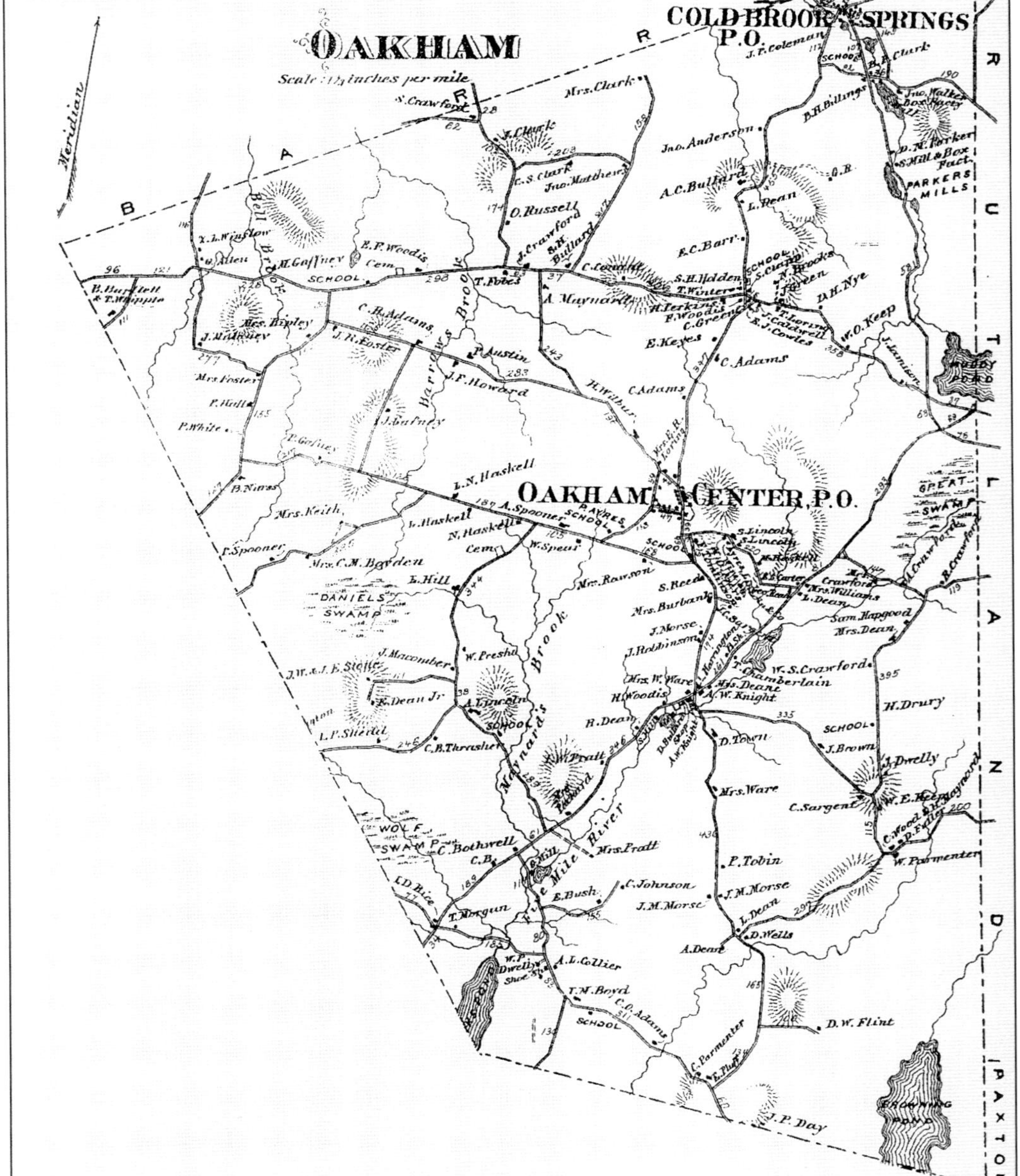

INTRODUCTION

During the early 1900s, several Oakham residents wrote histories of their families, about events of the day, and the history of the town. Most of their writings were published by the Oakham Historical Association. Well-known residents of that time, the authors included Henry P. and Henry B. Wright, Charles M. Packard, and Hiram Knight. What had never been done, until now, was a pictorial history of the town.

When the OHA decided to publish this book it was with the intent to organize the pictures held by the association and to provide information about the people and places seen in these pictures. After going through hundreds of photographs in our collection, word began to spread about our project. As our excitement grew with each newly discovered photograph, so did the interest of several residents. Soon we were receiving photos that had been locked away and only shared with individual families. Now was the time to dust off some of these photos and share them with everyone.

When we think of Oakham and its history, names like Allen, Lincoln, and Tomlinson stand out in our minds, and most of us recognize their homes. But how much do we know about the others? The Briggs, Crawfords, Dwellys, and Packards to name a few. Who these people were, where they lived and worked, and what they did in their free time is what we have tried to explain through the images found on the following pages.

The committee has spent countless hours researching each of the photographs and printed materials, trying to provide as much information as possible to the reader. Every time a photograph was reviewed something new was discovered that increased the group's interest. We hope that you too will find something new and interesting among the images we have chosen.

—The Oakham Historical Association

Committee: Jeffrey Young
Marcia Casault
Hazel Young
Eva Grimes
Wesley Dwelly
Don Linehan
Dennis Casault

One

Center of Town

The center of Oakham was first settled in the late 1700s. The first meetinghouse was built close to where the Congregational Church now stands. By the year 1800, the center even had an inn, which was later known as the Park View Inn.

In 1814 a new church/meetinghouse was erected. It is the same building we see today except that it faced south until 1845, when it was turned, raised, and moved to its current position. The building was raised to accommodate the town offices, which remained in the lower portion of the church until Memorial Hall was built in 1874.

Many businesses existed in the center through the years, as you will see in this chapter. There was a general store, a watch and jewelry store, telephone company, carriage shop, drugstore, and dentist office, among others. This was not unusual during this time period, as limited transportation created the need for each village to have businesses to serve its population.

As you will see, many of the homes and buildings used for businesses of that time still exist today, along with the church and Memorial Hall. One "newcomer" to the center is the library, which was built in 1907. So, although the businesses are long gone, much of the "look" of the center of Oakham remains.

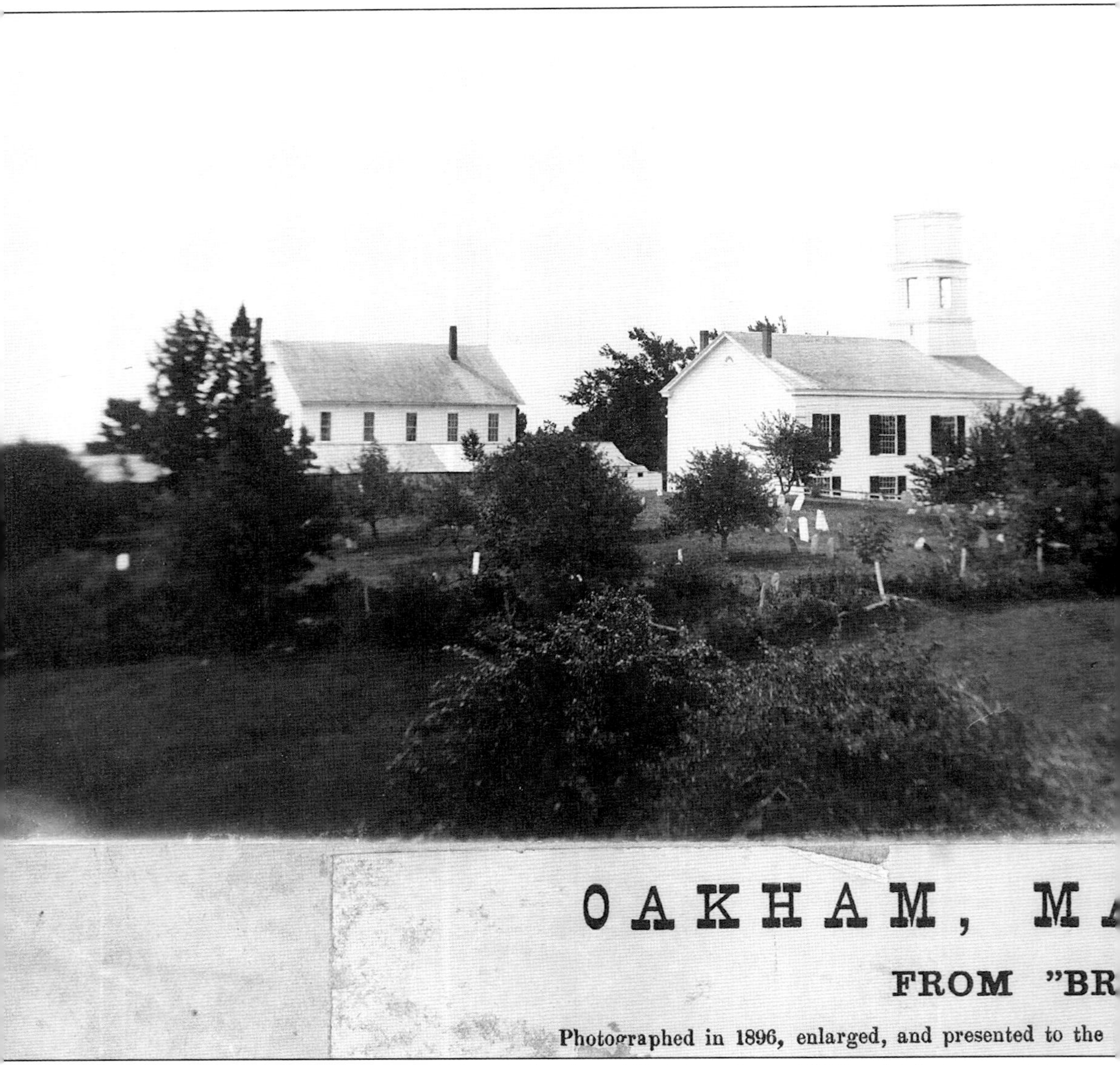

This photograph was taken by C.M. Packard in 1896 from Briggs' Hill, which is east of the cemetery and cheese factory. To the left of the church, the top of the horse sheds can be seen.

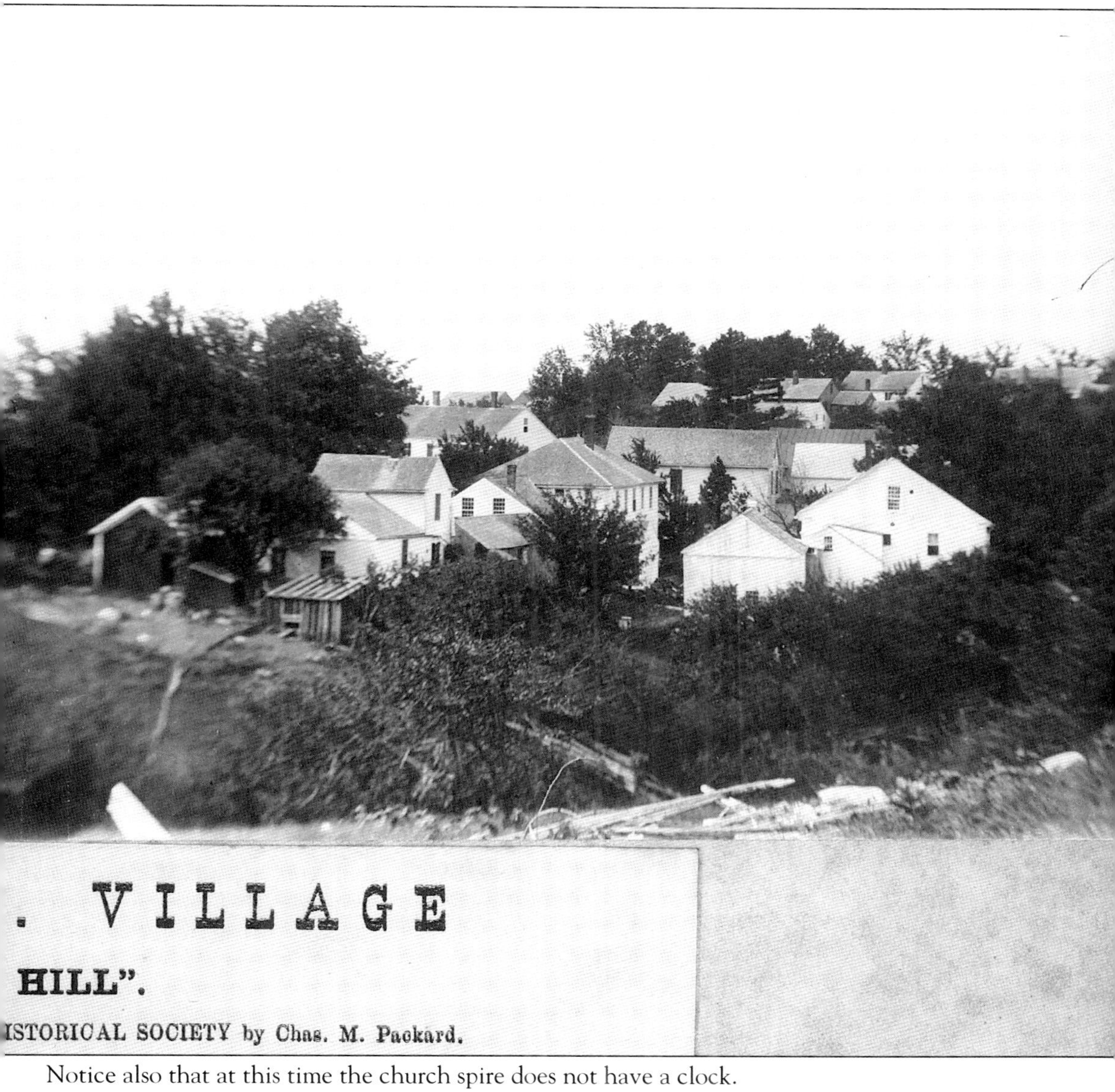

Notice also that at this time the church spire does not have a clock.

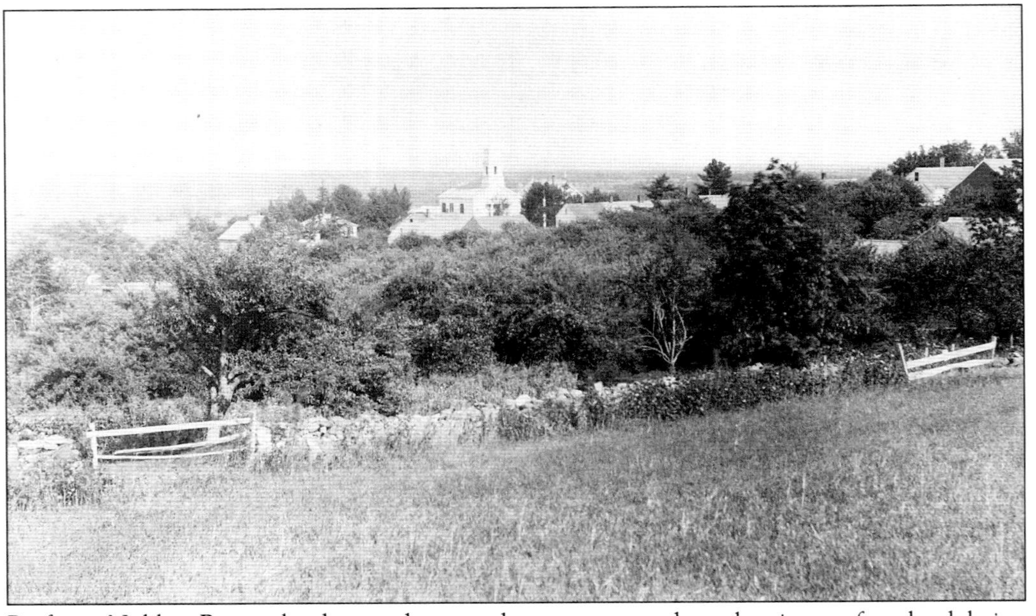

Professor Nobb, a Boston landscape photographer, was engaged to take pictures for a book being published of interesting views of Worcester County. When he came to Oakham in June 1894, he was taken to Prospect Hill, where it was said he became very excited. When he turned on his heel, he could count 17 church spires. The *Oakham Herald* of November 4, 1896, recounts, "a torchlight procession with drum corps and the big fire last Saturday night called out a crowd of 150" on Prospect Hill.

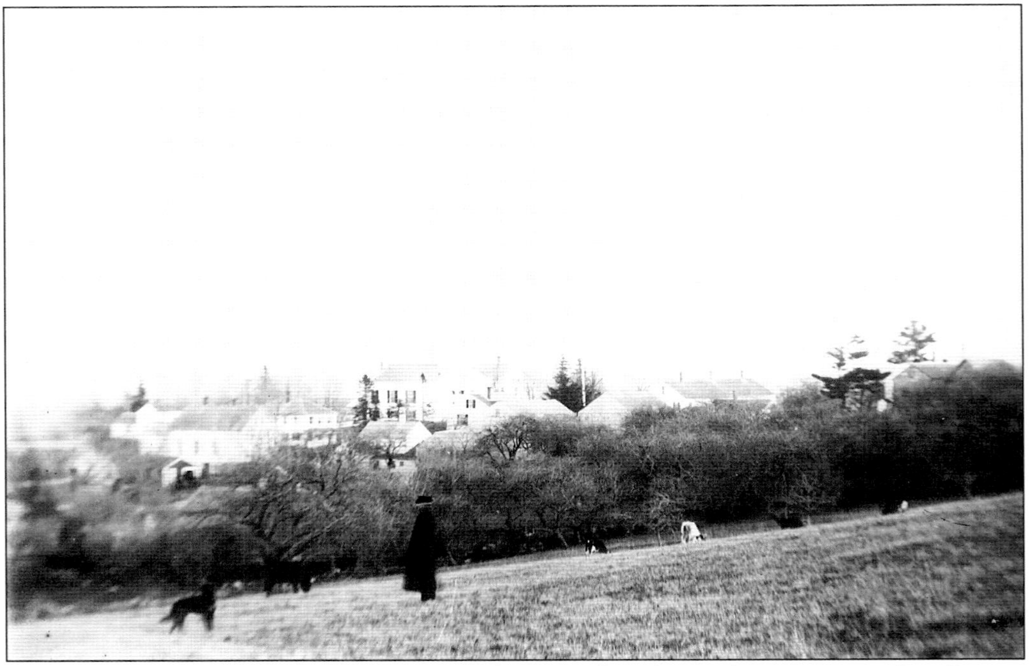

This is a similar view to the previous picture, but was taken during the winter months, allowing a better view of the center of town. The building with three chimneys is the Park View Inn.

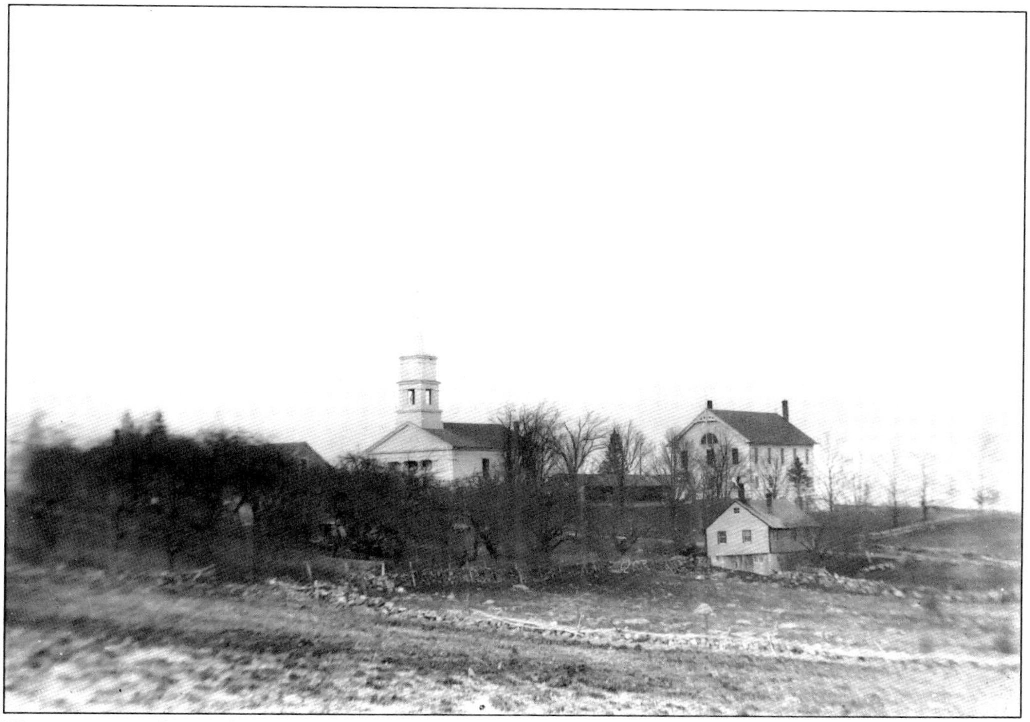

Here is a view from what is now right field in Wright Memorial Park. The small building nearest to us was used as a shop by various businesses over the years, among them a cobbler shop and the Holden Furnace Company.

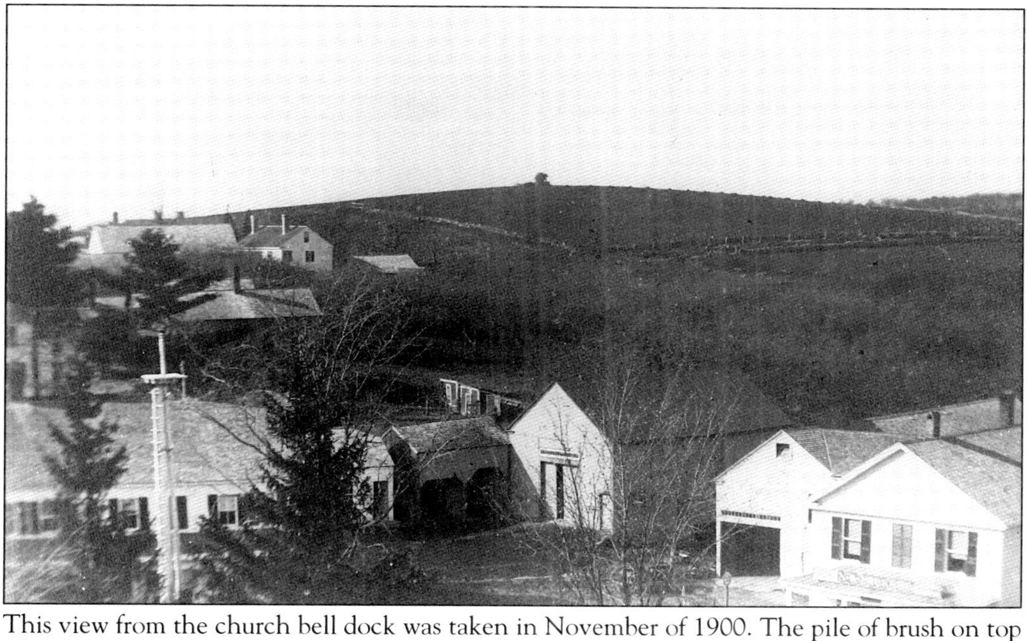

This view from the church bell dock was taken in November of 1900. The pile of brush on top of Prospect Hill was placed there by C.M. Packard due to the request that every town have a bonfire on their highest hill the evening of President McKinley's second election.

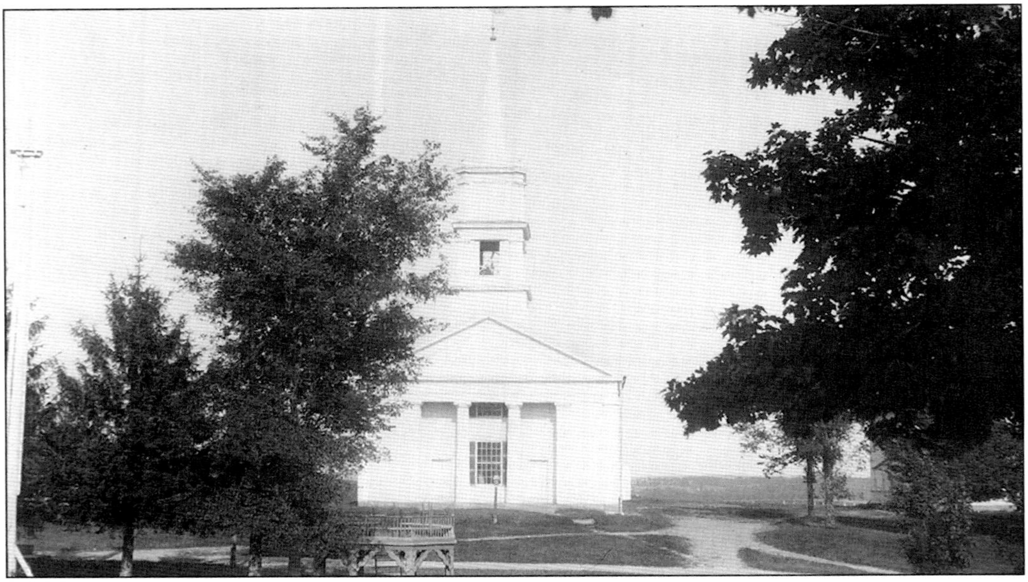

The church was built in 1814, replacing a smaller meetinghouse that had existed on the site. In 1845 it was moved 28 feet to the west and turned from facing south to its current position. At the time the building was moved it was raised to provide for a vestry, town hall, and selectmen's office below the main floor.

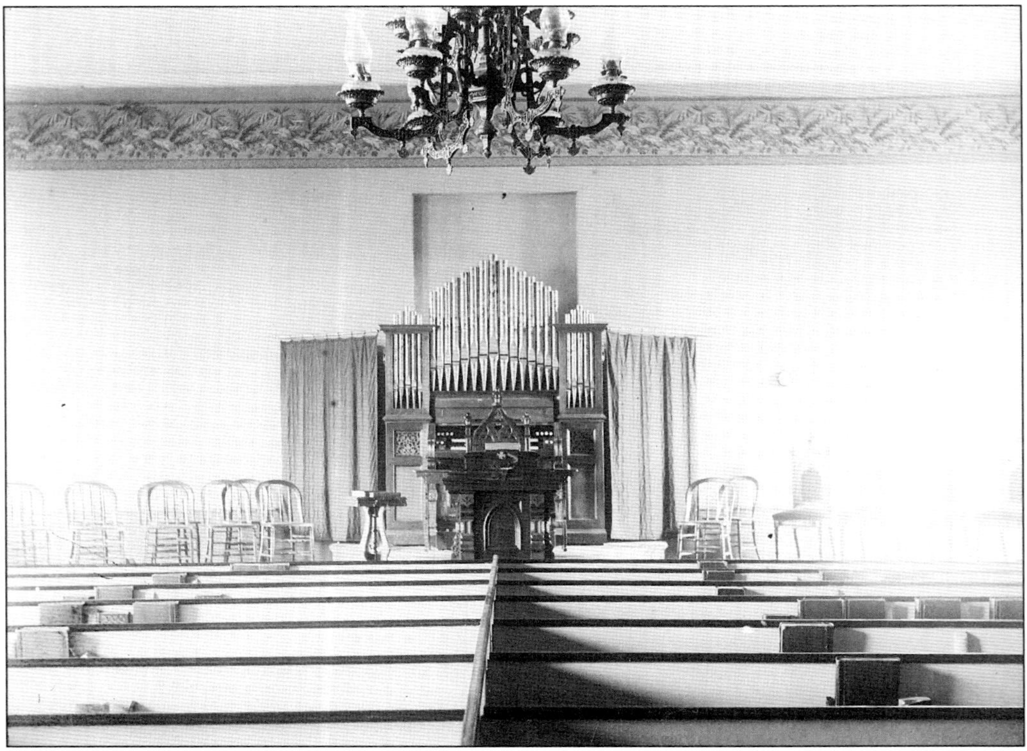

Pictured here is the interior of the Congregational church around the year 1900. The original pulpit was made of mahogany and built by John Morse.

This photograph was taken in 1905 during the installation of the clock in the church steeple. The four-faced clock was donated to the town by Lewis Dean.

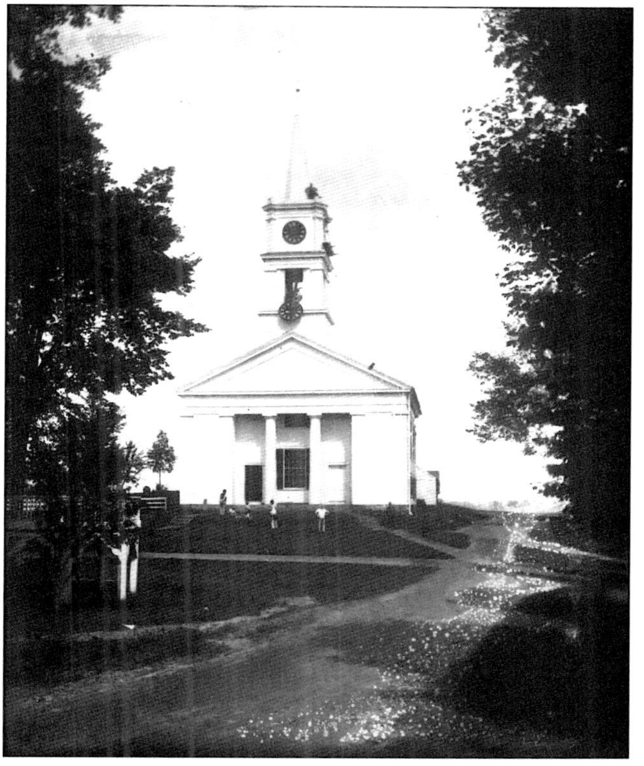

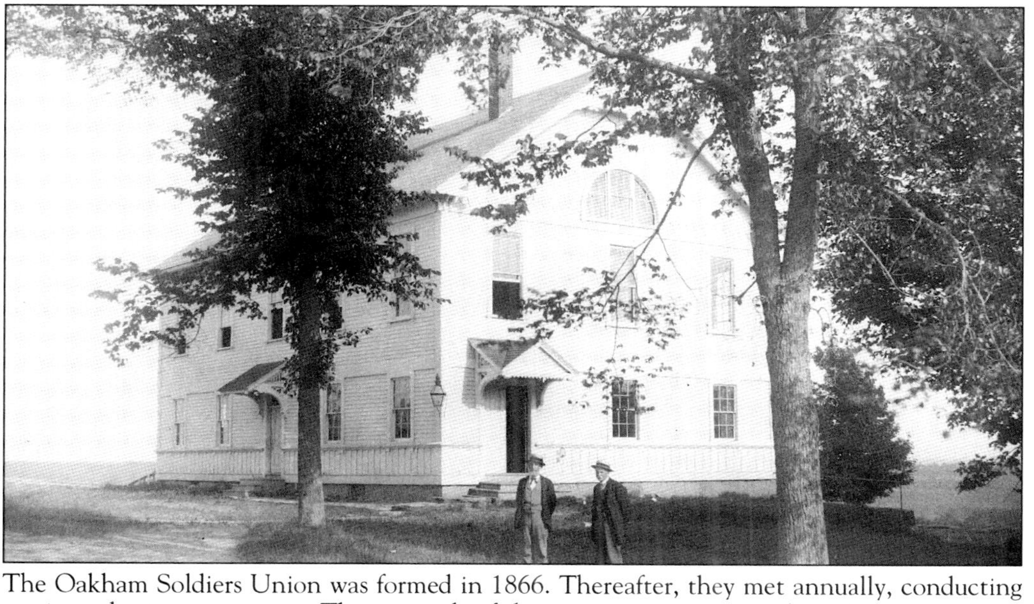

The Oakham Soldiers Union was formed in 1866. Thereafter, they met annually, conducting services, sharing supper, etc. The proceeds of these meetings were saved until about six years later, when they began to plan a soldiers memorial. By March of 1874, the town had voted $2,500 for the purpose of erecting a town hall and two school rooms in one building. The Soldiers Union contributed $1,200 toward the building and $200 for memorial tablets bearing the names of those who have served their country.

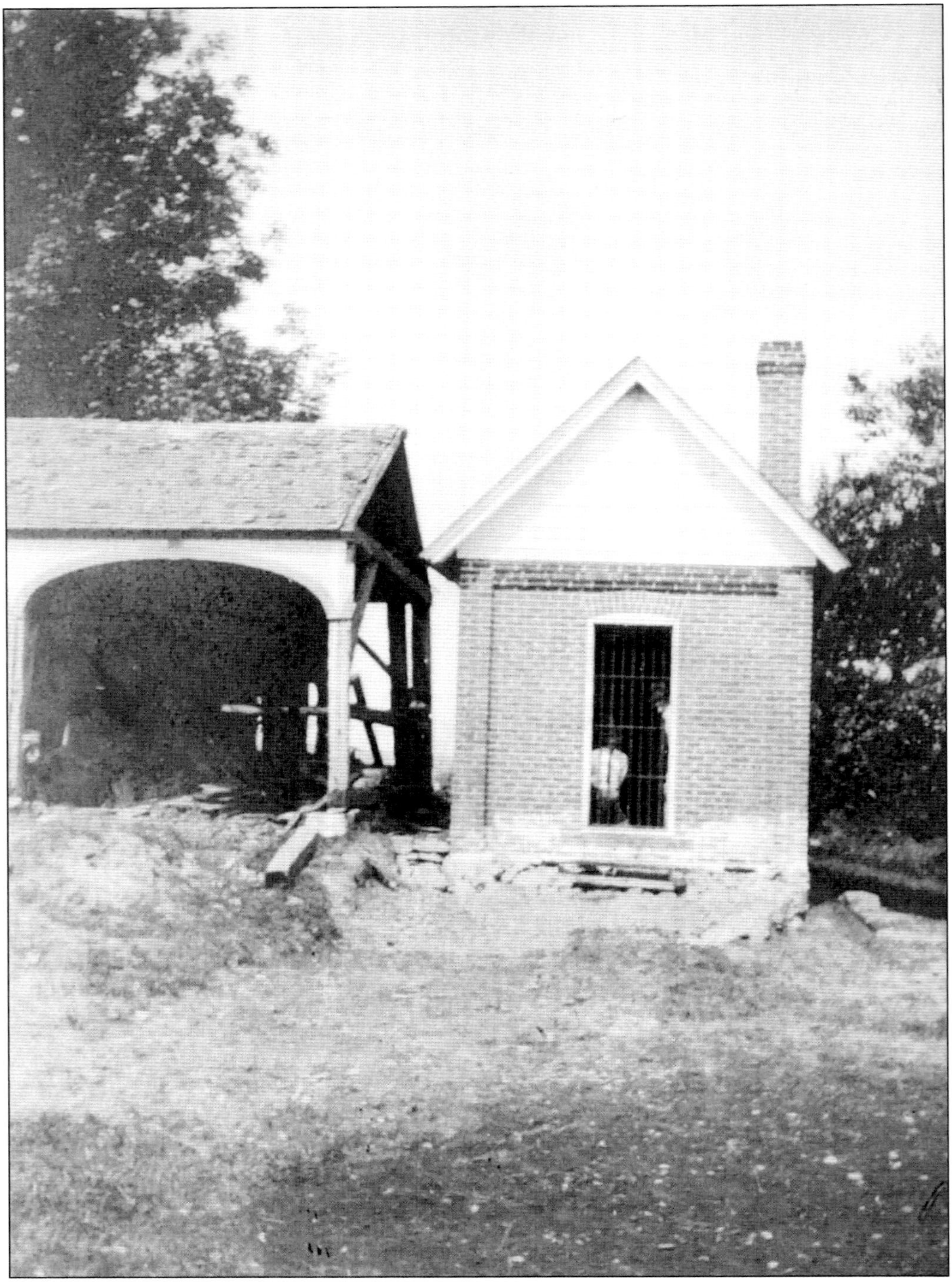

In the 1890s, when you went up the drive between the church and Memorial Hall, you would see what appeared to be a "gatehouse." This was the Tramp House, built in 1893 where the stocks once stood. In one instance that is recorded on November 4, 1893, five tramps spent the night here in what was commonly called the "cooler."

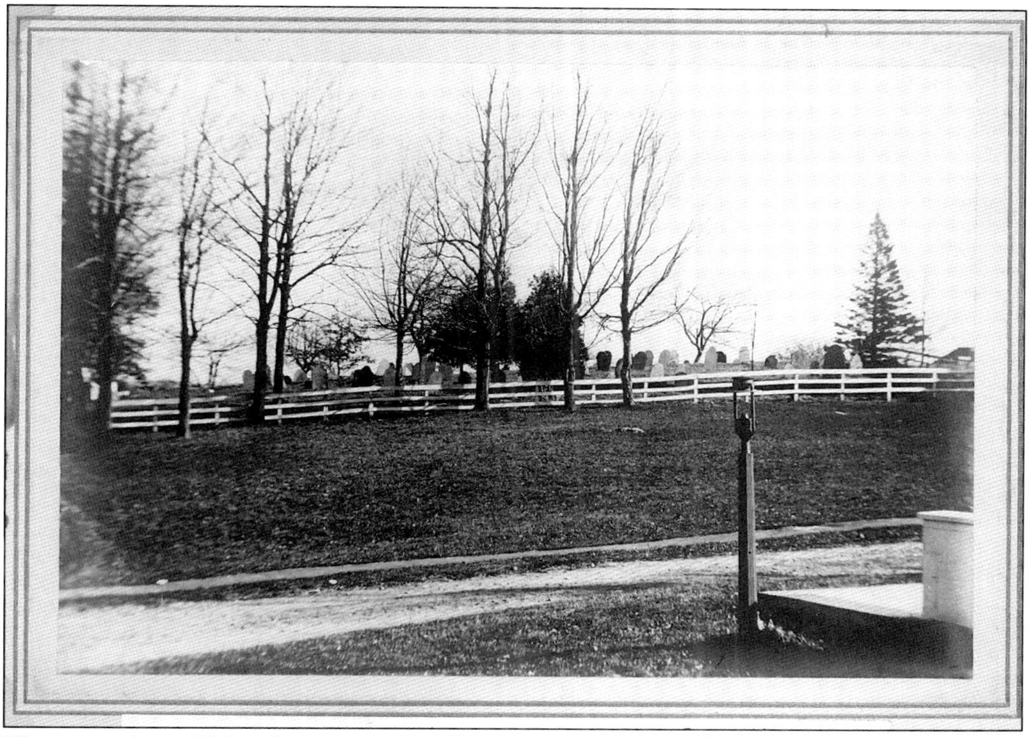

There are about 65 headstones in the old burying ground, or church cemetery. The earliest burial here was in 1770 (William Black and Samuel Crawford), and the last was in 1850 (Anna Bell). This photograph was taken *c.* 1900 from the front porch of the store/post office on the north end of the town common. Note the old-style kerosene street light and the weigh station in the right foreground.

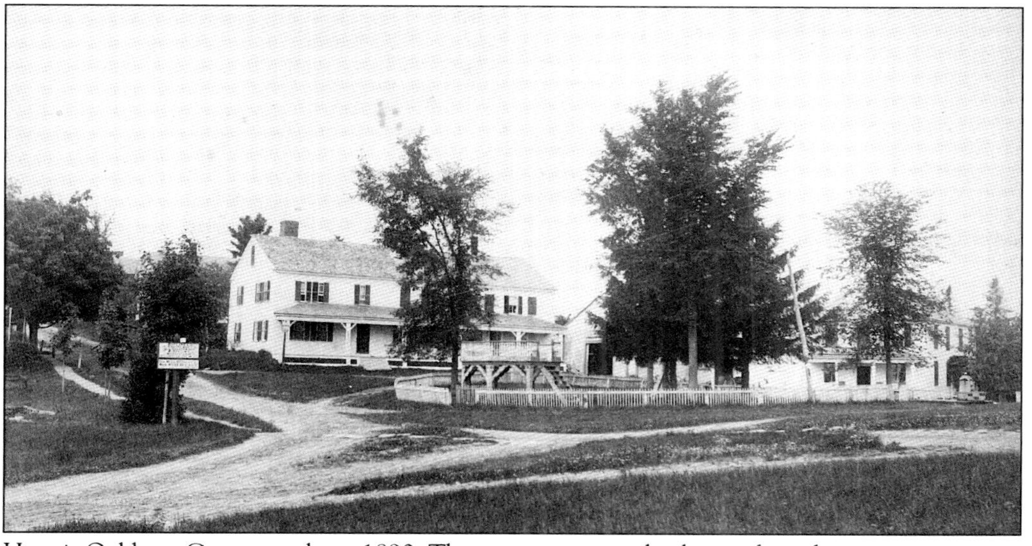

Here is Oakham Common about 1890. The common was a lot larger then than it is now, since the roads were narrower. There was room for a bandstand, picket fence, flagpole, a well, and several trees.

PACKARD'S STORE.

We have tried It and found it pays to divide profits with the customer.

MISCELLANEOUS.

10 pounds	Rolled Oats.		.25
10	"	Cooking Soda,	.25
10	"	Rye Meal,	.23
10	"	Granulated Meal,	.23
5	"	Rice,	.25
3	"	40 to 50 Prunes,	.25
4	"	Crackers,	.25
4	"	Dates,	.25
4	"	Pearl Tapioca,	.25
5	"	Corn Starch,	.25
3 cans	Tomatoes,		.25

The best St. Louis Flour this week (until we sell 10 bbls.) every barrel warranted $4.15
Haxal Flour, 4.75

Ready mixed Paints, White Lead and Oil constantly on hand at popular prices

Bargains this week in Remnant Prints, Ginghams, Outing Flannels.

25 bushels good eating potatoes for 50 cents per bushel.

Meat Market Department.

Beef, Steak, Round,	.14
" " Rump or Sirloin.	.20
" Roasts,	.10 to .14
" Boil,	.03 to .10
" Corned, Fancy Boneless Brisket,	10
" " Common,	.05 to .08
Pork Roast,	.12
Hams, whole or half,	.14 to .15
" sliced,	.20
Shoulders, smoked,	.11
Best Lump Butter, 3 to 5 pounds,	25

N. W. Packard, - Oakham.

This advertisement for Packard's Store was run in the May 9, 1900 edition of the *Oakham Herald*. Besides the prices being much lower than today, you will notice that the quantities are larger, probably due to people not shopping as frequently as today.

Here is a sales slip from Packard's Store for Mrs. Burt in 1899.

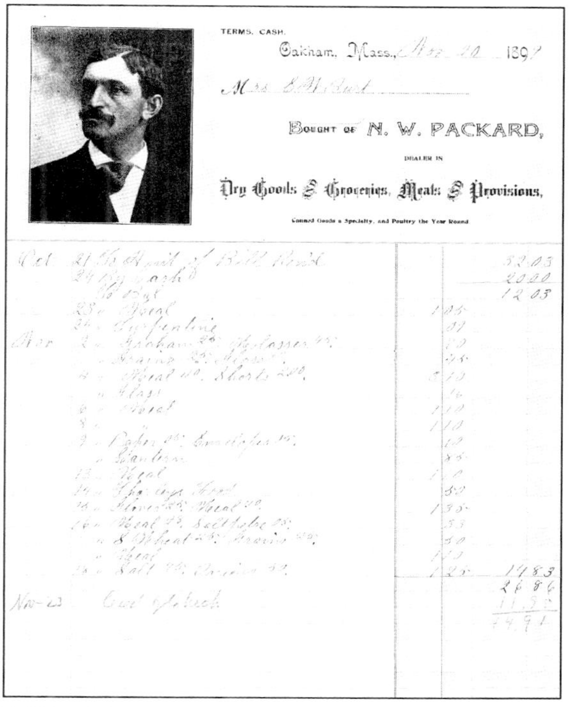

TERMS, CASH.

Oakham, Mass., 189

Bought of N. W. PACKARD,

DEALER IN

Dry Goods & Groceries, Meats & Provisions,

Canned Goods a Specialty, and Poultry the Year Round

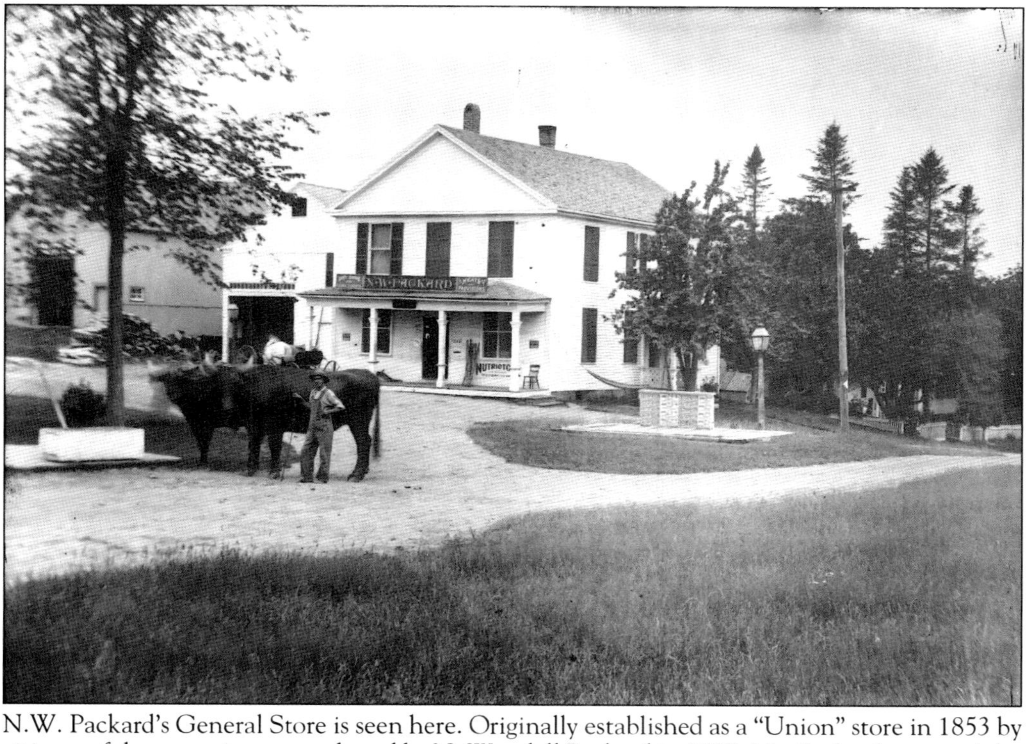

N.W. Packard's General Store is seen here. Originally established as a "Union" store in 1853 by citizens of the town, it was purchased by N. Wendell Packard in 1887. Mr. Packard operated the store through 1908, when it was purchased by George Butler.

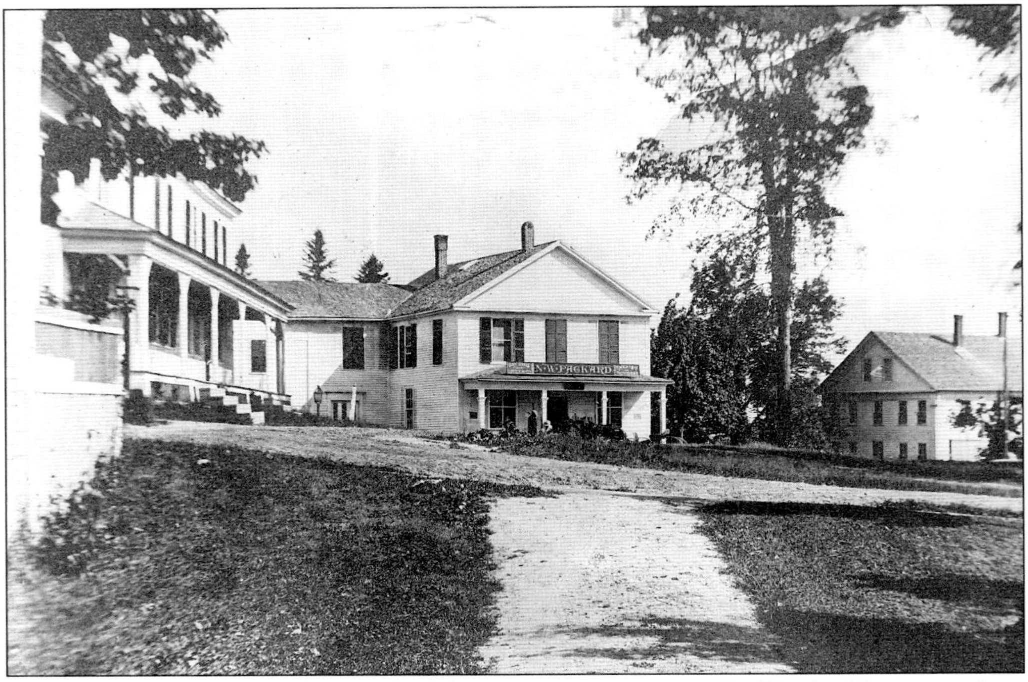

This is a view of the northern end of the town common in 1900. The buildings seen here are, from left to right: the Park View Inn, N.W. Packard's General Store and Post Office (note Fanny Ayres's horse and buggy in front), and Packard's tenement house (the former cheese factory).

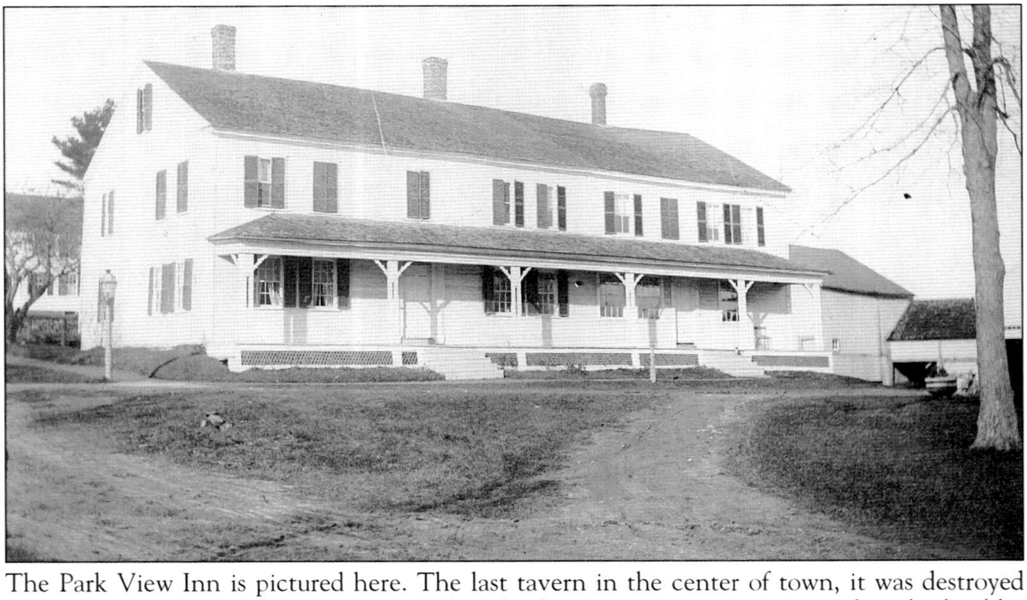

The Park View Inn is pictured here. The last tavern in the center of town, it was destroyed by fire in 1908. The inn was constructed in the late 1700s, as it is mentioned in the booklet "Independence Day in 1797." In this story, late in the day of the celebration, the militia was firing more salutes when one participant left his ramrod in the barrel and shot it over the heads of the spectators, where it landed on the roof of the inn.

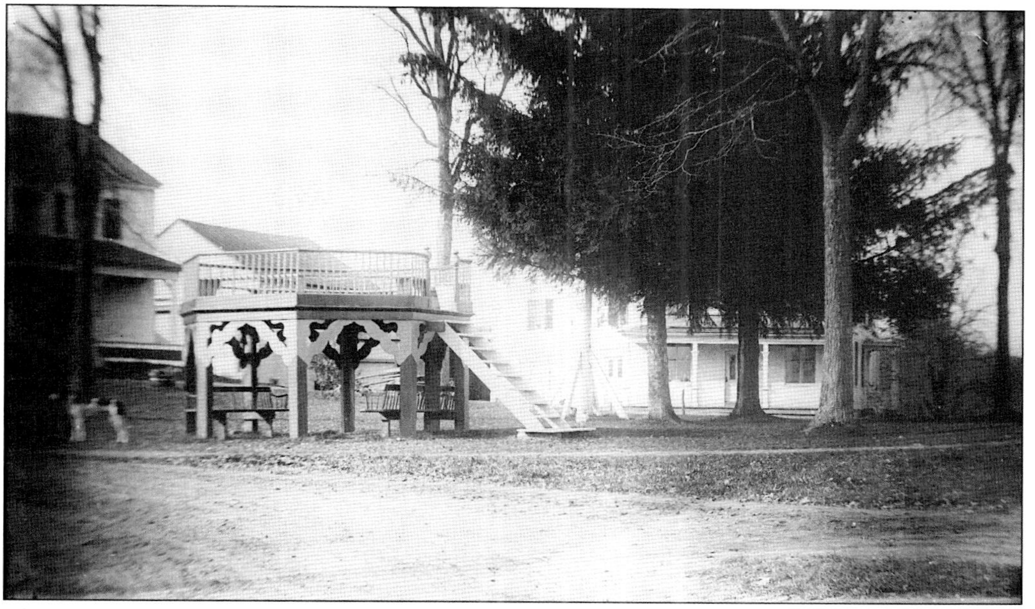

This is the bandstand on the common. The bandstand was dedicated September 5, 1877. There were several bands in existence in Oakham through the late 1800s, and the bandstand was erected to provide a place for concerts and for use during field days and other celebrations.

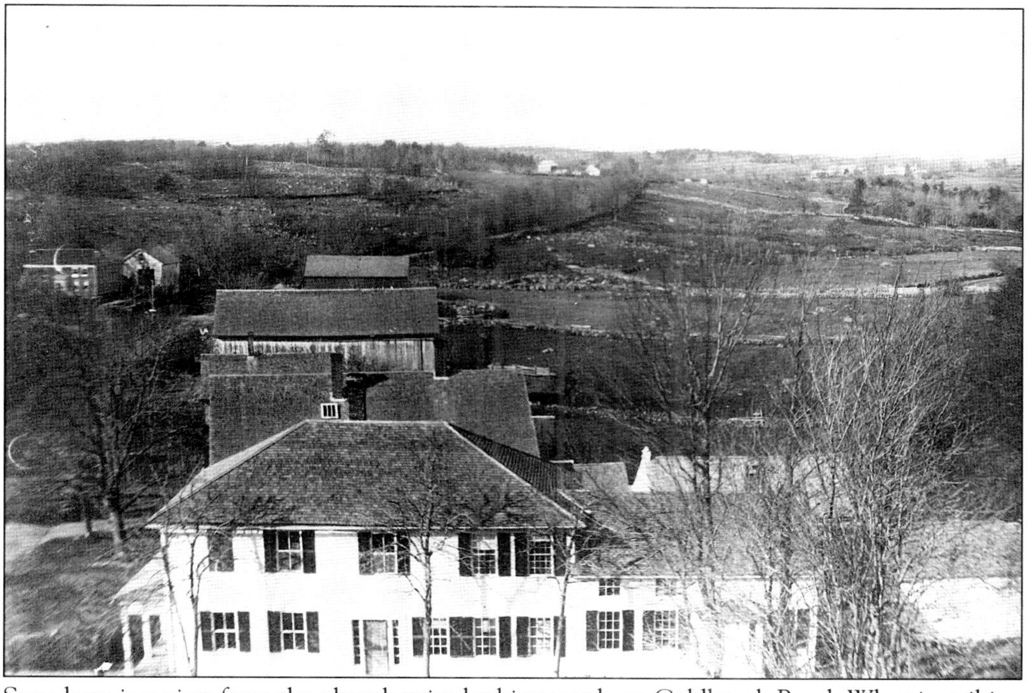

Seen here is a view from the church spire looking north up Coldbrook Road. What is striking about pictures such as this is the lack of trees at the time, which afforded a great view. The field in the upper left portion of the picture is where the Oakham Center School now stands.

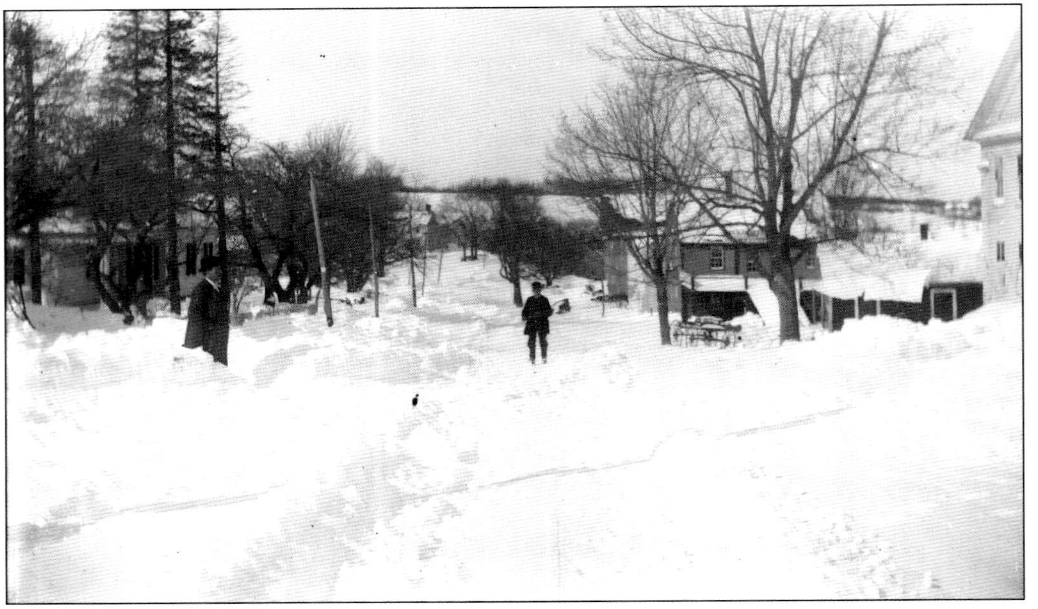

This winter scene is looking north on Coldbrook Road from near the common.

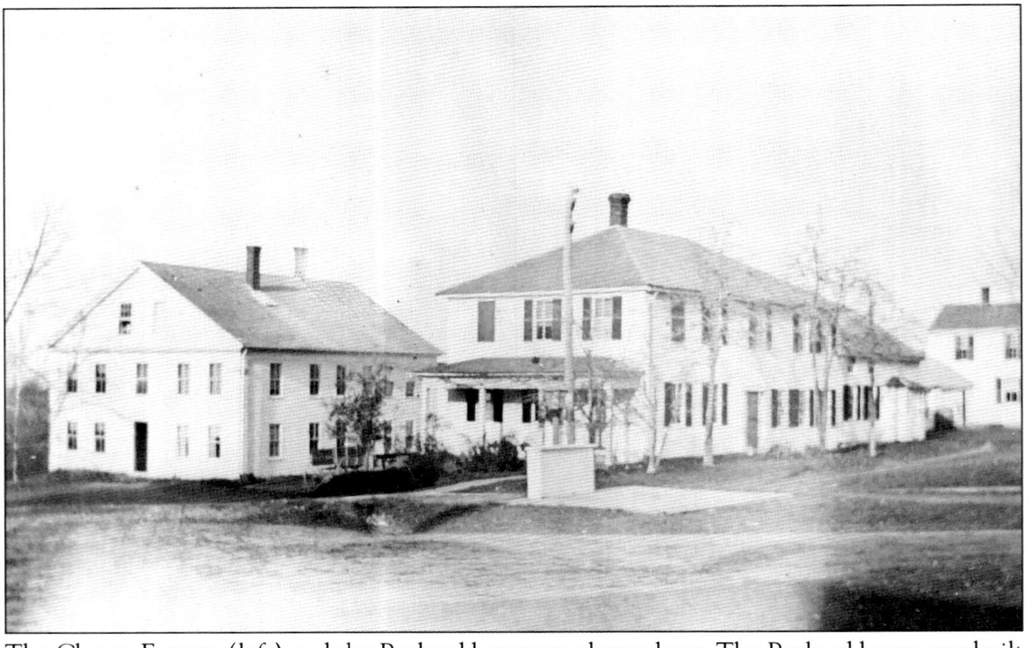

The Cheese Factory (left) and the Packard house are shown here. The Packard house was built in 1828 as a one-story building and used as a school until 1836. A second story was then added, and the building had various uses through the years, such as: a straw and hat shop, carriage shop, doctor and dentist office, and, from 1851 to 1865, the Oakham High School. The Cheese Factory was originally built near Coldbrook in 1832, and was purchased and moved to this site by James Conant and Isaac Rice to be used as a Methodist church. The building was later sold to Alonzo Lincoln, who used it as a cheese factory. This cheese became known as "Methodist Cheese," and was very popular in Boston.

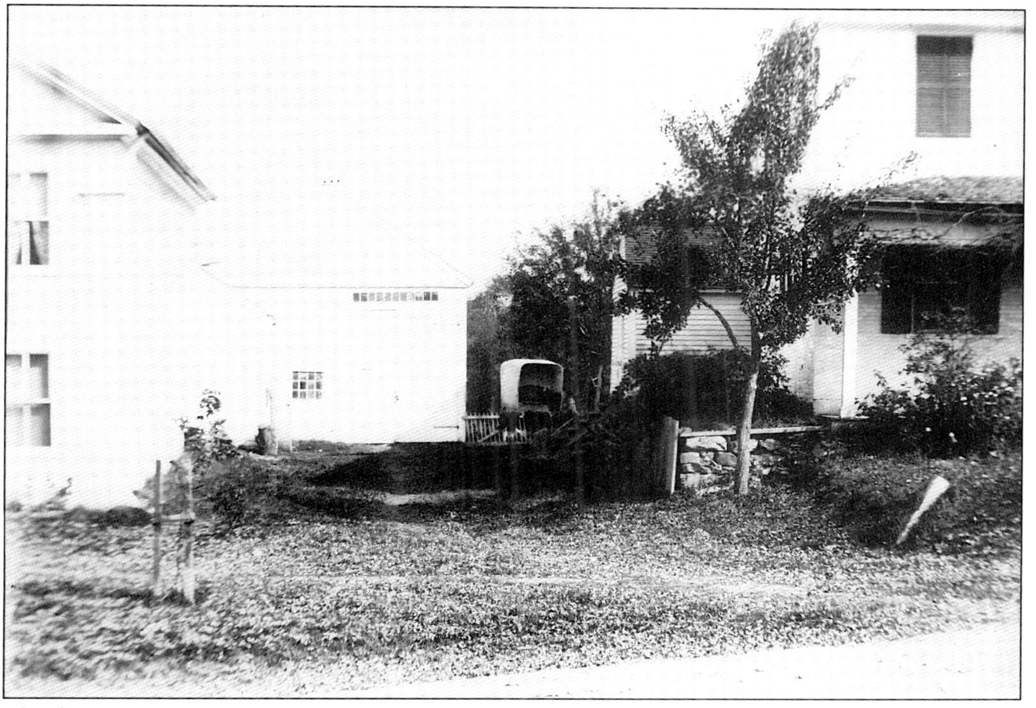

This barn and carriage was located between the Cheese Factory and the Packard house.

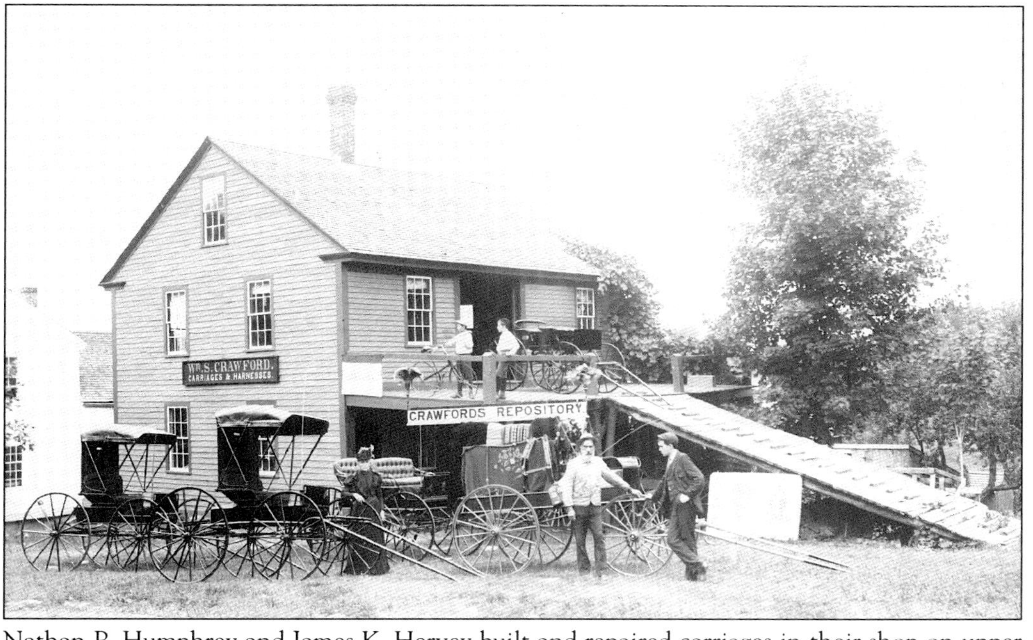

Nathan P. Humphrey and James K. Hervey built and repaired carriages in their shop on upper Maple Street. The business was later moved to the brick house off the common that once was a schoolhouse. When Mr. Hervey sold out his share to his partner, the business was moved to William Crawford's shop a short distance north on Coldbrook Road. Mr. Crawford then carried on the business.

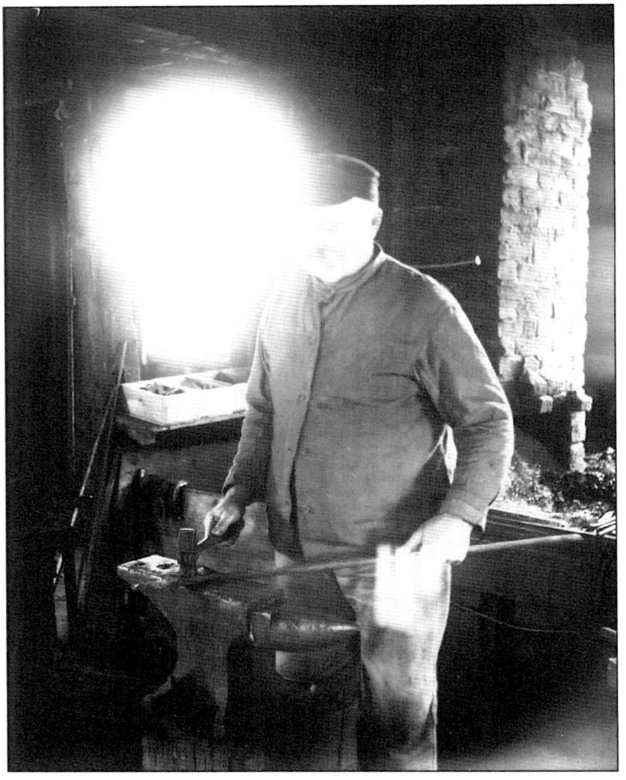

James Babbitt is seen here in his blacksmith shop.

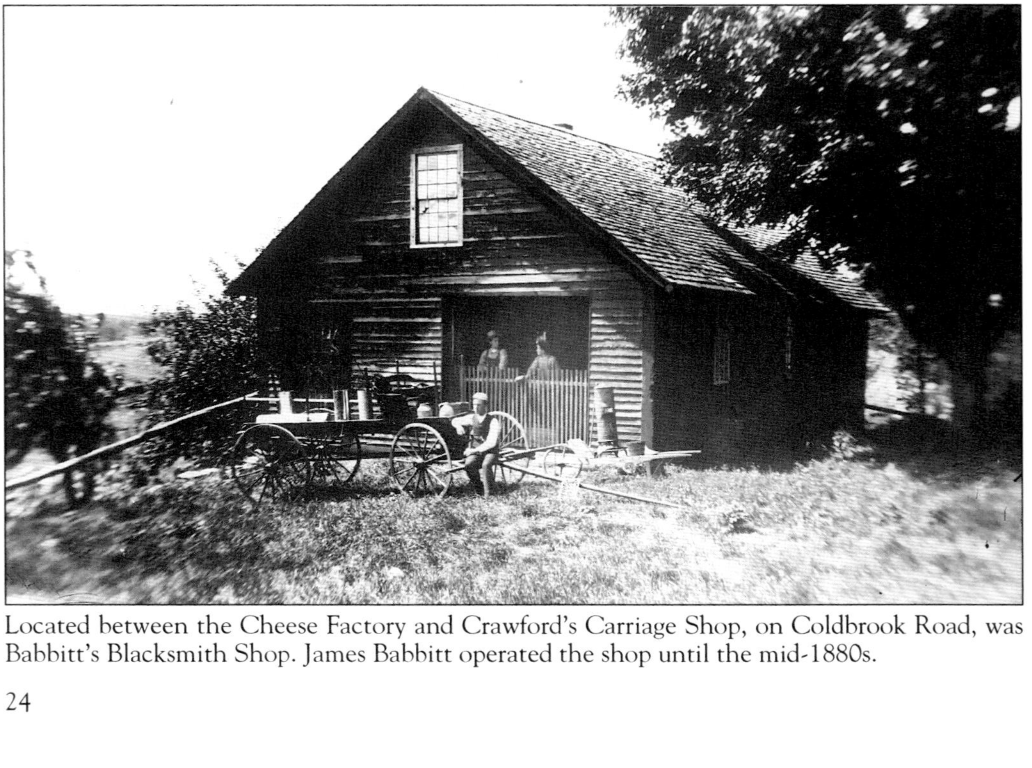

Located between the Cheese Factory and Crawford's Carriage Shop, on Coldbrook Road, was Babbitt's Blacksmith Shop. James Babbitt operated the shop until the mid-1880s.

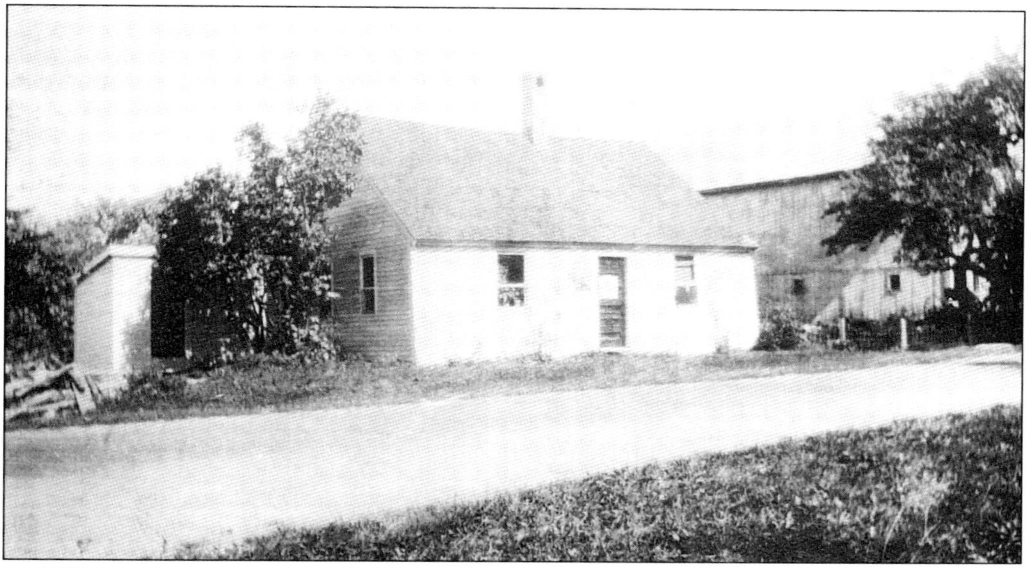

In 1797, two houses, a meetinghouse, and a tavern made up the center of town. The Rose Cottage, built by Jonathan Bullard, was one of the two houses. At one time a water-powered wood shop on the property made wooden pegs, which were used at that time instead of nails. A tailor shop was operated by Peter Foley during the time he lived here. This residence is located at 68 Coldbrook Road.

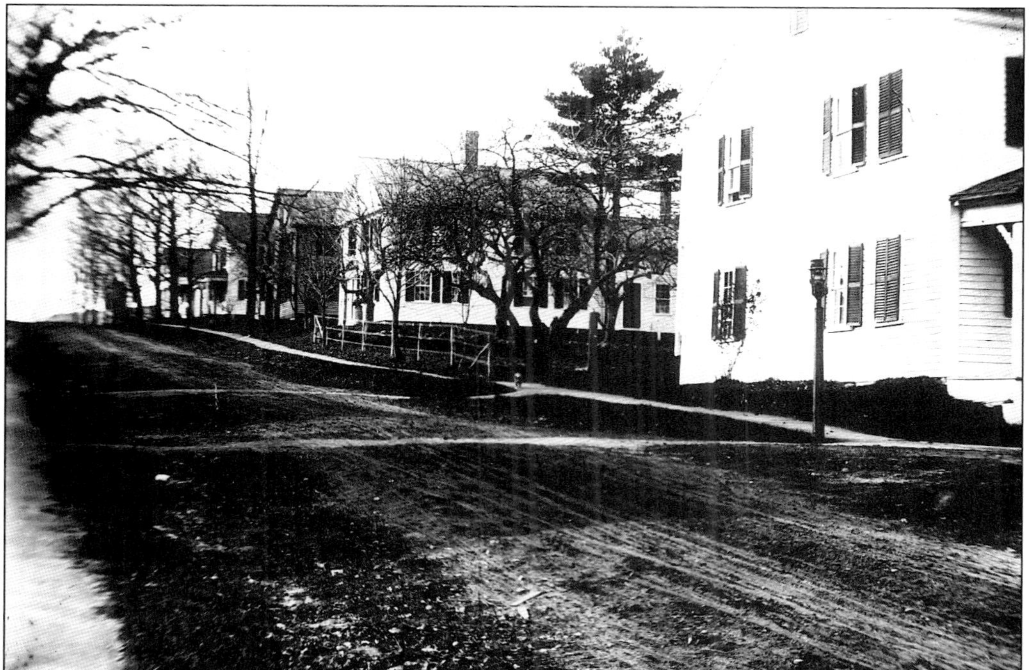

Pictured here is the north side of Maple Street. From right to left are: the Park View Inn, "Hillsite"—the home of the Spooner family, the Sargeant home, the parsonage, and the Jesse Allen home.

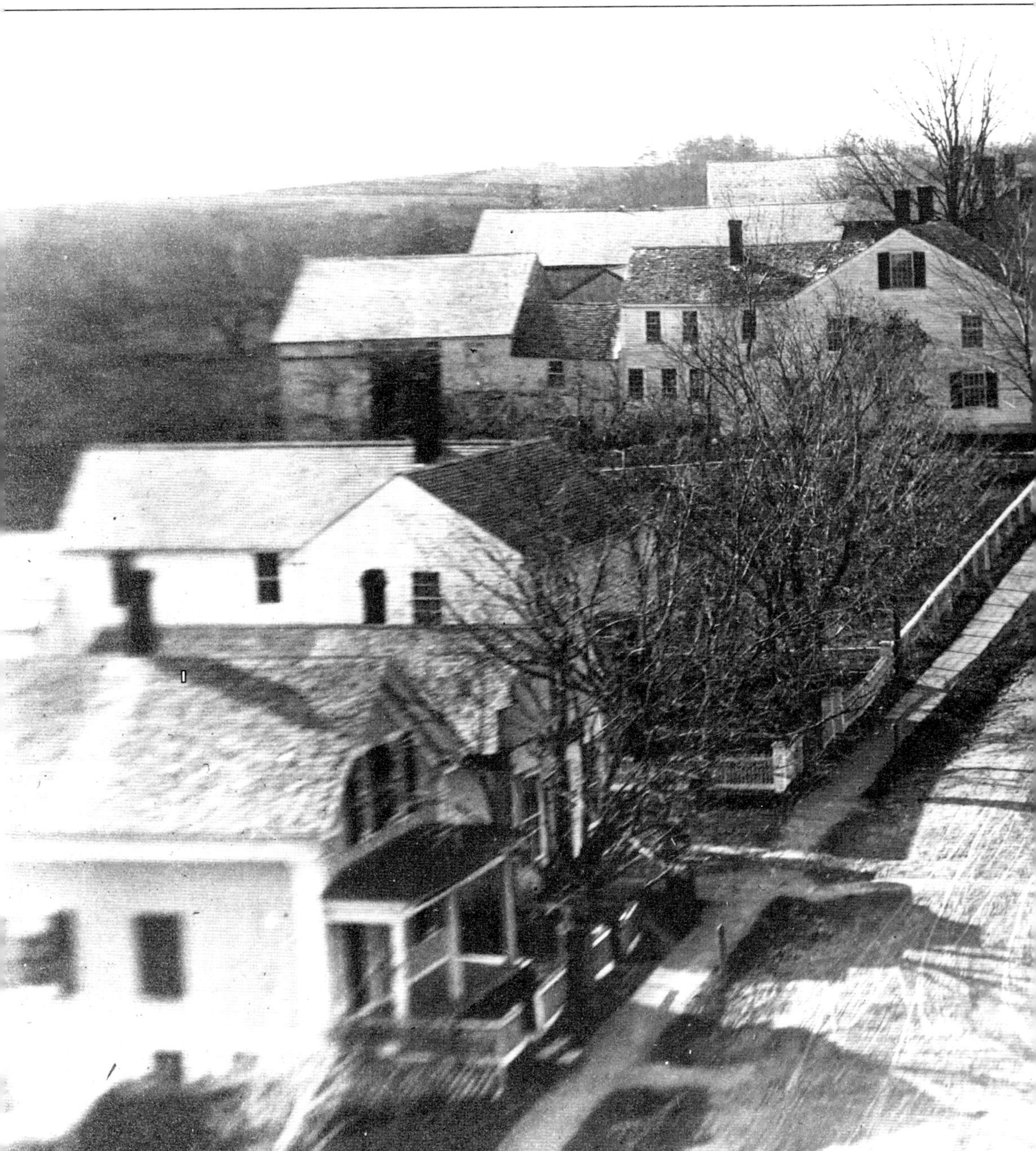

Maple Street is shown here as it looked in November 1900. The photo was taken from the church bell dock by C.M. Packard.

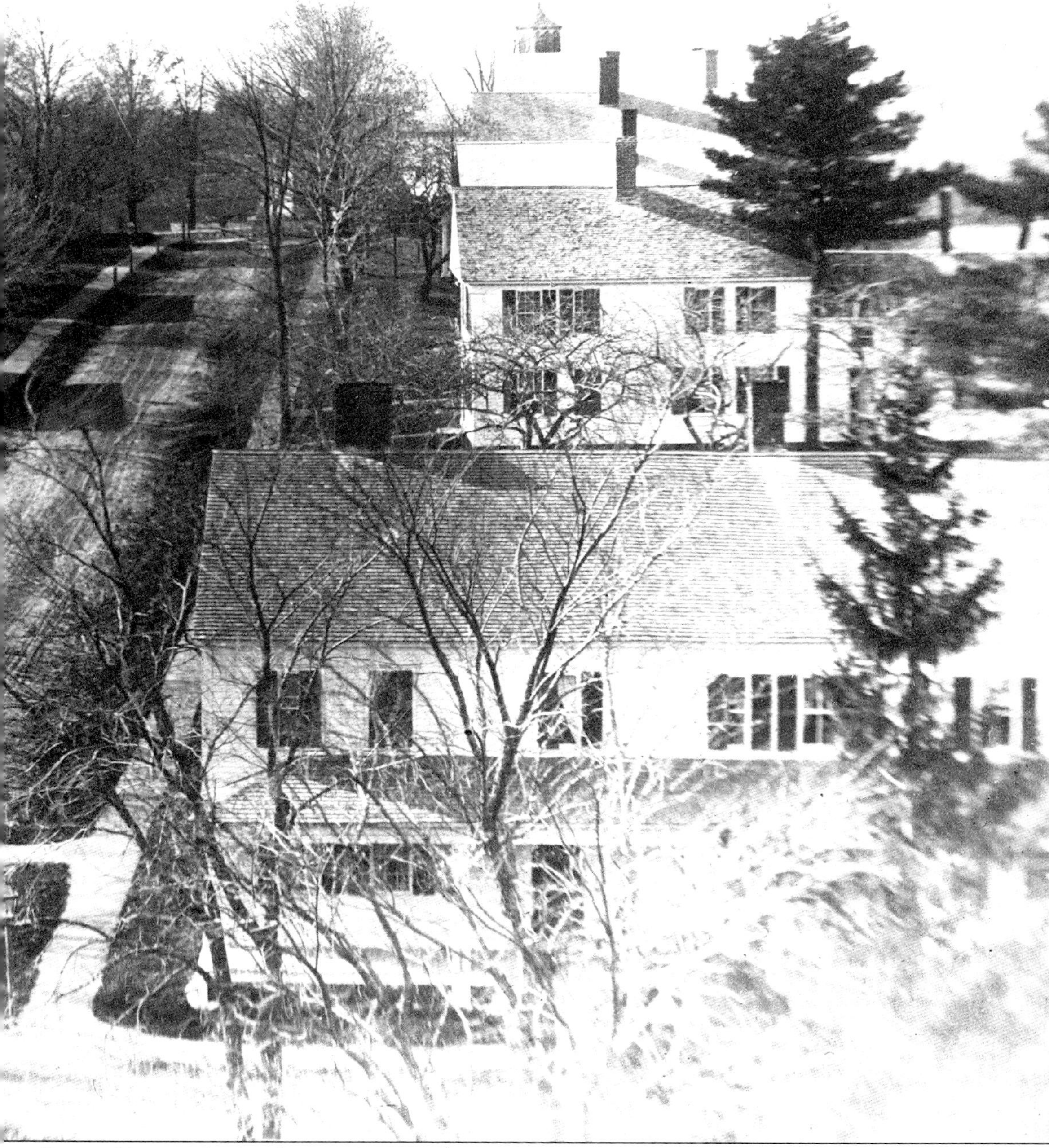

Pictured here is the Stephen M. Sargeant home. Originally built and owned by Hosea Crawford around 1830, Mr. Sargeant purchased the property from Irene Clapp in the 1860s in order to expand his business. To the right of the house can be seen his shop/laboratory where he manufactured flavoring and extracts.

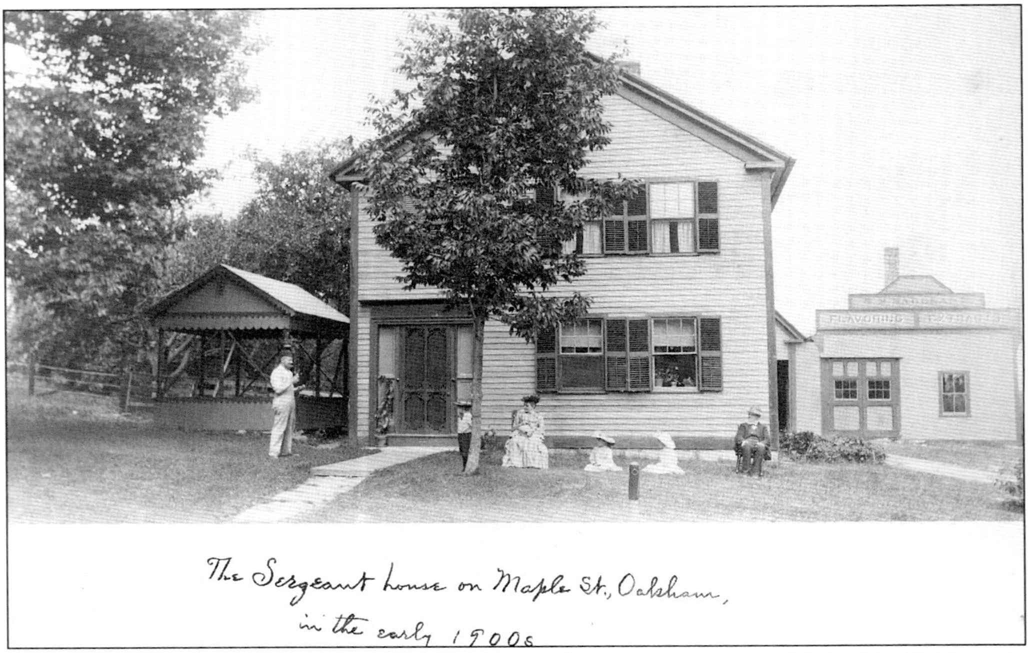

Stephen M. Sargeant is at work in his laboratory. The company was established in Oakham in 1865 and prospered here for many years, eventually moving to Worcester in the early 1900s. In the foreground are some of the bottled fruit flavorings and extracts that the company sold.

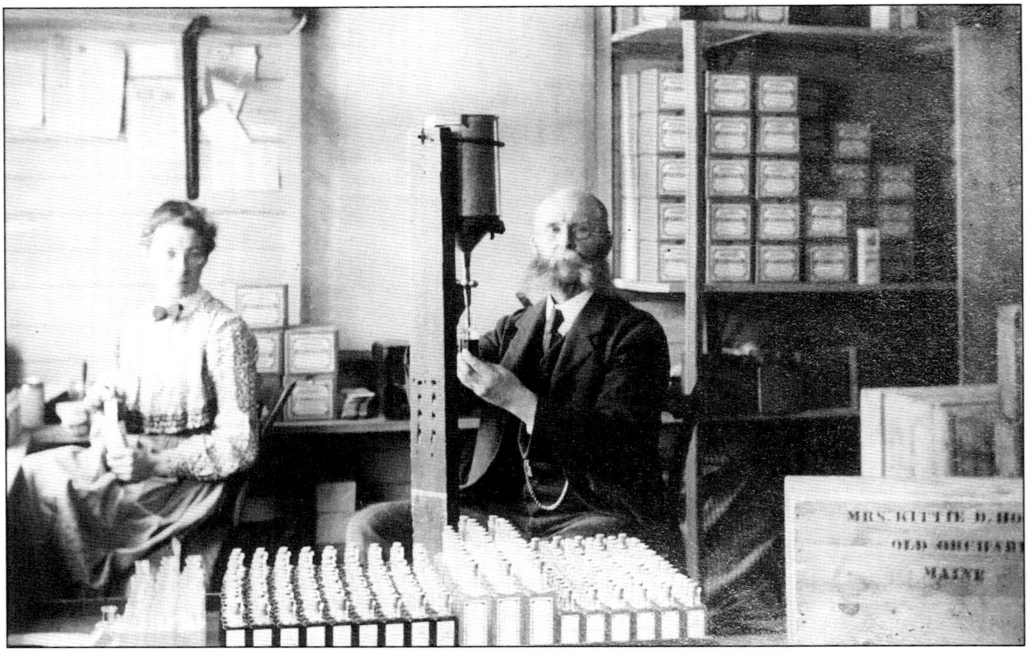

Seen here is Deacon Jesse Allen, son of Deacon James Allen and grandson of Deacon Jesse (the elder) Allen. Deacon Jesse, the younger, was very involved in the social and governing activities of the town. During the year 1900 he held the following positions: town clerk, overseer of the poor, school committee member, cemetery committee member, library trustee, treasurer, and tree warden.

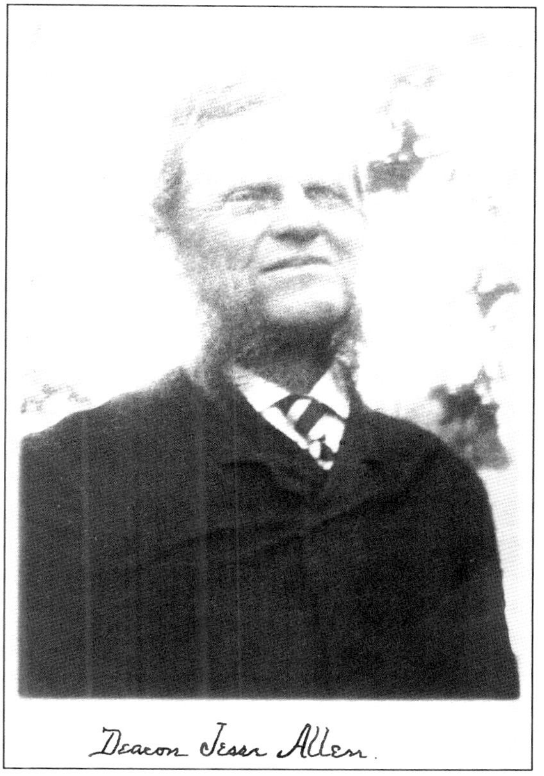

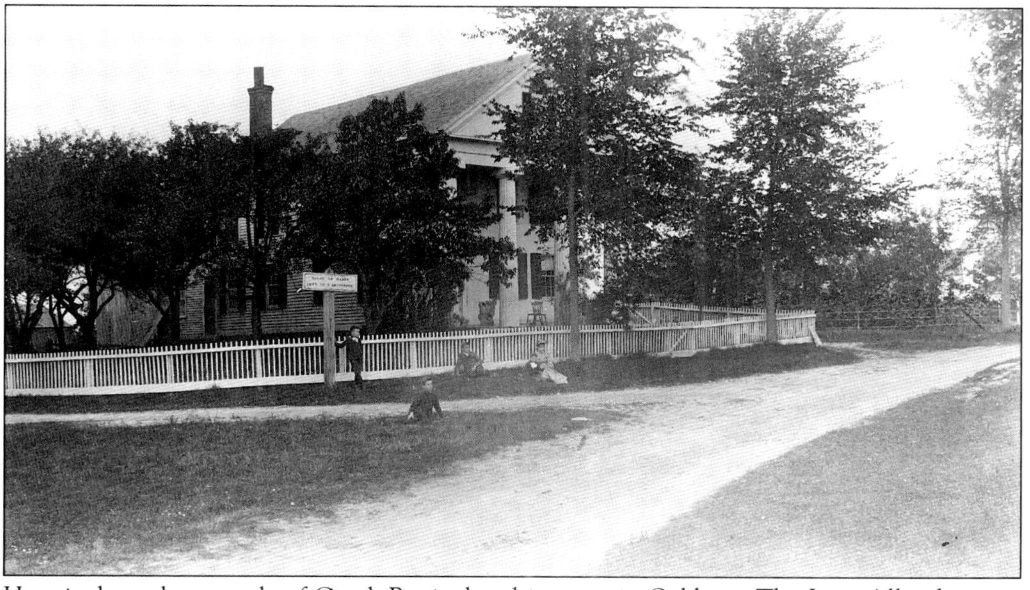

Here is the only example of Greek Revival architecture in Oakham. The Jesse Allen home is located at 56 Maple Street. It was built around 1836 by Phineas Morton. James Allen purchased the property in 1858, and members of his family lived there for the next 64 years. The present row of maple trees on the western border of the property was a gift to the home owner in 1934 from their neighbors.

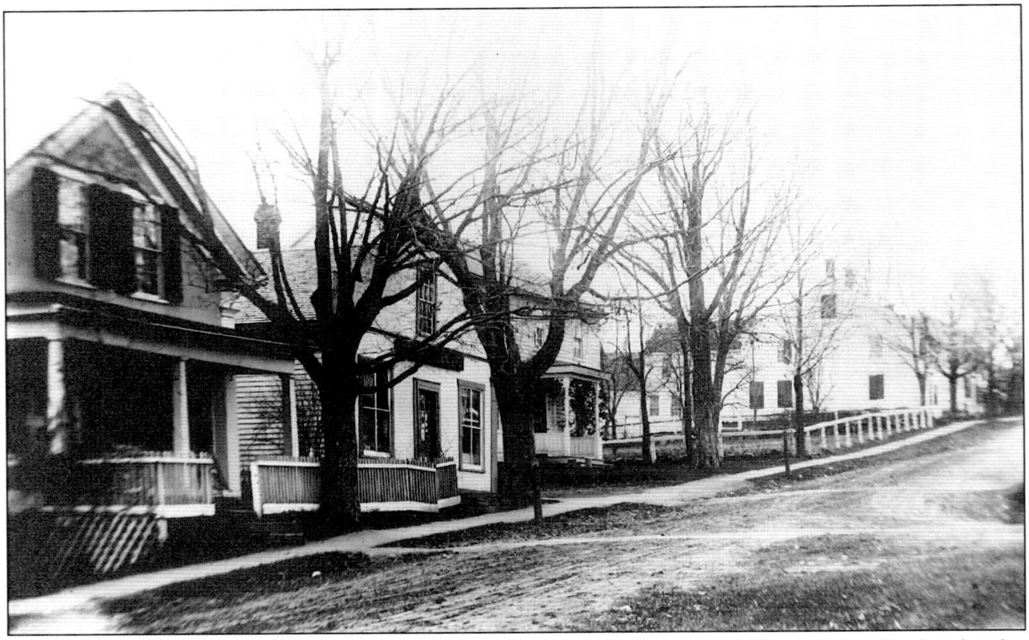

This is the south side of Maple Street. The photo was taken in 1900 by C.M. Packard. The first house on the left is the Tottingham house, followed by the store owned by F.S. Conant, Conant's house, and the home of Martha Mateona's heirs.

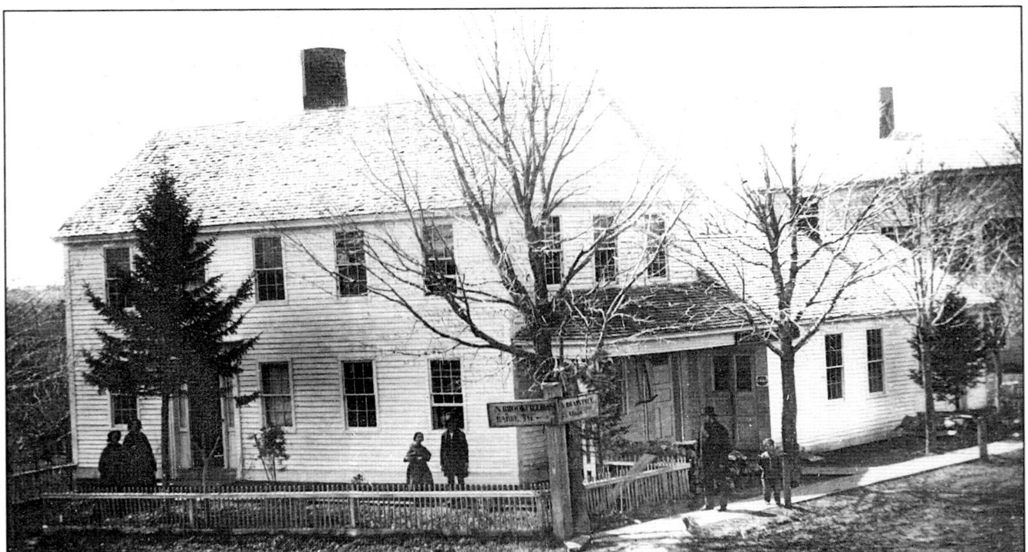

In 1834, the house lot on the corner of Maple Street and Coldbrook Road was purchased by Samuel Henry who, in 1835, built the house and shop seen here in this *c.* 1880 photograph. Between 1835 and 1855, Mr. Henry lived in the house and operated a succession of businesses from the shop: carriage trimming, harness making, drugstore, and dentist office. In 1855, Mr. Henry sold the house and shop to his druggist, Deacon Cheney Reed, who continued to operate the drugstore until his death in 1866. The buildings were destroyed by fire in 1886, and the property was sold to the Fairbank family, who later donated it to the town for the library.

Pictured here is Celia Fobes, one of the contributors to the construction of the library. She was married to Hiram Fobes, the tenth and youngest child of Perez Fobes. Hiram was raised in Oakham and later lived and owned a business in Worcester.

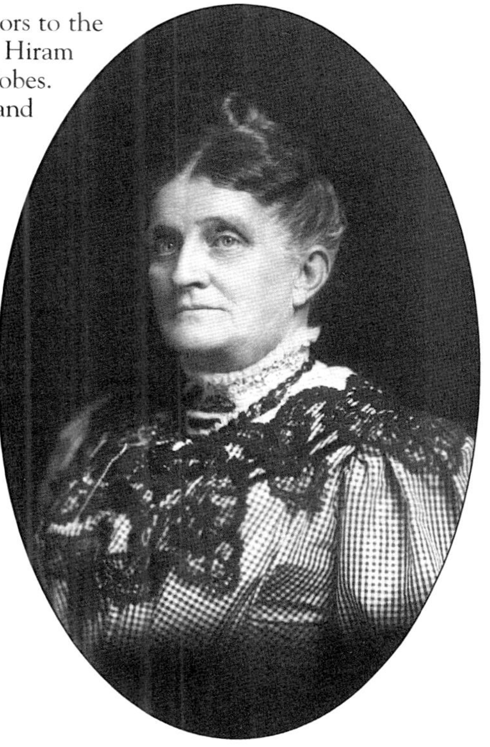

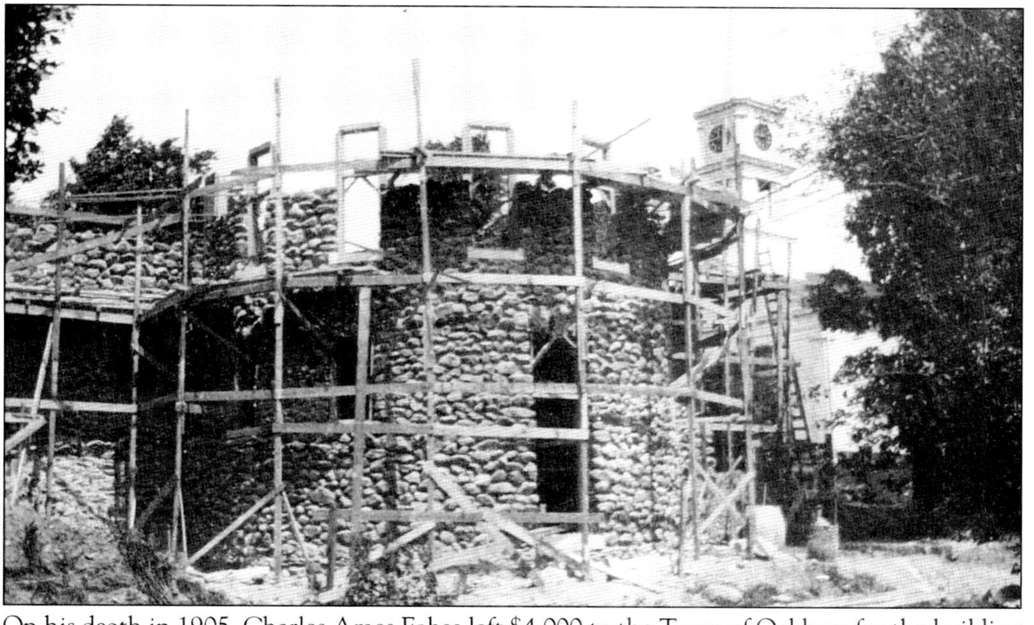

On his death in 1905, Charles Ames Fobes left $4,000 to the Town of Oakham for the building of a library. In the following year, Celia Fobes and Harriet Fobes Gifford supplemented that amount with gifts of $3,000 each. This photograph shows the rear of the library during a pause in construction for the cornerstone ceremony in August of 1907. The cornerstone was taken from the old Fobes farm, the current site of the Oakham Historical Museum.

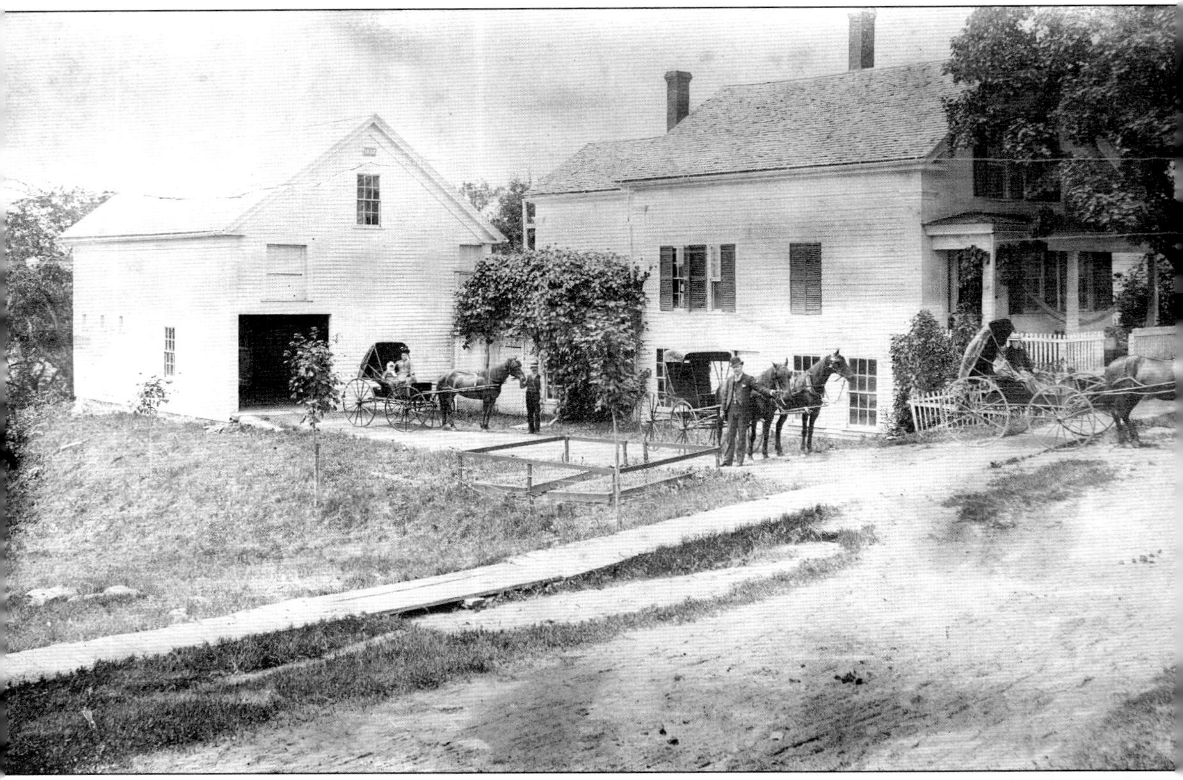

Located at 17 Maple Street, this home was built by James W. Packard in 1848. Packard served as the town's first librarian, keeping a supply of books in his home until 1882. The home is more commonly known as the residence of Omer D. Tottingham, a tinner who peddled his wares in surrounding towns. The sign above the barn window reads 1887. For a time this was also the residence of Dr. Elishu L. Sawyer, who is pictured in the carriage on the right.

This is the window of the F.S. Conant store. Specializing in clocks, watches, and jewelry, the store also sold many other household items. Later in 1903, the building was used by the Conant and Parker Telephone Company. The telephone business continued to operate out of this building until 1956, when the business was purchased by the New England Telephone Company. It was the last local telephone company in the state.

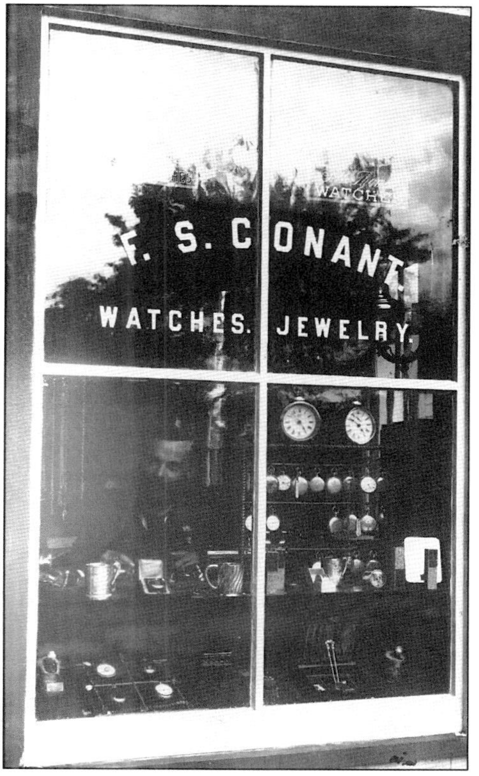

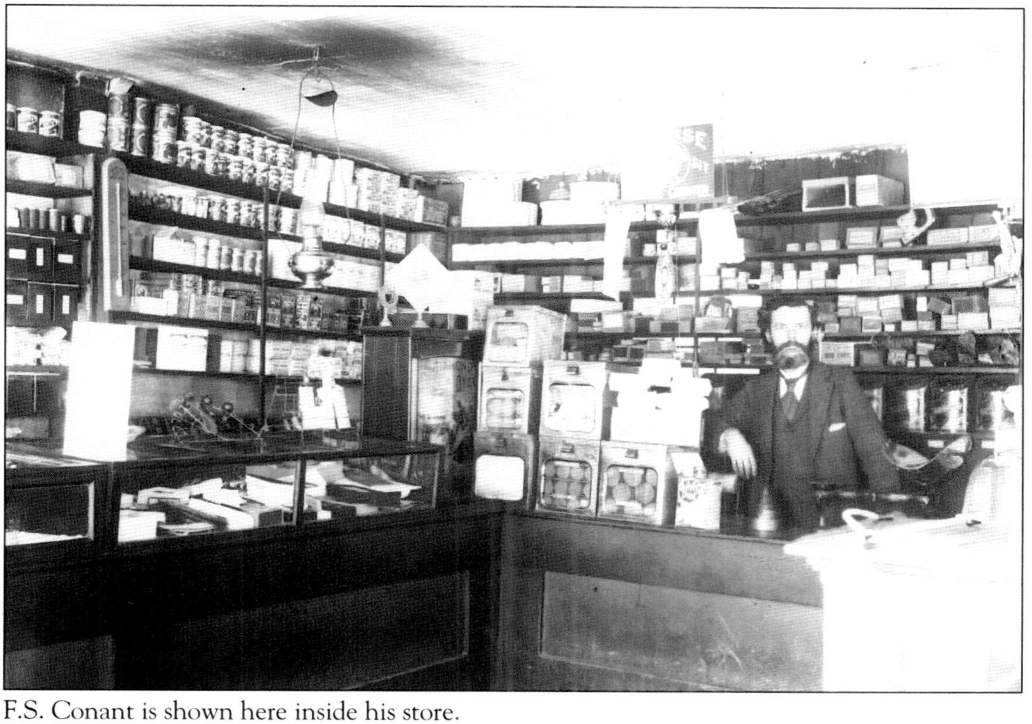

F.S. Conant is shown here inside his store.

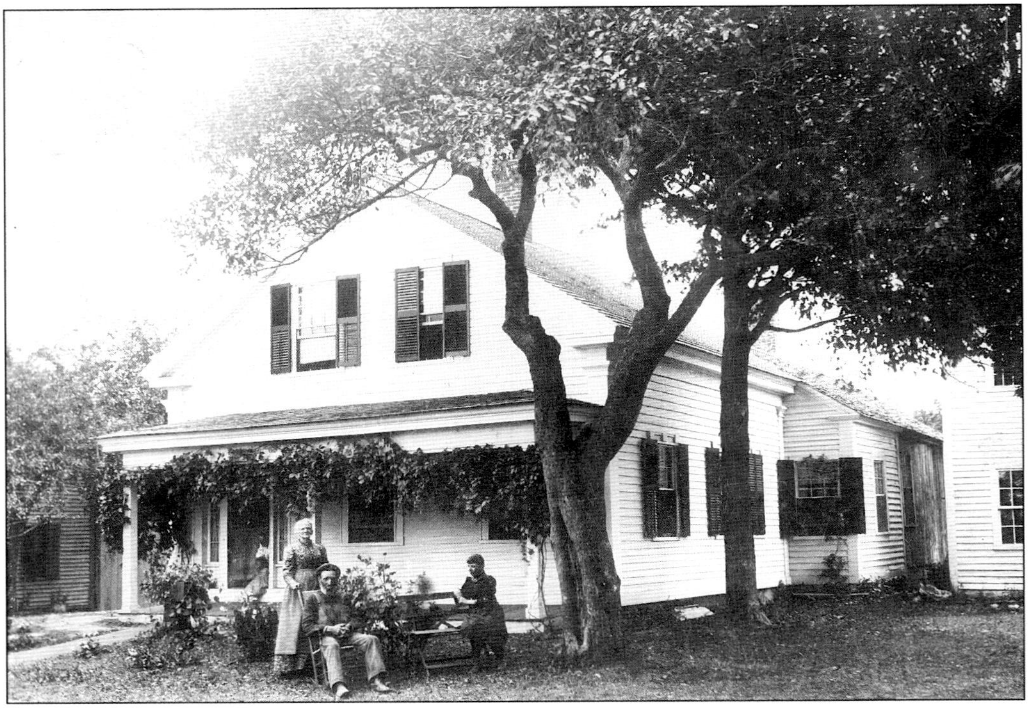

Built before 1846 by John W. Ayres, this house is located at 43 Maple Street. For several summers the home was used by the Henry P. Wright family as a summer home. Pictured here, from left to right, are Charlotte Packard Gleason, Charles A. Gleason, and one of their eight children.

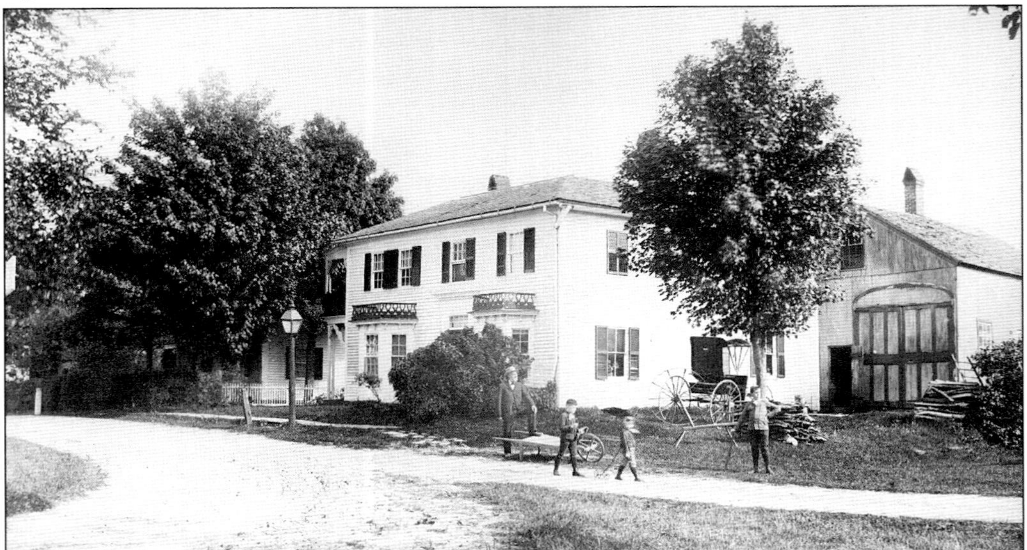

Built around 1810, this residence was occupied by the Armory J. Holden family beginning in 1869. Mr. Holden built the "Holden Wood Furnace" at the site behind the present library and later at a shop located on Rutland Road. The home is located at 67 Maple Street, and the photo was taken around 1888.

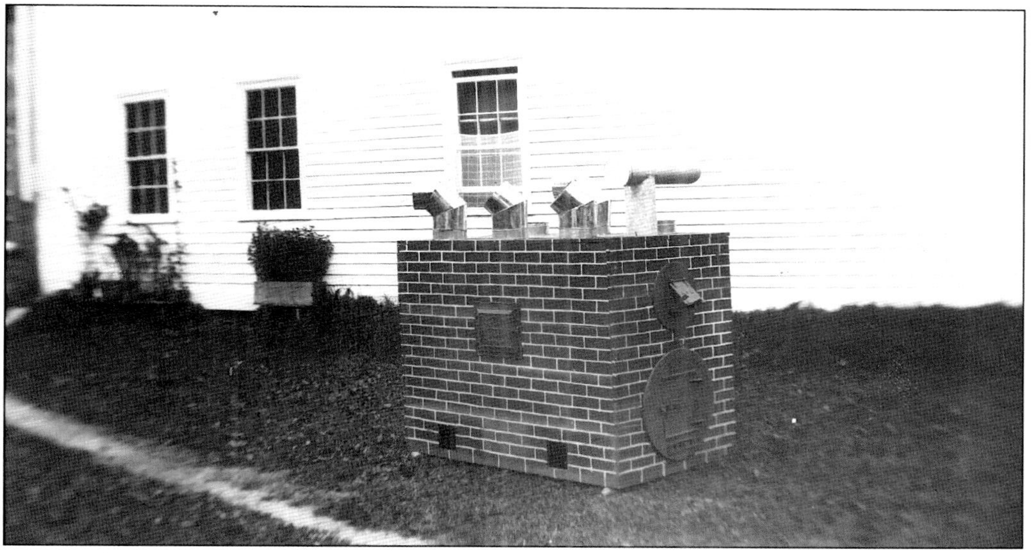

A completed Holden Wood Furnace is ready for installation. The furnace invented by A.J. Holden of Oakham, and patented in 1887, was installed in many buildings in central Massachusetts.

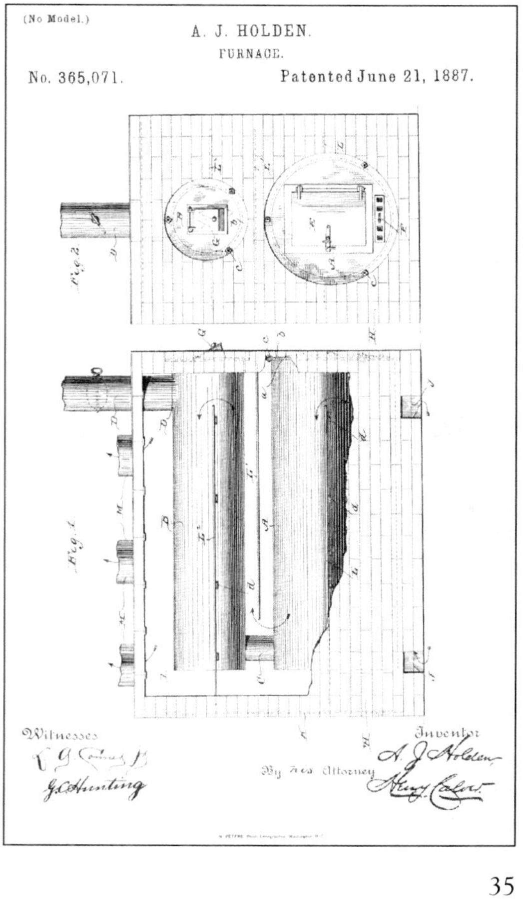

The patent diagram of the Holden Wood Furnace is shown here. The furnace was billed as fuel efficient and clean burning.

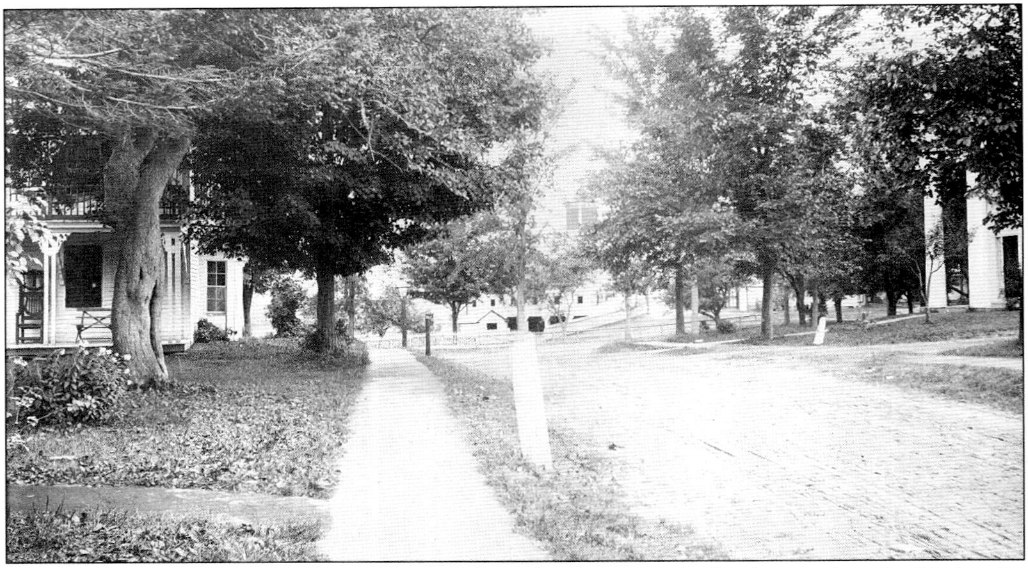

This is a view looking west from the top of Maple Street. In the background is the Fairbank's barn. Parts of the Holden home (left) and the Allen home (right) can be seen.

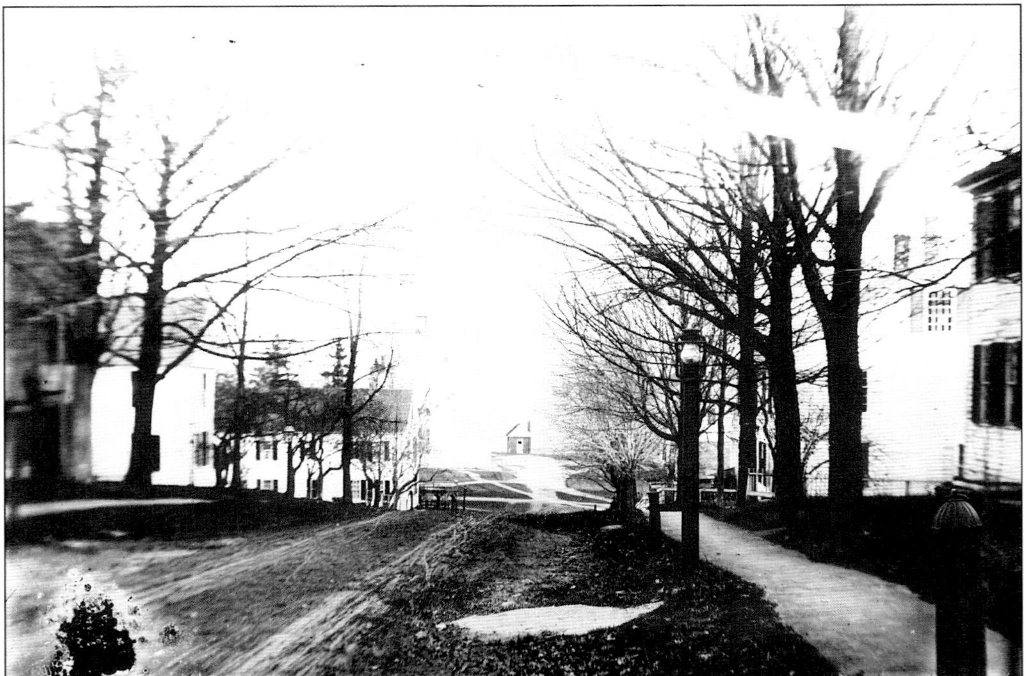

Looking down Maple Street from the top, you can clearly see the Tramp House in the center of the picture. Also visible are the sidewalks, lined with hitching posts and kerosene lamps.

Two

Coldbrook Springs

During the mid-1700s, the families of James, James Jr., Joseph Craige, and those of Aaron and Solomon Parmenter settled in the northern part of Oakham. A few years later a tavern and sawmill were in operation. Within the next one hundred years a gristmill, a basket shop, another sawmill, two railroad stations, and two hotels operated in the village of Coldbrook Springs. For many years the village was the most populous part of town.

The Boston and Maine and the Boston and Albany railroads not only brought goods to and from the town, but also visitors from near and far to partake in the "healing" waters of the springs. The village was connected to the rest of the town not only by postal deliveries, but by the services of the Conant and Parker Telephone Company, which was established in the late 1800s.

Unfortunately, in the early 1900s, the need for water by cities in the eastern part of the state resulted in the closing of the schools and businesses, and the relocation of residents to nearby towns. By the 1930s, nearly every building had been torn down or moved. What once was a bustling, thriving village is no more.

The village of Coldbrook Springs is no longer a place, but only a part of the memories of those that once lived there. This chapter is, in a way, a tribute to those who remember the village, and to those who want to keep that memory alive.

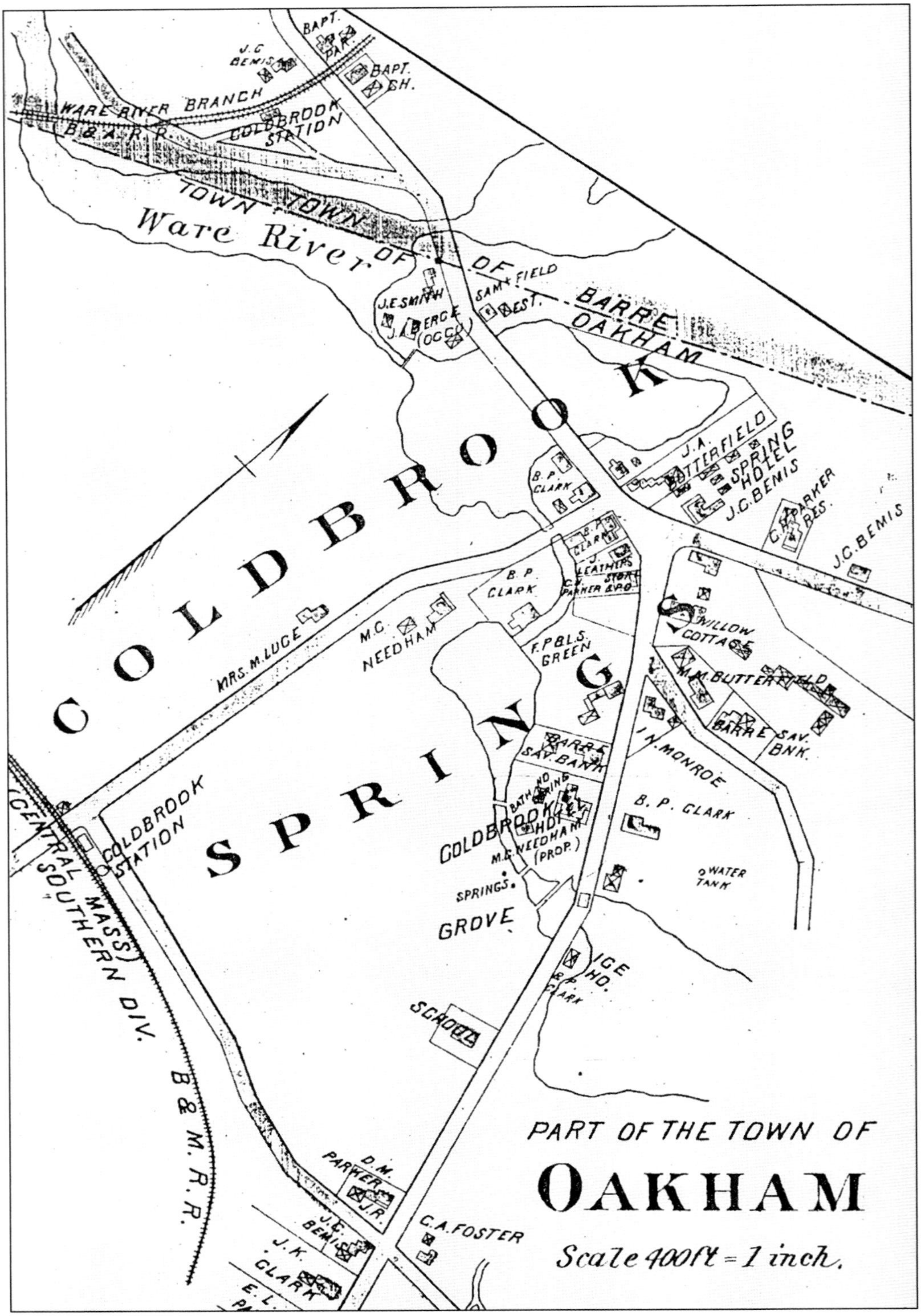

Pictured above is a map of Coldbrook Springs.

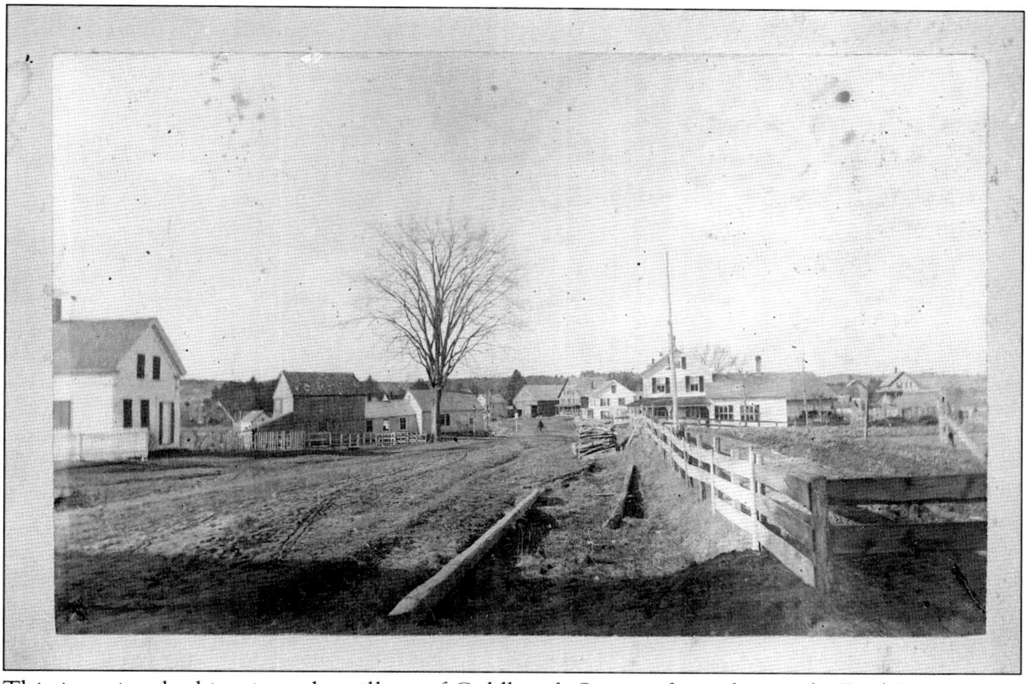

This is a view looking into the village of Coldbrook Springs from the south. Fred Parmenter's house and barn are just left of the center, and the Cody home is across the street on the right.

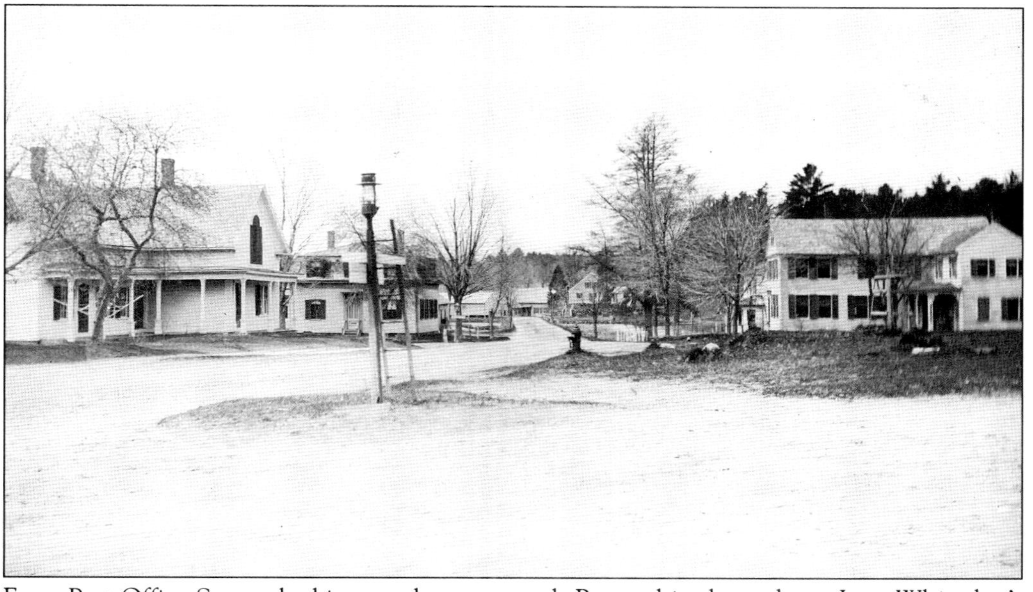

From Post Office Square looking northwest towards Barre, this photo shows Iona Whittaker's home on the left, the Herbert "Honey" Wilbur home with the "Honey" sign out front, and the Frank Winslow home on the right. Winslow owned land toward Barre Falls, which had a spring on it. He piped the water to the hydrant, pictured here in the center, and provided water free of charge to residents.

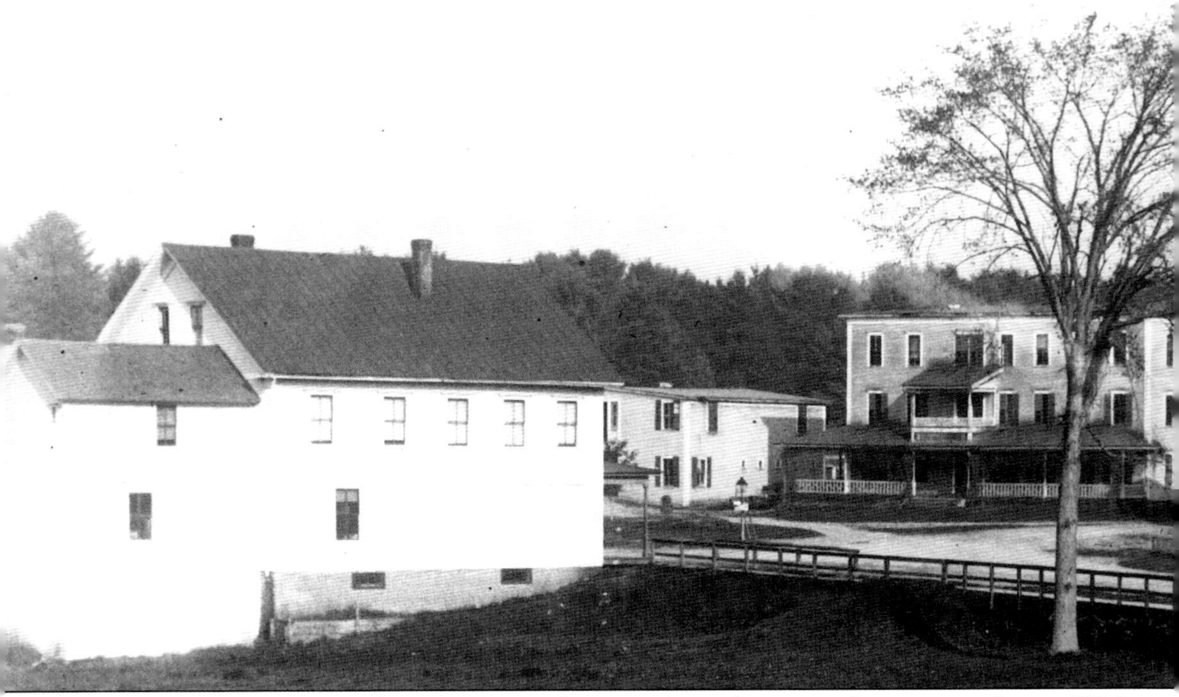

Coldbrook Springs was the area of town that grew faster than any other section of town. With the main road to Worcester and two railroads passing through, the village of Coldbrook Springs provided its residents with the means of connecting to the rest of the state. Pictured here are,

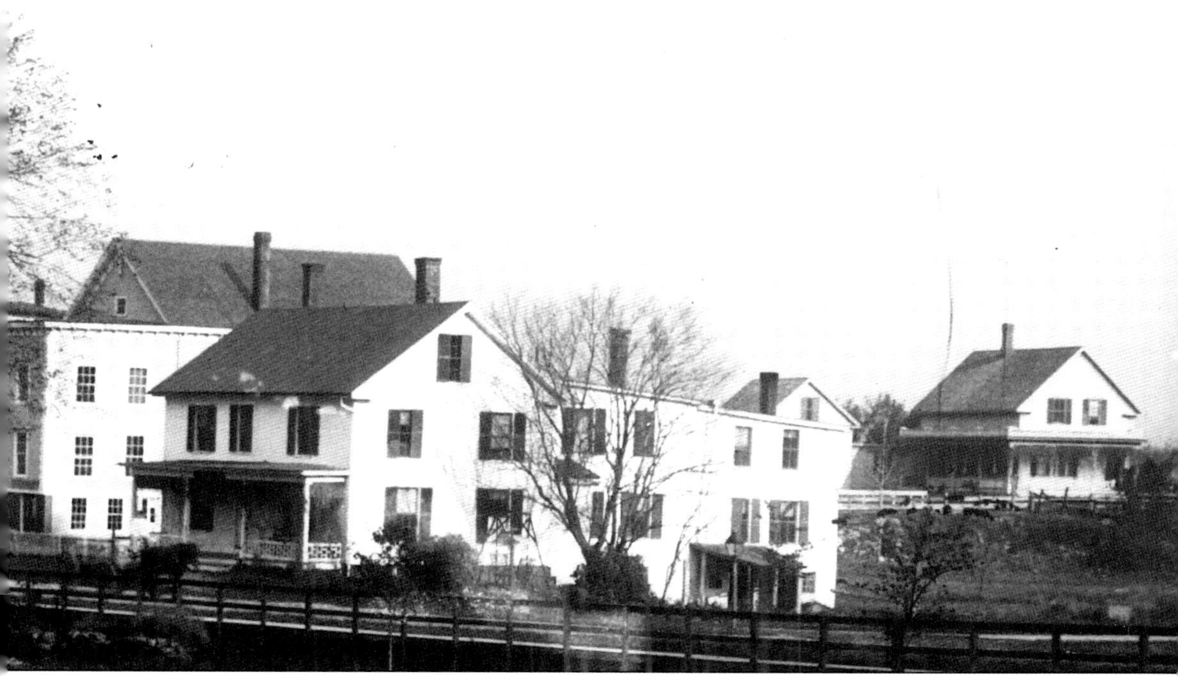

Parker's Store (on the left), the Eagle Inn (behind the tree), and the home of Harry Parker (on the far right).

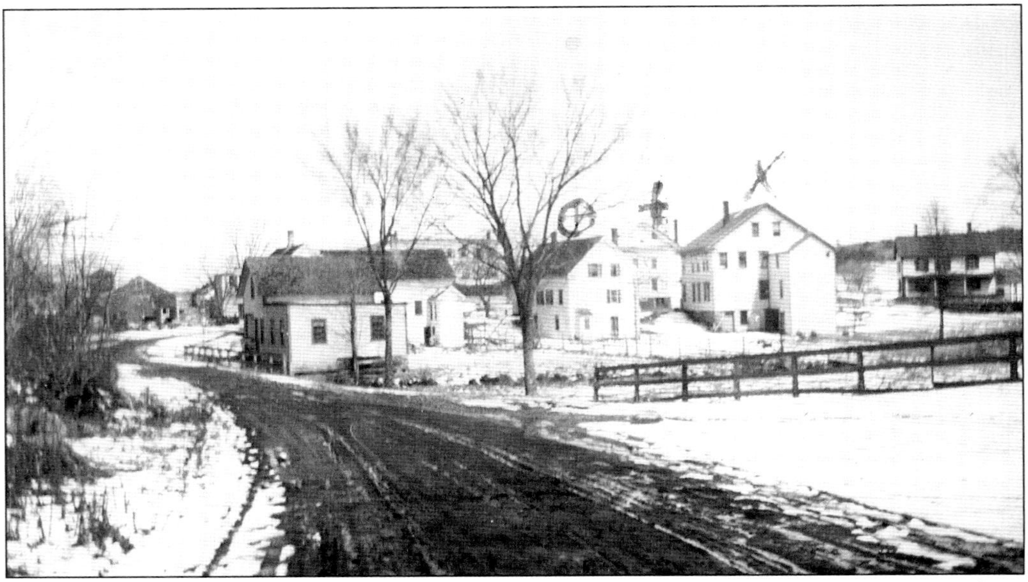

Looking northeast towards Post Office Square from Coldbrook Road, this photo shows, from left to right, the Winslow's barn, Iona Whittaker's shop, an unidentified house, the Harwood Ripka house, Redmen's Hall, Parker's Store, and the Webber home.

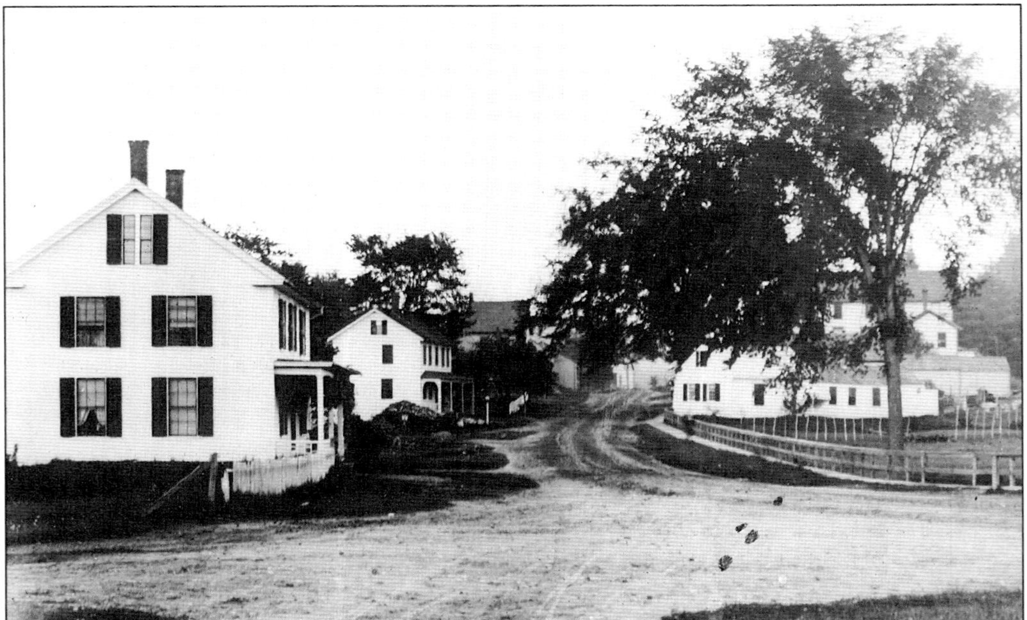

Main Street looking southeast shows, from left to right, the Cody home, an unidentified house, the Moss home, and the Parmenter house.

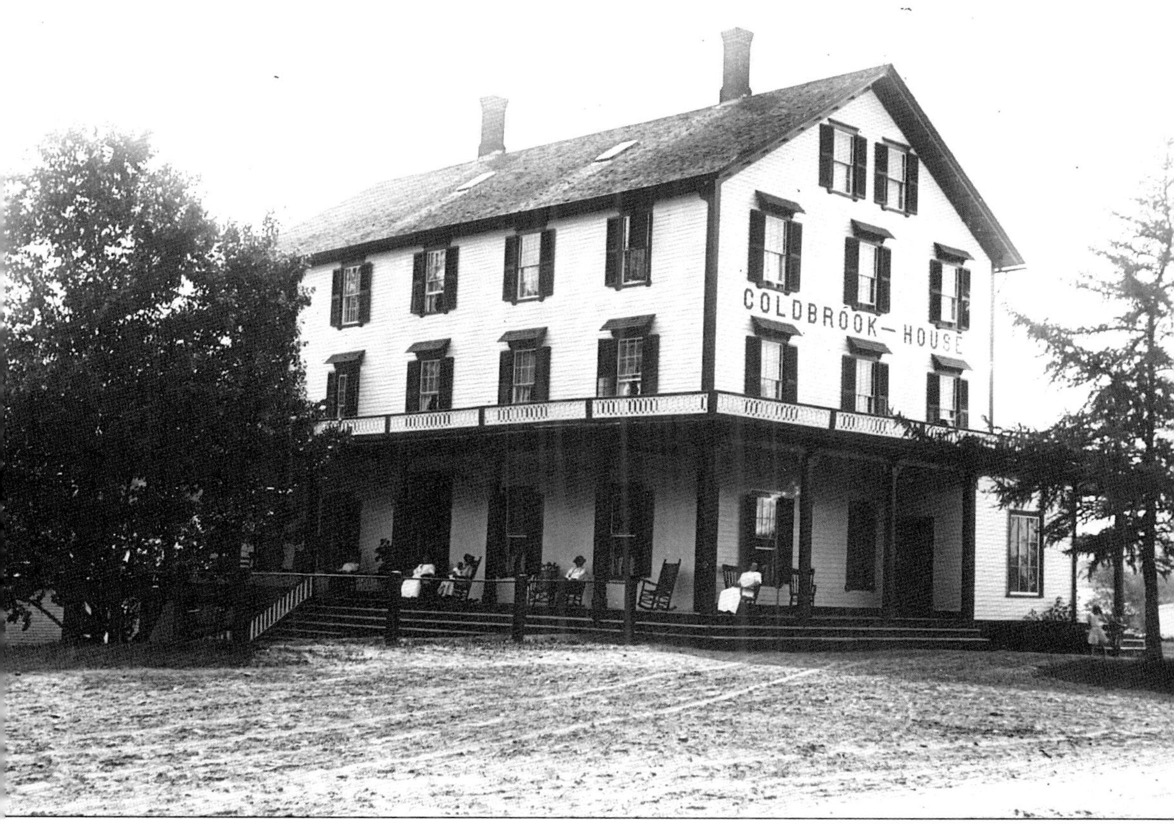

The Coldbrook House was built in 1867 to provide rooms for the countless tourists that came to take advantage of the springs. The hotel had 32 rooms and catered to the needs of the patrons in almost every way. George Davis operated the hotel during its early years. Monroe C. Needham purchased the hotel in 1897 and operated it until 1917.

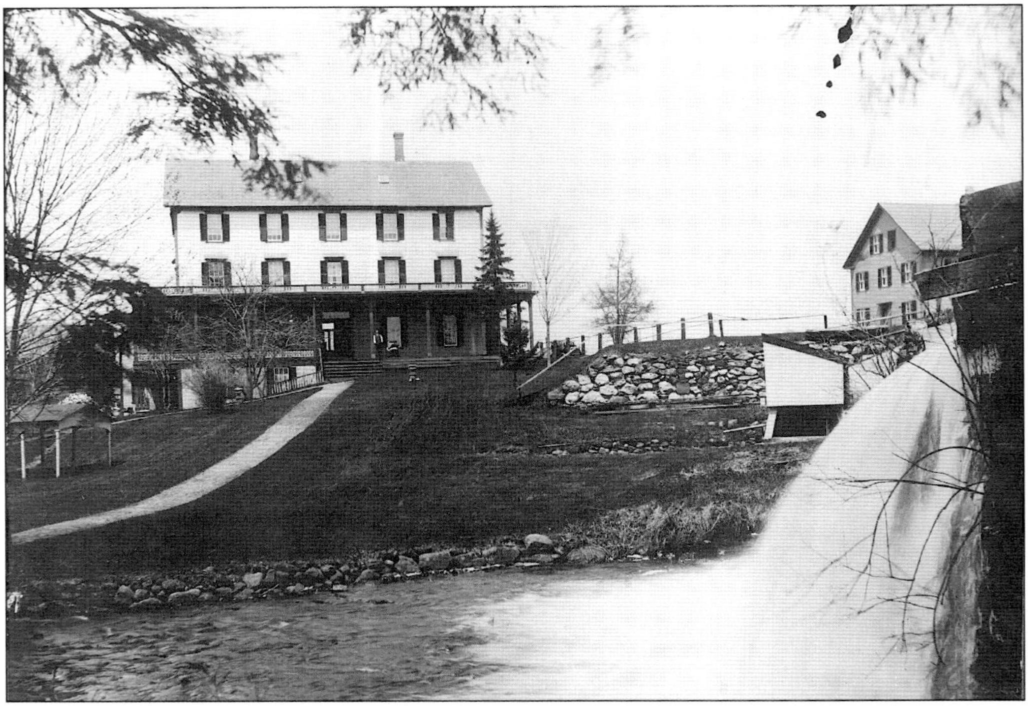

The front of the Coldbrook House shows the pathway leading to the springs where visitors enjoyed the "healing" waters. The building on the right once housed a bowling alley. It is said that while Ken Wilkins was walking across the bridge, he slipped and fell into the brook. He was not hurt in the mishap.

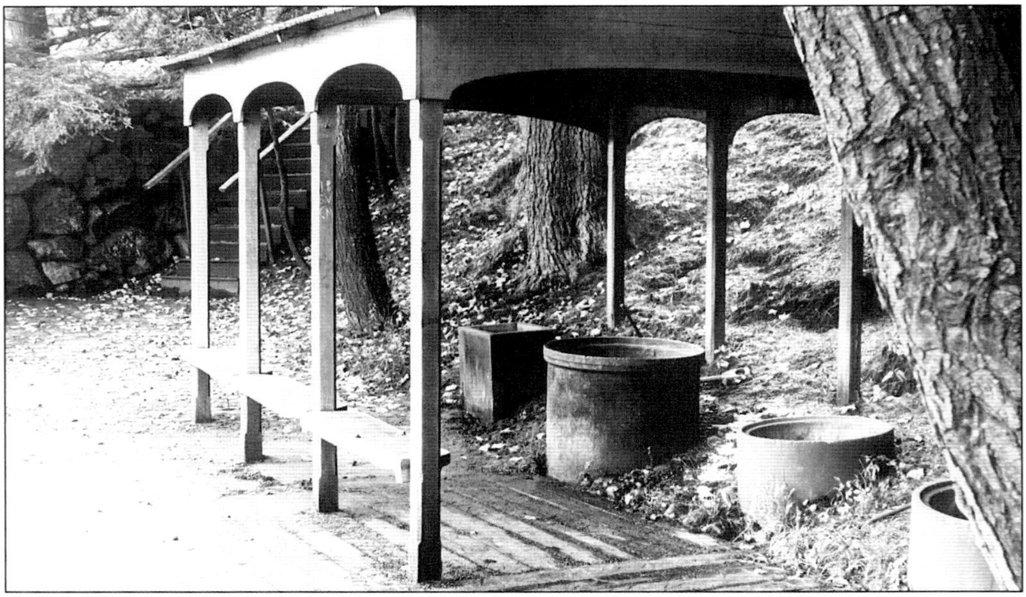

The popular "springs" of Coldbrook attracted tourists as early as 1873. Supposedly the water was used to treat a variety of diseases, particularly those diseases "peculiar to women."

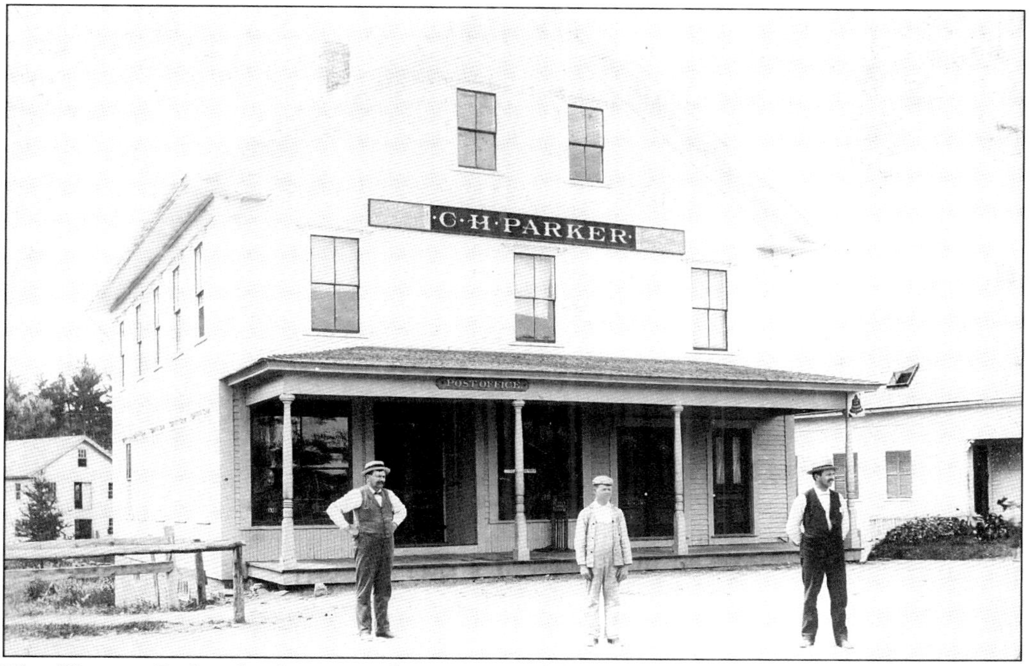

The Clarence Parker family operated a store in Coldbrook Springs for 40 years. Clarence Parker purchased the business in 1887 and his grandson Earle was the last of the family to operate the business, when it was sold to a Worcester company a few years before the village was taken over by the state. The Parker Store also housed the post office for the village of Coldbrook Springs, and in later years part of the Conant and Parker Telephone Company. Part of the basket shop is shown on the left, and a portion of Fred Ripka's home is on the right.

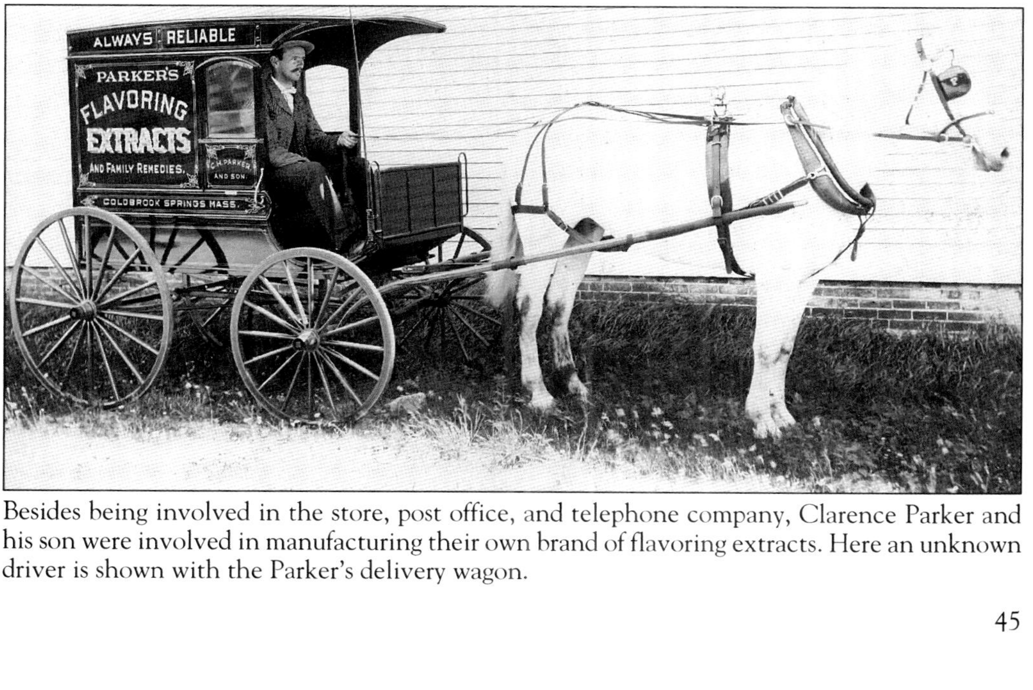

Besides being involved in the store, post office, and telephone company, Clarence Parker and his son were involved in manufacturing their own brand of flavoring extracts. Here an unknown driver is shown with the Parker's delivery wagon.

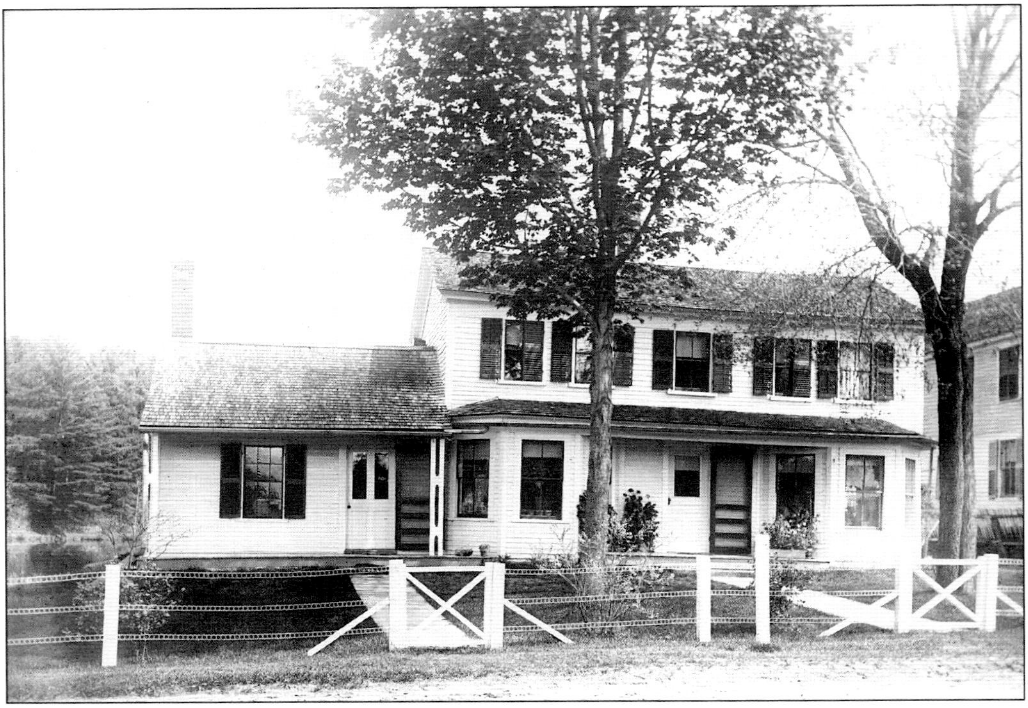

Pictured above is the Clarence H. Parker home in Coldbrook.

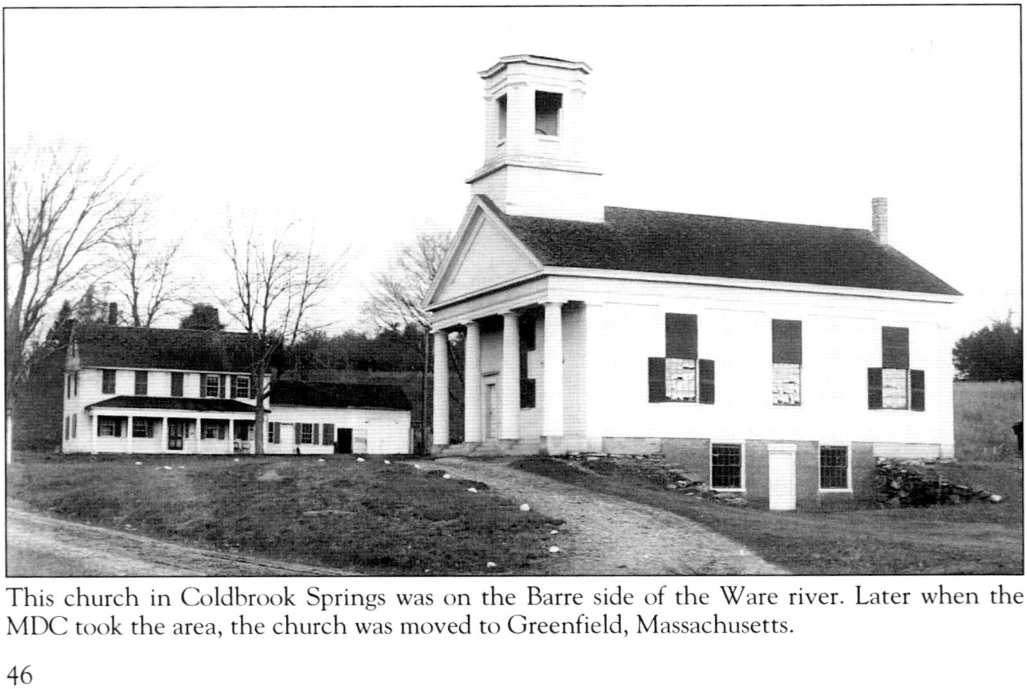

This church in Coldbrook Springs was on the Barre side of the Ware river. Later when the MDC took the area, the church was moved to Greenfield, Massachusetts.

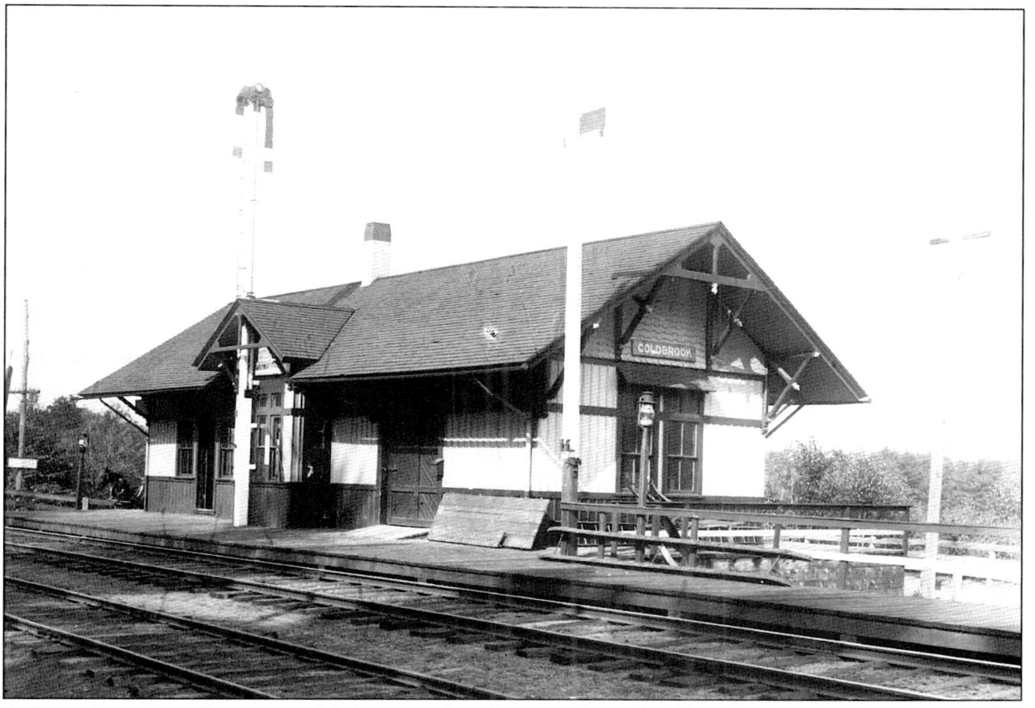

A branch of the Boston and Maine railroad opened in Coldbrook Springs in 1887. Trains were an important means of transportation in the late 1800s, carrying passengers and freight faster than the conventional stage. During the early years, eight trains a day passed through this station.

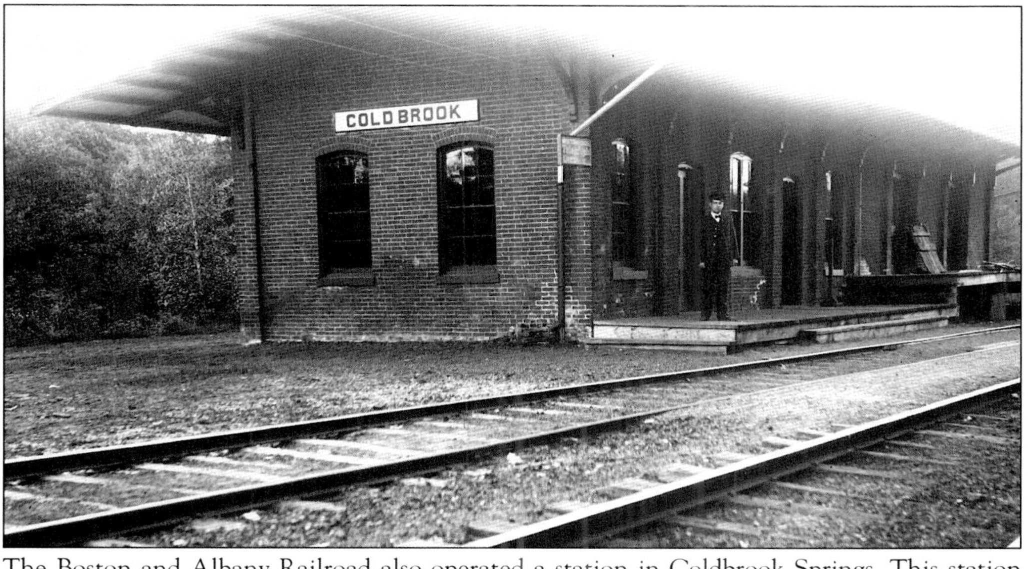

The Boston and Albany Railroad also operated a station in Coldbrook Springs. This station opened in 1873, providing mostly passenger service. The first station agent, James C. Bemis, served in that capacity for 28 years.

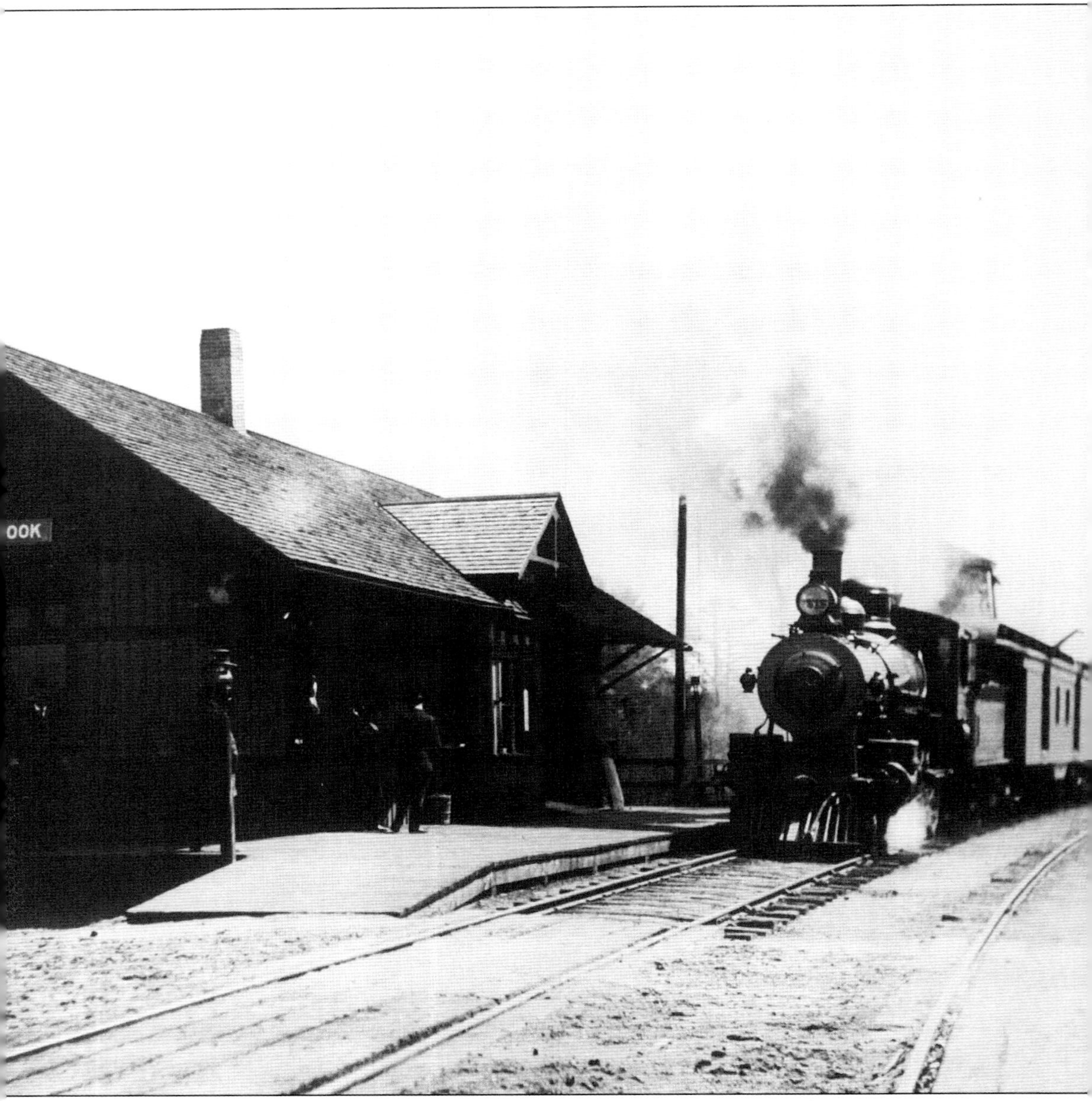

Another view of the B and M railroad station in Coldbrook Springs shows an engine coming in. This station was located on the road leading to Oakham Center, about one half mile south of the Coldbrook Village.

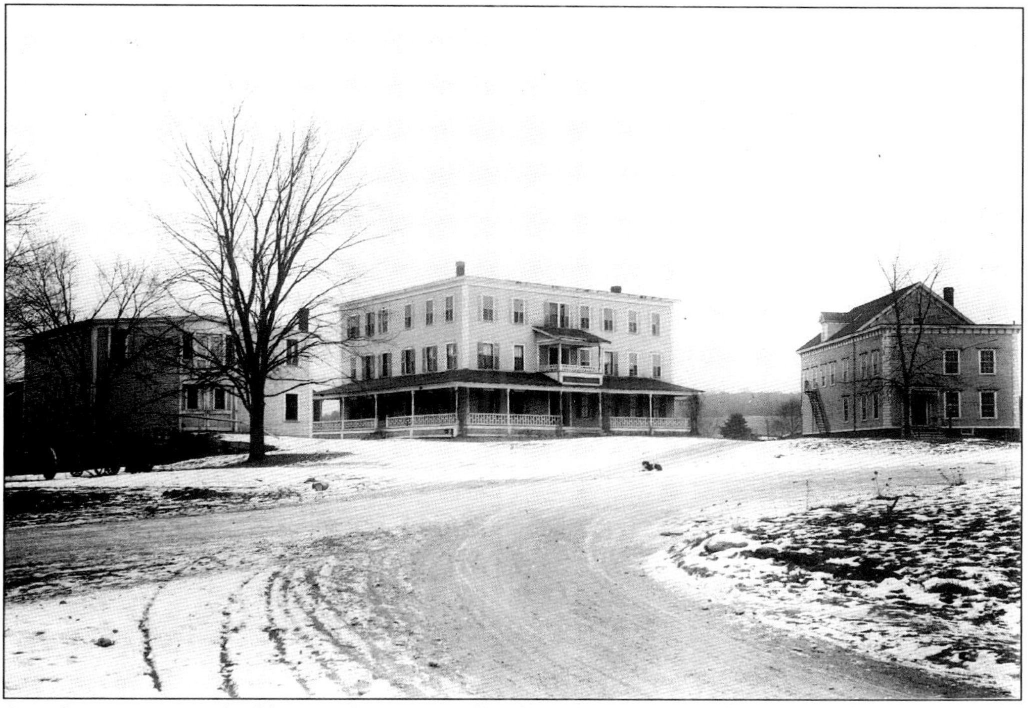

Another prominent building in the center of Coldbrook Springs was the Eagle Inn. The original inn was destroyed by fire in 1885, and was replaced with this building. To the left is a livery stable, operated by owners of the inn. Clark's, or Redmen's Hall, is on the right.

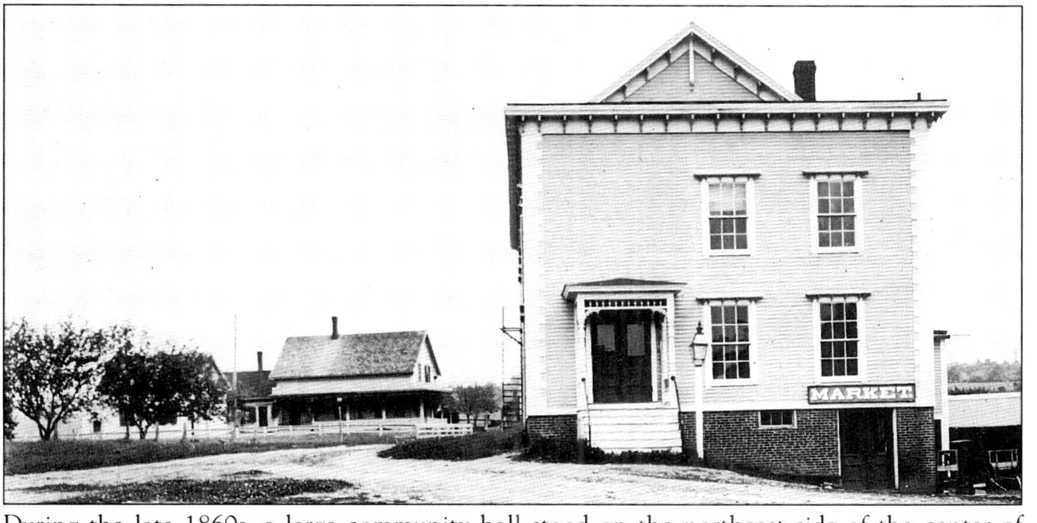

During the late 1860s, a large community hall stood on the northeast side of the center of Coldbrook Springs. When the hall was destroyed by fire in the early 1890s, the owner, Benjamin Clark, constructed this building in 1893. While Mr. Clark operated a market in the basement of the building he rented out the two upper floors to area organizations. During the early 1900s, the Wannanapan Tribe Number 141 of the International Order of Red Men purchased the building, which was used by local organizations for meetings, programs, and dances. Harry Parker's home is on the left.

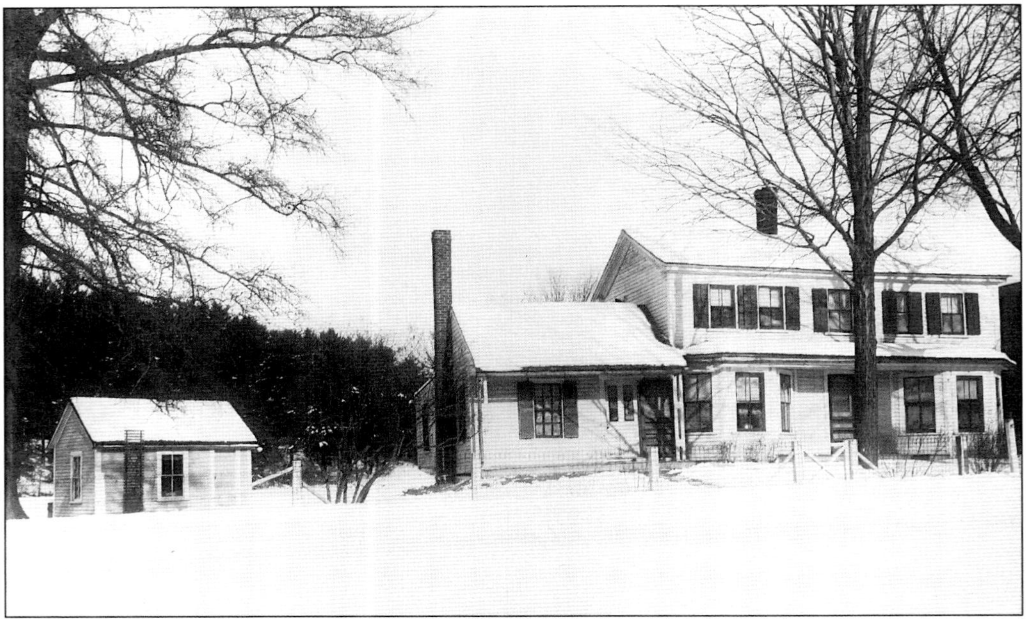

When first married, Earle and Eleanor Parker resided in the rooms upstairs from his grandfather's store. A few years later, Earle had this home built on the main road running through the village.

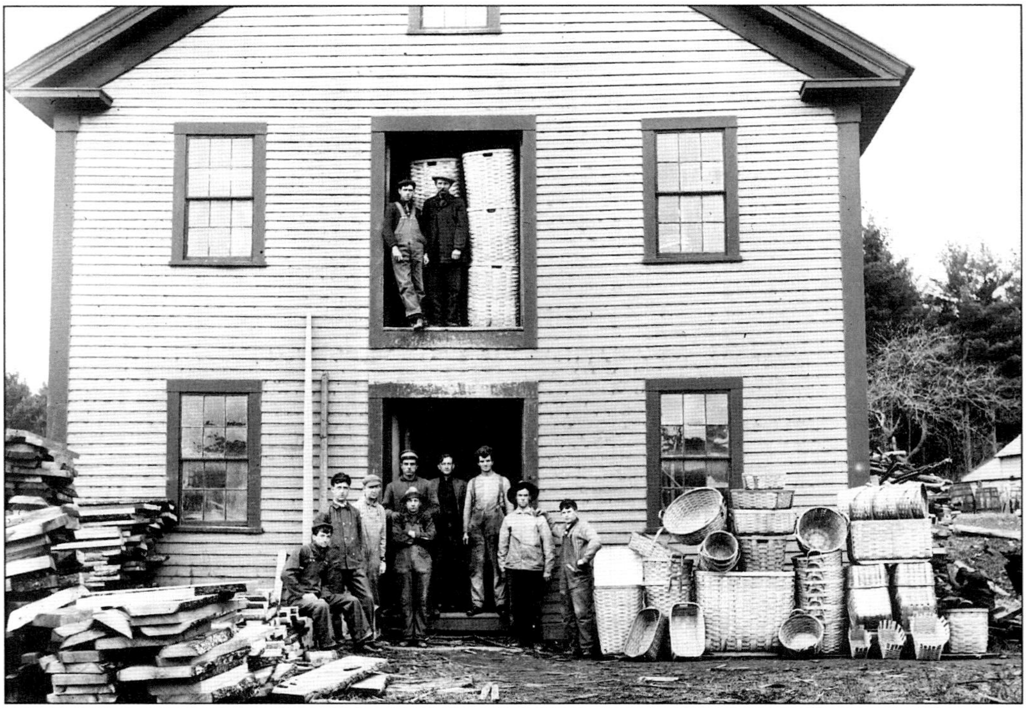

Using water for power near Muddy Pond, the Coldbrook Basket Company made baskets of all sizes and shapes. Providing employment for area residents, the mill manufactured baskets of white oak.

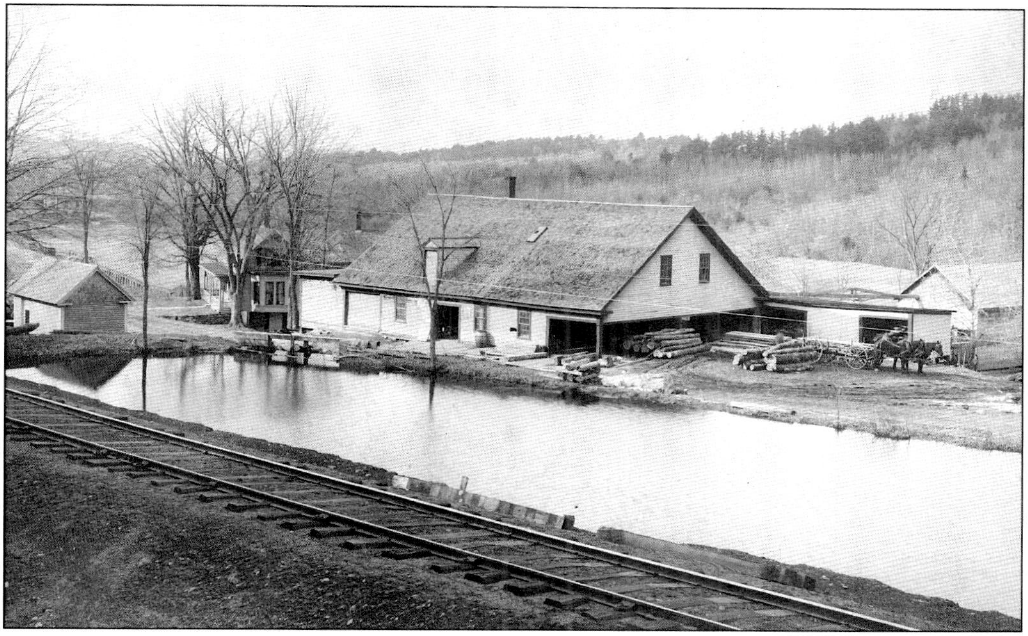

Providing lumber for nearby residents, the Parker Saw Mill was located off the main road leading to Worcester, just south of the Coldbrook House.

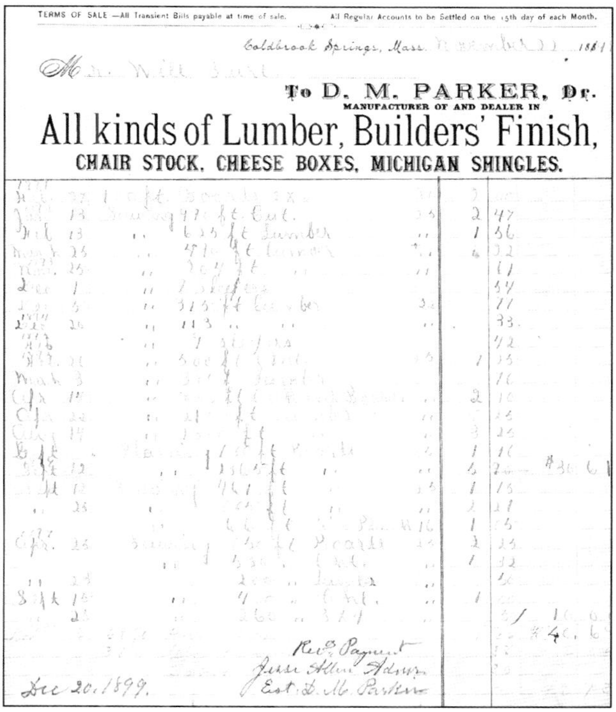

TERMS OF SALE —All Transient Bills payable at time of sale. All Regular Accounts to be Settled on the 15th day of each Month.

Coldbrook Springs, Mass. 189

M

To D. M. PARKER, Dr.

MANUFACTURER OF AND DEALER IN

All kinds of Lumber, Builders' Finish,

CHAIR STOCK, CHEESE BOXES, MICHIGAN SHINGLES.

This sales slip from Parker Sawmill, dated November 22, 1898, shows 100 feet of 2-by-6-foot boards sold for $2 and 850 feet of boards sawed for $2.25.

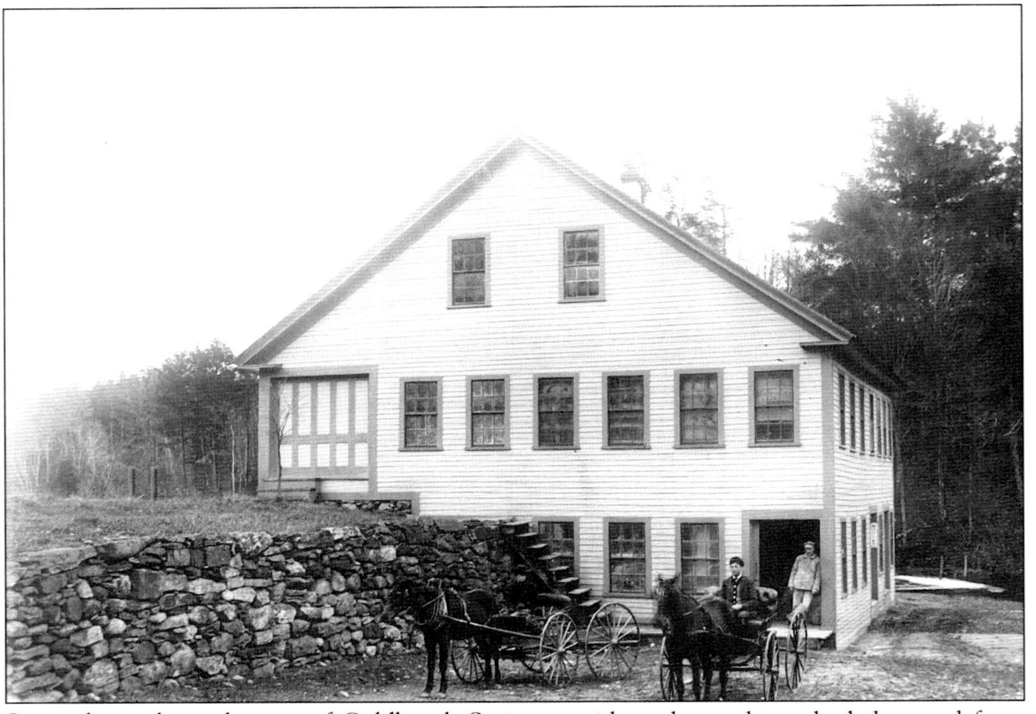

Since the early settlement of Coldbrook Springs, residents have always had the need for a gristmill in order to grind corn, rye, and wheat to feed family and livestock. This gristmill was located south of the Ware River.

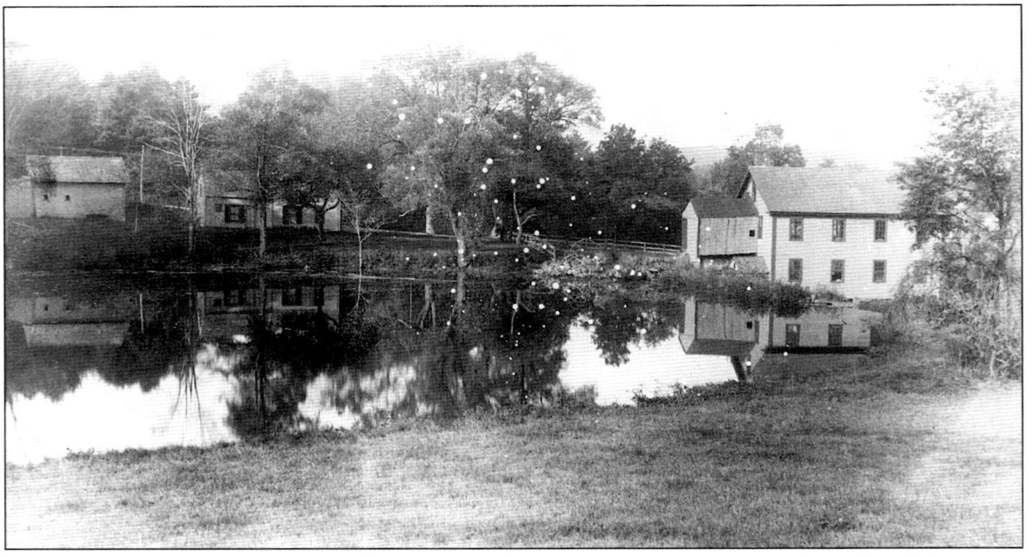

Providing an important source of energy, this brook, which empties into the Ware River, was dammed up to power the gristmill. It was common practice to dam brooks and rivers, and these man-made ponds were often dug with the assistance of hired help and oxen.

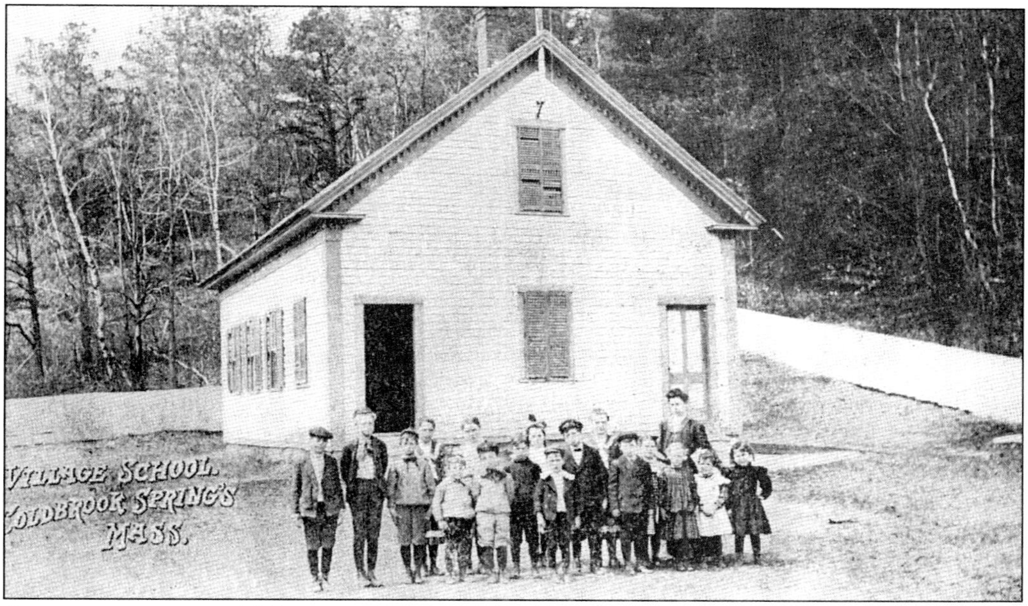

At a town meeting in 1768, a committee was chosen to divide the town into five school districts. District number five included the North Four Corners and the village of Coldbrook Springs. This schoolhouse was located on the main road leading from Barre to Worcester, south of the Coldbrook House Hotel. This school remained open until 1930, when the state took over the village for watershed purposes.

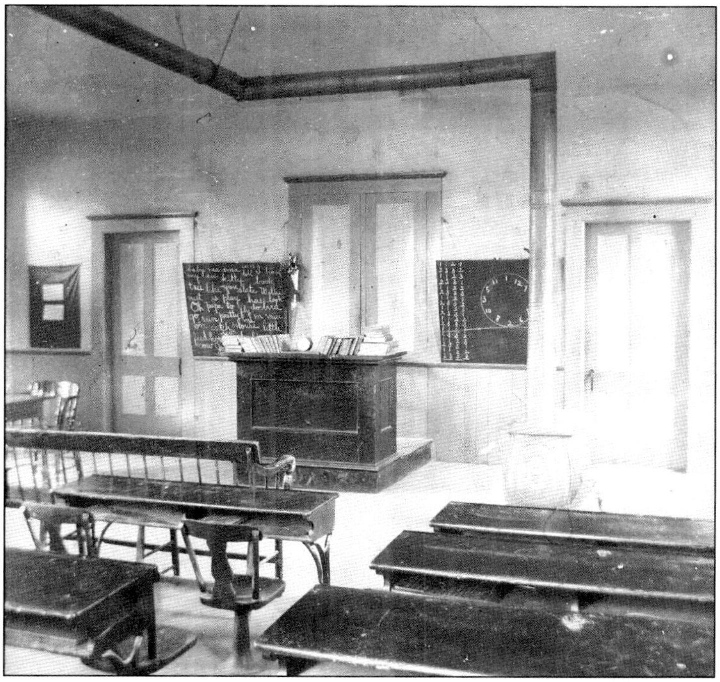

This early view of the interior of the Coldbrook Springs school shows the teacher's desk at the front of the room. During this time students shared desks. It is hard to believe that the small wood stove would radiate enough heat through the long chimney pipe to keep the children warm during their long hours of studying.

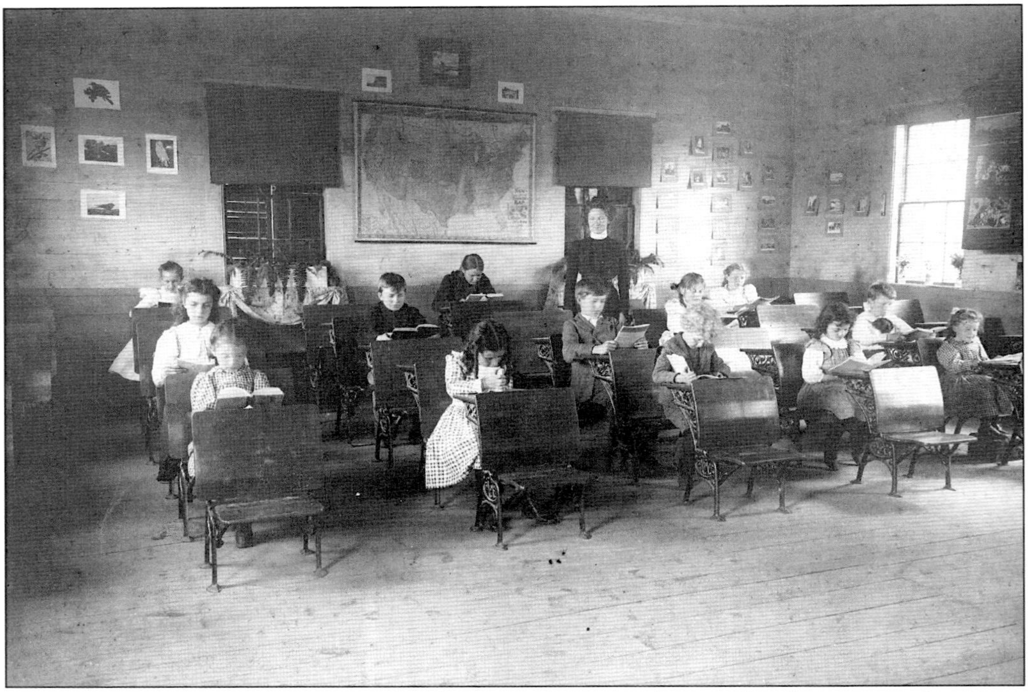

This more recent view of the same school shows a classroom decorated with a variety of teaching aids. Pictures of the birds on the left, a map of the United States, and individual desks for the students all helped to make this a more comfortable environment. With their teacher, Miss Minnie Mellen, looking over their shoulders, these unidentified students are hard at work.

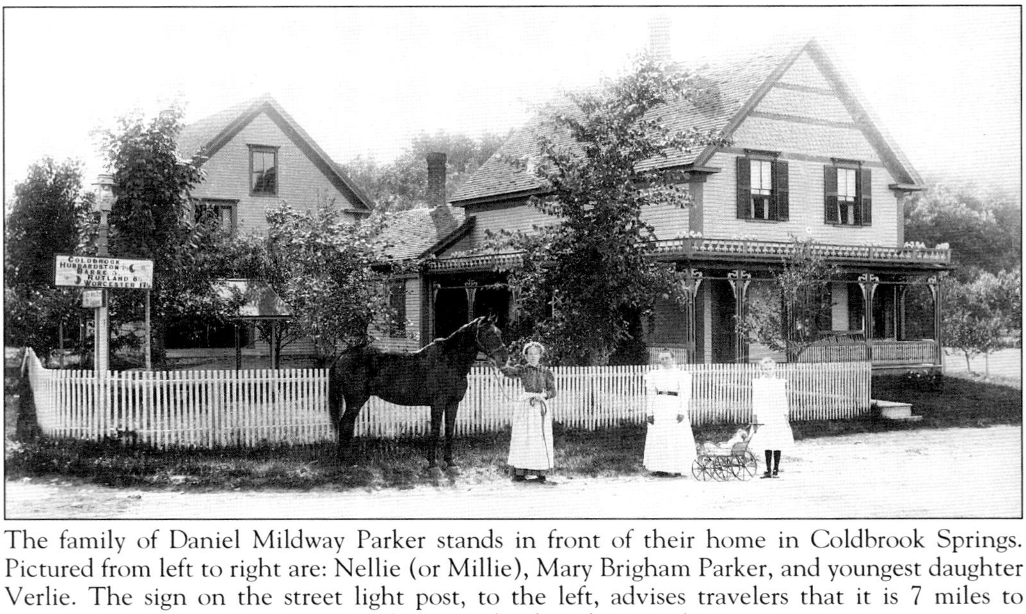

The family of Daniel Mildway Parker stands in front of their home in Coldbrook Springs. Pictured from left to right are: Nellie (or Millie), Mary Brigham Parker, and youngest daughter Verlie. The sign on the street light post, to the left, advises travelers that it is 7 miles to Hubbardston, 5 miles to Barre, 6 miles to Rutland, and 17.5 miles to Worcester.

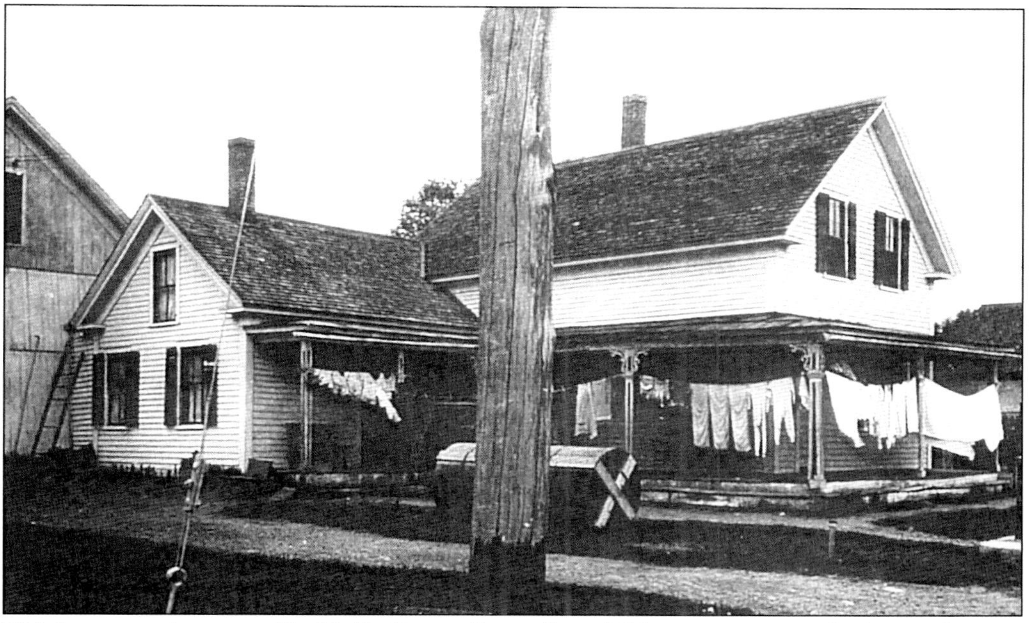

This house was last owned by Nellie Potter. Four of her children were among the last students to attend the Coldbrook Village School. They now have many descendants living in the Oakham-Barre area.

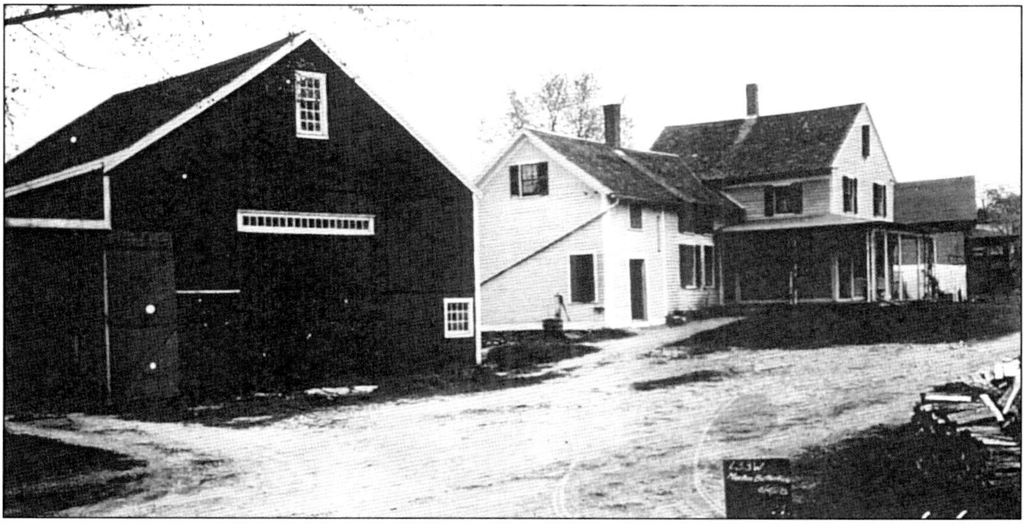

Located near the Parker Store, this home was purchased by Marcus Morton Butterfield at auction for the sum of $225.

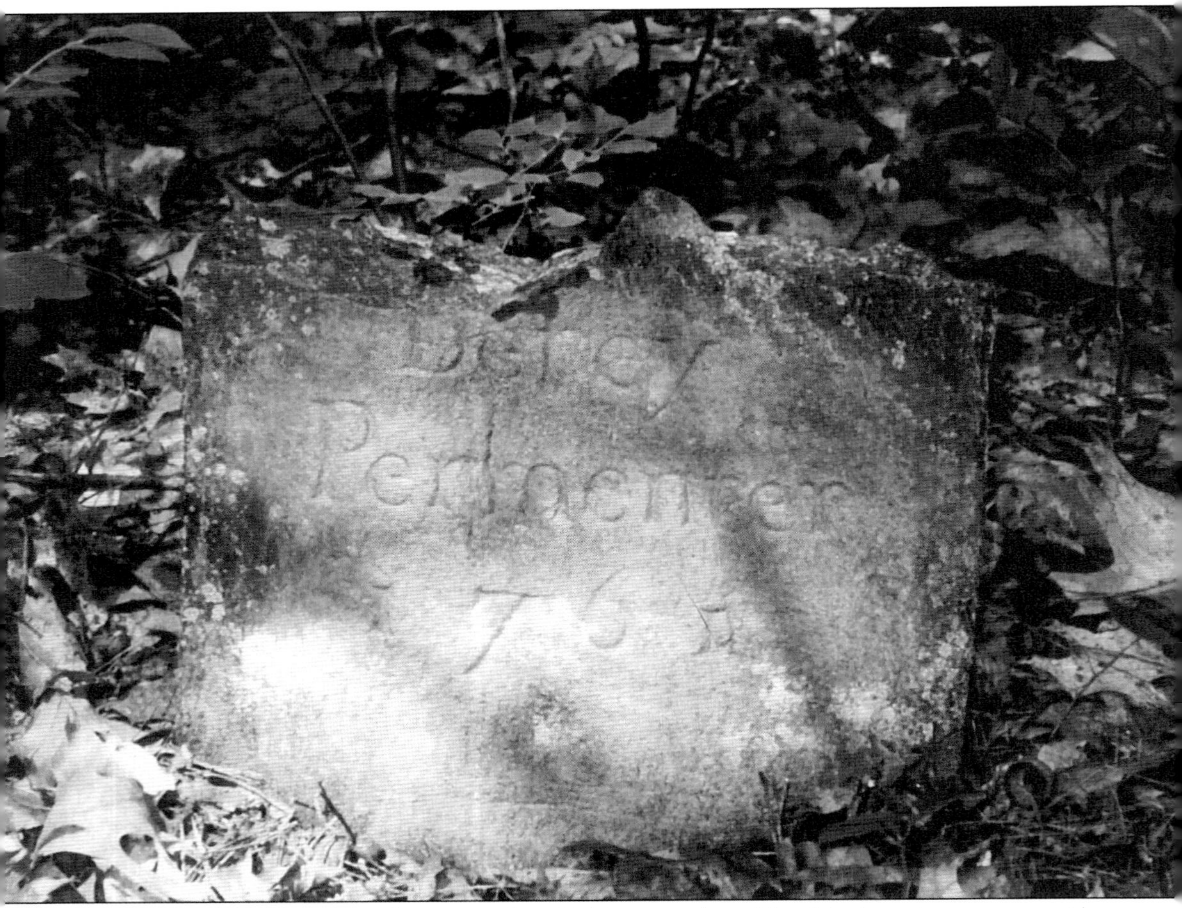

Shortly after the first settlers arrived in Oakham, a plot of land in lot nine was set aside as a burial ground. Betty Parmenter, daughter of Solomon and Elizabeth, was the first Oakham resident to be buried in town. As Betty's footstone shows, she died at the age of seven.

Three

Government and Schools

When the town was being formed, town meetings were held frequently—often two months apart—to decide the very basic questions of governing a town. By the year 1900, the manner by which the needs of the town would be addressed had been developed. Now there was an annual town meeting with an occasional "special" during the year.

The warrant for the town meeting of March 1900 had many of the same articles that we vote on each year when we go to the town meeting. In addition to those, the 136 voters who attended the annual town meeting of 1900 had three more decisions to make. They were asked for a "yes" or "no" vote in answer to the question, "Shall license be granted for the sale of intoxicating liquors in this town?" Article 20 was written "to see what measures the town will adopt in providing for a town seal." Article 22 asked to unite with other towns and hire a superintendent of schools.

Schools were very important to the people of Oakham. The town was incorporated in 1762. By 1769 a school was erected southeast of where the library now stands. This was before Ware Corner Road extended to the center of town. From that time until all students attended school in Memorial Hall, there had been 11 more schools for the education of the children of Oakham. These were:

1. Center School II—"off the common"
2. East Center—area of Tomlinson and Hapgood Roads
3. West Center—New Braintree Road
4. Old Southwest—Lincoln Road
5. Southwest—area of Lincoln and North Brookfield Roads
6. East Hill—East Hill Road
7. Old West—Old Turnpike Road
8. West Brick—still standing on Old Turnpike Road
9. North—area of North Brookfield and Rutland Roads
10. Old North—Coldbrook Springs village
11. North—Coldbrook Springs village

Treasurer's Report.

Dr.

To cash balance,	$1596 21	
Use of Town Hall,	31 50	
Sale of school supplies,	4 64	
J. Leyden, auctioneer's license,	2 00	
H. P. Austin, auctioneer's license,	2 00	
D. R. Dean, butcher's license,	1 00	
Borrowed from Worcester County Institution for Savings,	800 00	
Education state children,	46 50	
Mrs. Rugg, ashes,	2 00	
Matthew Walker, trial justice,	3 90	
Mortar, lime and hair,	4 15	
Transportation state children,	62 00	
High school tuition refunded,	65 50	
Mass. school fund,	559 18	
Tuition of Boston children,	108 00	
Corporation tax,	7 97	
National bank tax,	37 97	
State aid refunded,	256 00	
Dog tax refunded,	179 08	
Interest on bank deposits,	13 23	
Wm. S. Crawford, collector,	3892 67	
		$7675 50

Cr.

Paid by vote of the town,	$9 89	
By paying Selectmen's orders,	5906 86	
Cash on hand,	1758 75	
		$7675 50
Pine Grove cemetery trust fund (Rev. Geo. H. Gould),	$100 00	

Respectfully submitted,

JESSE ALLEN,

Treasurer.

Pictured above is the Treasurer's Report from the Annual Town Report fot the year 1900. The only thing in common between this fiscal year 1899 report and the anticipated expenditures of the Town of Oakham for fiscal year 1999 is the number seven. Whereas "they" spent $7,675.50 that year, we have a budget approaching $1.7 million. What a difference a hundred years makes.

TOWN OFFICERS FOR 1899.

TOWN CLERK:

JESSE ALLEN.

SELECTMEN:

C. H. PARKER, D. R. DEAN, JAMES LEYDEN.

ASSESSORS:

H. W. LINCOLN, S. H. BULLARD, WM. GAFFNEY.

OVERSEERS OF THE POOR:

JESSE ALLEN, WM. S. CRAWFORD, WM. S. SPEAR.

COLLECTOR:

WM. S. CRAWFORD.

TREASURER:

JESSE ALLEN.

CONSTABLES:

WM. S. CRAWFORD, W. R. DEAN,
H. P. AUSTIN, WM. GAFFNEY.

AUDITOR:

WALTER M. ROBINSON.

FENCE VIEWERS:

JESSE ALLEN, A. C. BULLARD, L. N. HASKELL.

SURVEYORS OF LUMBER:

D. R. DEAN.

As can be seen, our forbears devised a form of government that has served us well. To this day, we have the same offices conducting the town's business. Only the complexity of their positions and the rate of their compensation has changed.

6

Paid pens and holders,	$0 25	
Express on reports,	25	
Stamps, etc.,	1 00	
		$79 30

ASSESSORS.

Paid Assessors for services :		
H. W. Lincoln,	$32 50	
S. H. Bullard,	27 50	
Wm. Gaffney,	23 75	
Canvassing blanks,	1 50	
Printing reports,	16 25	
Postage,	3 00	
		104 .50

AUDITOR.

Paid auditor for services, Wm. M. Robinson,		15 00

SUPPORT OF PAUPERS.

Paid overseers of poor,		219 85

SCHOOL EXPENSE.

Paid school committee,		1885 63

STREET LAMPS.

Paid Charles Geoffrey,	$11 57	
F. S. Conant, oil,	1 55	
C. N. Ayres,	11 00	
		24 12

Coldbrook Springs.

Myron A. Butterfield,	10 50	
C. H. Parker & Son,	3 85	
		14 35

SUPERINTENDENT OF STREETS.

Paid W. A. Nye, highways,	$1000 00	
Opening roads,	778 15	
		1778 15

The sum of $219.85 paid for the support of paupers reflects the cost of $2.11 per week to have someone at the poor farm. The school expense of $1,885.63 covered the operation of six schools. The average salary for a teacher was $256. Fuel (wood) cost about $12 per year. The janitor received $10. The street lamps were kerosene lamps set upon poles. A person was hired to light them each evening and to extinguish them each morning. Mr. Nye, the superintendent of streets, received $321.95 of the $1,000 listed. Seventeen others shared $648.73 and supplies cost $29.32.

4

Polls.	Names. / Description of Property.	Tax.
1	Arnold, Russell	16 62
	2 horses 100, 1 cow 30, 1 two-year-old 20, house and barn 600, Fitts land 26a 250, homestead 1a 75.	
	Ayres, Miss Louisa.	Exempt.
	house and barn 400, house lot ½a 100.	
	Ayres, Miss Kate	3 40
	house 250.	
1	Ayres, John W.	10 50
	house and barn 400, homestead ½a 25, Coldbrook lot 1a 100, Macomber lot 11a 100.	
1	Austin, H. P.	2 00
1	Allen, James C	31 04
	1 horse 25, 7 cows 210, house and barn 1000, house lot 1a 300, homestead 15a 600.	
1	Bemis, James C	101 62
	3 horses 150, 1 cow 30, 2 swine 20, pony 25, 2 carriages 50, hotel, barn and shed, blacksmith shop and ice house 5000, slaughter house 300, Knights house and barn 850, homestead 13a 700, house lot ½a 100, Green lot 4a 100.	
1	Bothwell, Cheney	47 97
	2 horses 75, 4 cows 95, 5 two-year-olds 85, house, barn and shed 800, mill privilege 500, homestead 75a 1300, Partridge lot 40a 250, Clark lot 10a 125, Boyden lot 25a 150.	
1	Briggs, Geo. N.	118 42
	5 horses 375, 2 oxen 125, 25 cows 750, 7 two-year-olds 140, 2 one-year-olds 25, 1 bull 20, house, 3 barns and shop 1700, Bigelow house and barn 500, homestead 68a 3500, Knox lot 12a 325, Henry lot 6a 75, Drury lot 6a 250, Noyes lot 30a 400, Wilbur lot 5a 50, Bigelow house lot ½a 100, Ayres lot 1a 100, Corner lot 5a 125.	
1	Bullard, H. D.	2 21
	1 bicycle 15.	

This is a page from the Valuation and Taxes booklet for the year 1901. George N. Briggs was the largest taxpayer this year. He paid $118.42, for he owned two houses, four barns, a shop, five horses, two oxen, 35 cattle, and 133 acres. Times have changed. Bicycles were valued at $10 to $15. The men paid a poll tax of $2. The Evangelical Congregational Society paid a tax on their "parsonage, house and barn." It would appear that single women and widows were exempted from paying taxes on property valued up to $500, which often included their house and barn.

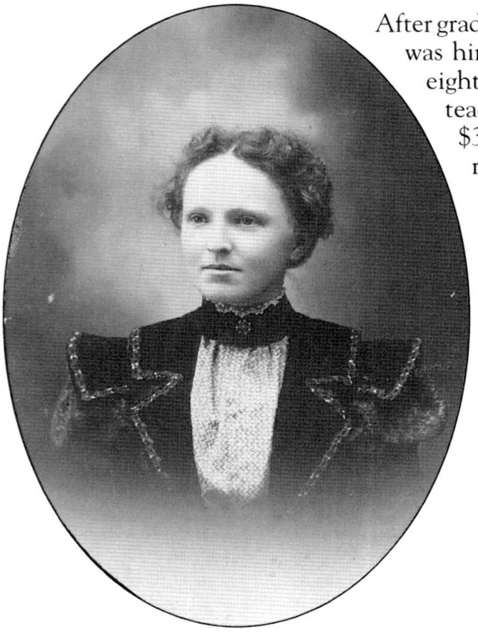

After graduating from high school in 1896, Florence Bothwell was hired to teach grammar school (grades five through eight) at the school in Memorial Hall. She began her teaching career the fall of 1897. In 1900 she received $320 for teaching that school year. Many in town remember her well, for she taught each year until her retirement in 1949.

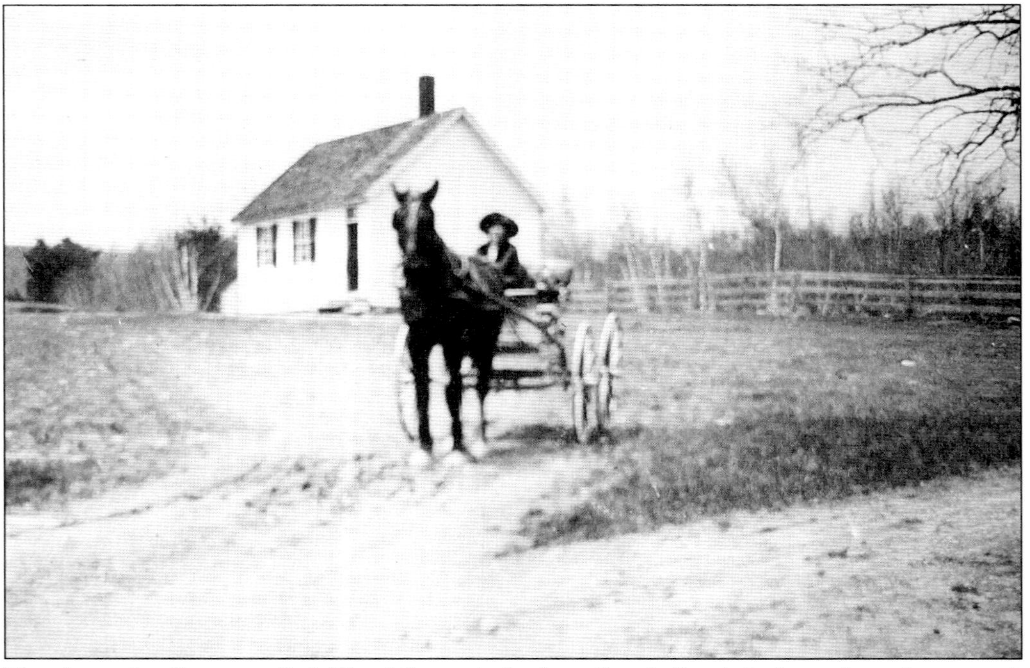

The first schoolhouse called "South" was indeed on South Road. It burned to the ground, becoming the first, and fortunately the last, schoolhouse to burn in the town of Oakham. Its replacement, pictured here, was built on the land of Cheney Bothwell at the intersection of Lincoln and North Brookfield Roads. According to the Town Report for 1899, it cost $11 to heat and $9.05 to care for the house that year.

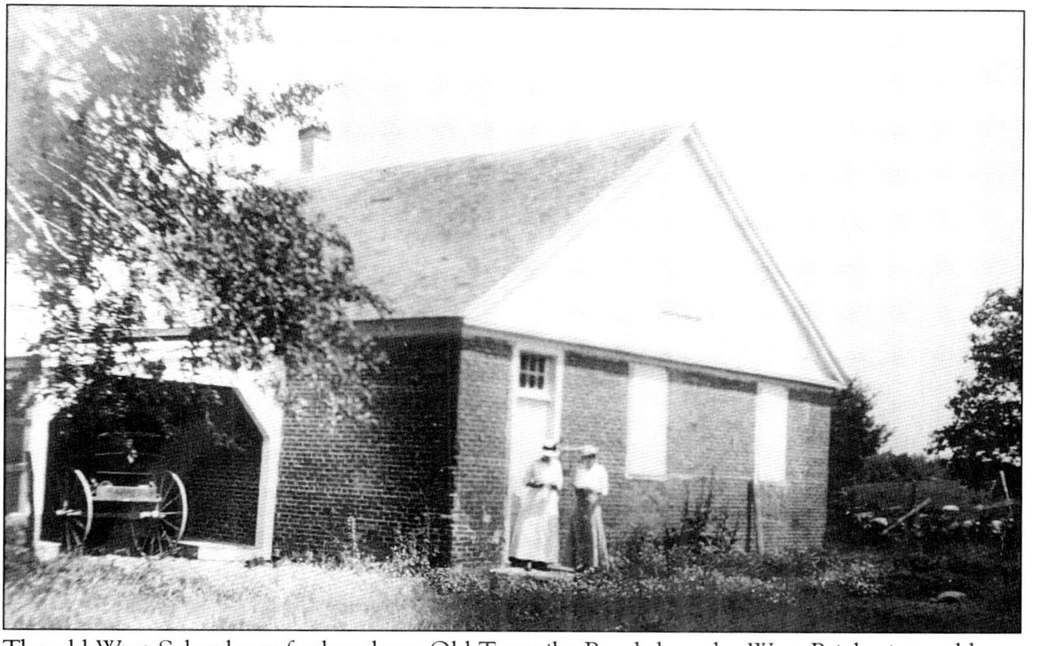

The old West School was farther down Old Turnpike Road than the West Brick pictured here. Old West was on the opposite side of the road beyond the Scott Road intersection. The school committee of 1851 said of the west district, "it is presumed they will not long remain without as good a schoolhouse as any other." The 1853 report mentions, " . . . a good schoolhouse much to the credit of the west district." It was during this time that the brick schoolhouse was constructed. In 1918, with only 11 children attending, it was recommended that the school be closed. It closed in June 1920. The West Brick has survived to this day as it was when first built.

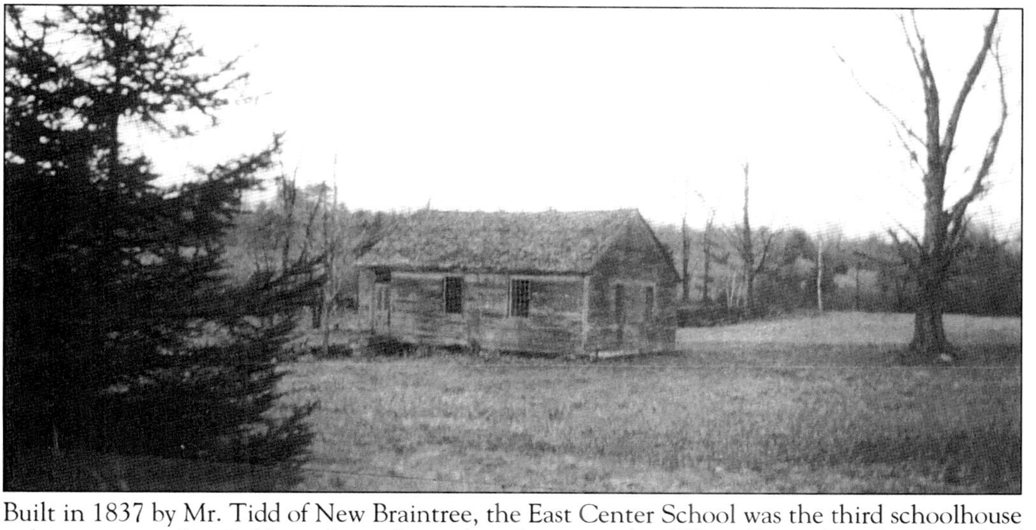

Built in 1837 by Mr. Tidd of New Braintree, the East Center School was the third schoolhouse to be constructed in Oakham. It was located on the west side of Ware Corner Road and north of Tomlinson Road. When first opened, Sullivan Dean was the teacher. There were 58 students. Other teachers were J. Haskell Allen, Leonard P. Lovell, Henry P. Wright, and Lizzie J. Bullard. The school closed in 1875 when the school rooms in the newly constructed Memorial Hall became available.

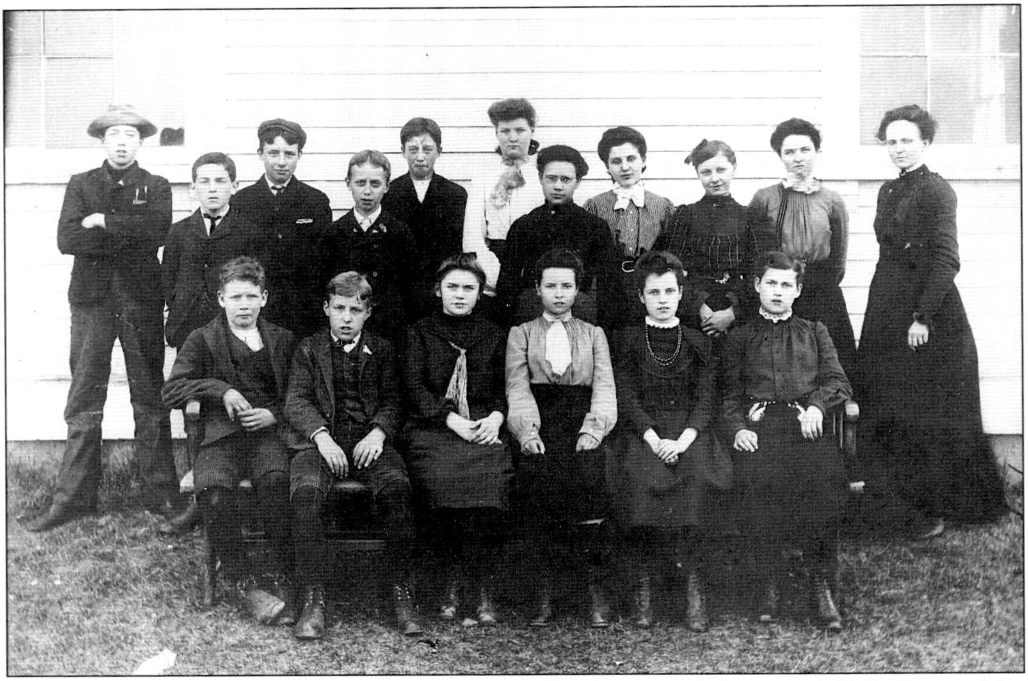

Florence Bothwell is the teacher in this photograph taken outside Memorial Hall. Some of the family names may be familiar to you: Angier, Burt, Clifford, Conant, Dean, Dexter, Draper, Duncan, Loring, Mader, O'Donnell, and Thrasher.

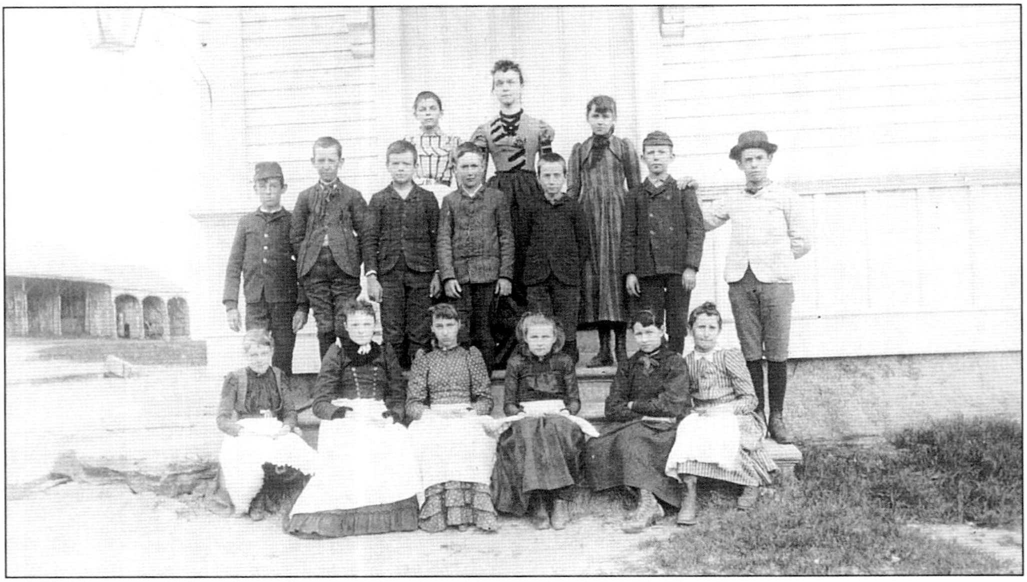

Taken around 1892, this picture is evidence that "times" were changing. Some skirts are floor length—others are shorter. A few boys have long pants—others knee length. Regardless of which length skirt, the girls wore high laced shoes. To the left of the school, notice the carriage sheds.

Four

Recreation

In the late 1800s people began to have more free time. At that time though, people needed to provide for their own entertainment, since this was before the advent of radio, television, movies, professional sports, etc. The people of Oakham entertained themselves through such activities as music, the theater, and baseball.

Baseball, the "national pastime," received that nickname not due to the number of fans the professional leagues attracted, but because each town and village had its own team. Oakham had its own baseball team. The players were residents of the town, and they played teams from Rutland, Spencer, Barre, and North Brookfield. Spectators were charged admission, from which the visiting team received their agreed upon share, which was used for equipment and travel.

Those interested in the theater formed groups that produced plays, the most notable being the Oakham Dramatic Club. These groups worked many hours creating sets and costumes and rehearsing for shows that most often were only presented once or twice. Memorial Hall was used as the theater.

The musically inclined residents joined bands, often sponsored by a prosperous businessman. Thus we had Packard's Brass Band and Crawford's Cornet Band, and later the Oakham Cornet Band. These bands were prominently featured at the Field Day exercises as well as other parades.

The Field Day programs were organized by the Oakham Village Improvement Society and began in the 1890s. These events were well attended by residents of Oakham and surrounding towns. The programs had a very full schedule from morning until evening and included all of the activities mentioned above—bands in the parade, baseball in the afternoon, and plays during the evening.

So, although today we have many more entertainment outlets available, we may have lost some of the community spirit that existed one hundred years ago.

Sixth Field Day, Oakham Village Improvement Society,

Wednesday, Aug. 23, 1899.

OFFICIAL PROGRAM

10.00 A. M. ——GRAND PARADE, forming as follows:

Chief Marshall and Aids,
Packard's Brass Band.

DIVISION I, "War."

Armed and mounted Rough Riders,
Aguinaldo and Filipinos,
Filipino Light Artillery,
Collection of Captured Animals.

DIVISION II, "Peace"

Coaches and Decorated Teams,
Decorated Floats,
Trades Procession,

DIVISION III,

Grand Miscellaneous Affair,
Happy Family,
Antiques and Horribles

11.00 — Charge of Rough Riders on Insurgent Block House on the Common.

SYNOPSIS. Gathering of Filipinos–Proclamation by Aguinaldo–Camp scene–Approach of Rough Riders Scouts—Their capture–War Dance by Filipinos about the prisoner–First charge of the Rough Riders–The repulse–Final charge of the Rough Riders and capture of the blockhouse. – Old Glory swing to the breeze.

11.45–Awarding of the prizes for the best decorated coaches from the Grand Stand. Singing, by Sunbonnet Chorus.

12 M.–2P. M –Dinner in vestry of church.
50 cents per plate, Children, 25 cents.

1.00–6.00 P. M. continuous High class Vaudeville Performance in Memorial Hall by the Alabama Minstrels and Cake Walk Company, Management of Irving Mullett.
Admission, 15 cents. Children, 10 cents.
Introducing the following attractions:

ALABAMA MINSTRELS,
in their new and original First Part. New songs and jokes.

BILLY WEEKS,
the daring slack wire walker, introducing his latest and thrilling balancing act.

PAT CARNEY,
Banjo Comique, in his popular comic and musical acts.

HENRY CUMMINGS,
Accordian Soloist.

MRS. MAMIE BOYD,
the sweet voiced singer, in new songs.

ROLAND DAVIS,
Boy Vocalist.

MISS RUTH BRIGGS,
the popular ballard singer.

ASHOD & LORING,
"the Dago and the Dutchman'
in an eccentric comedy sketch.

GREEN & REED,
Musical Artists.

Our Big Feauture. The cream of the profession in a genuine

CAKE WALK,
Black Diamond, leader .Introducing new steps and pleasing novelties. Don't miss it. This feature alone is worth the price of admission. Watch for Little Gracie, the Child Cake Walker,

NYE & MULLETT,
End Men and Cake Walkers.

Part of the program for the Sixth Field Day was held in 1899 and was organized by the Oakham Village Improvement Society. Events began at 10 a.m. and continued through the evening with time out for dinner and supper. There was a "Charge of the Rough Riders" exhibition at 11 a.m., 1899 being the year after the Spanish-American War. Notice the athletic events and baseball game, along with the afternoon entertainment and play at 8 p.m.

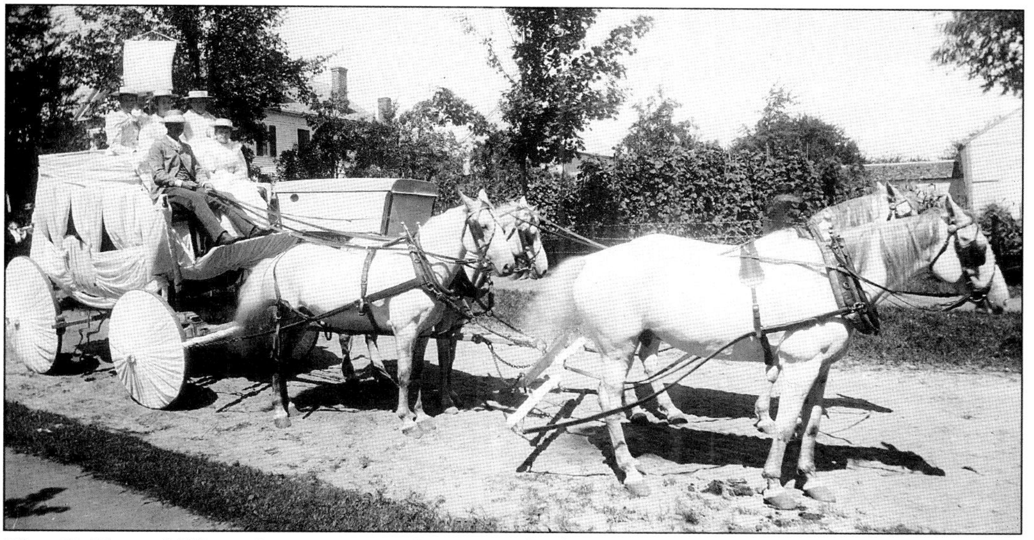

The Oakham Village Improvement Society, which organized the Field Day exercises, also supplied a float for the parade. The Oakham Village Improvement Society was formed in 1891 for the sole purpose of beautifying the streets in Oakham. The Field Day exercises were used as a fund-raiser by the society, which spent much of the proceeds in building and repairing sidewalks in town.

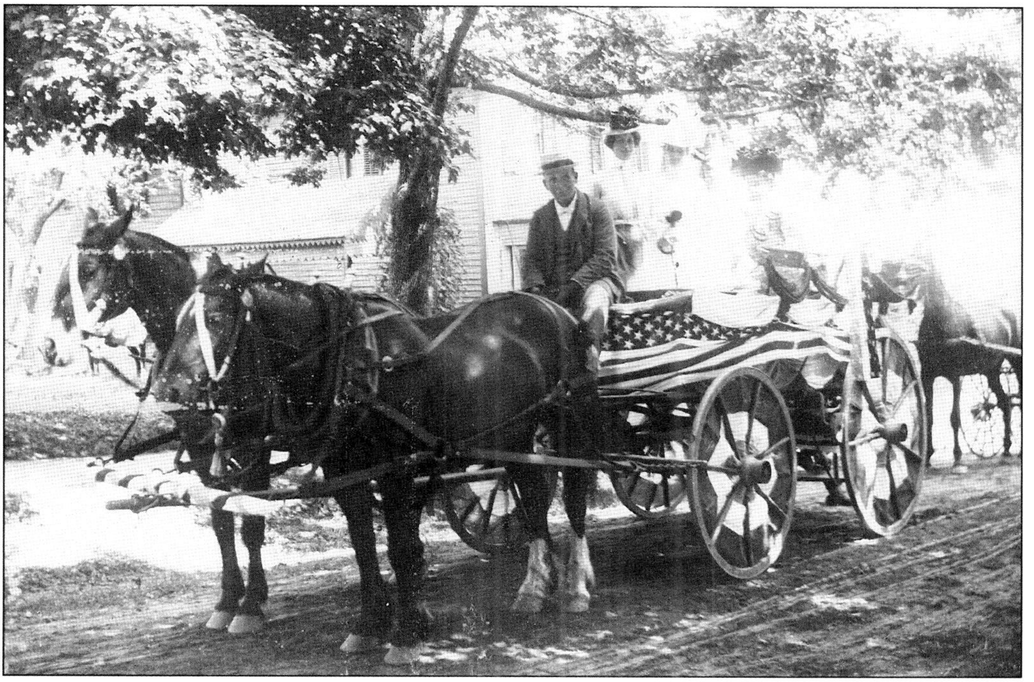

One of the parade floats in the Field Day parade of August 1900 is shown here. The driver is Sylvester Haskell of Oakham. The other occupants of the wagon are Jennie Woodruff, Martha Abbott, Alice Allen, Lora Wilbur, Ruth Prouty, Grace Wilbur, Lou Wilbur, and Elizabeth Brown.

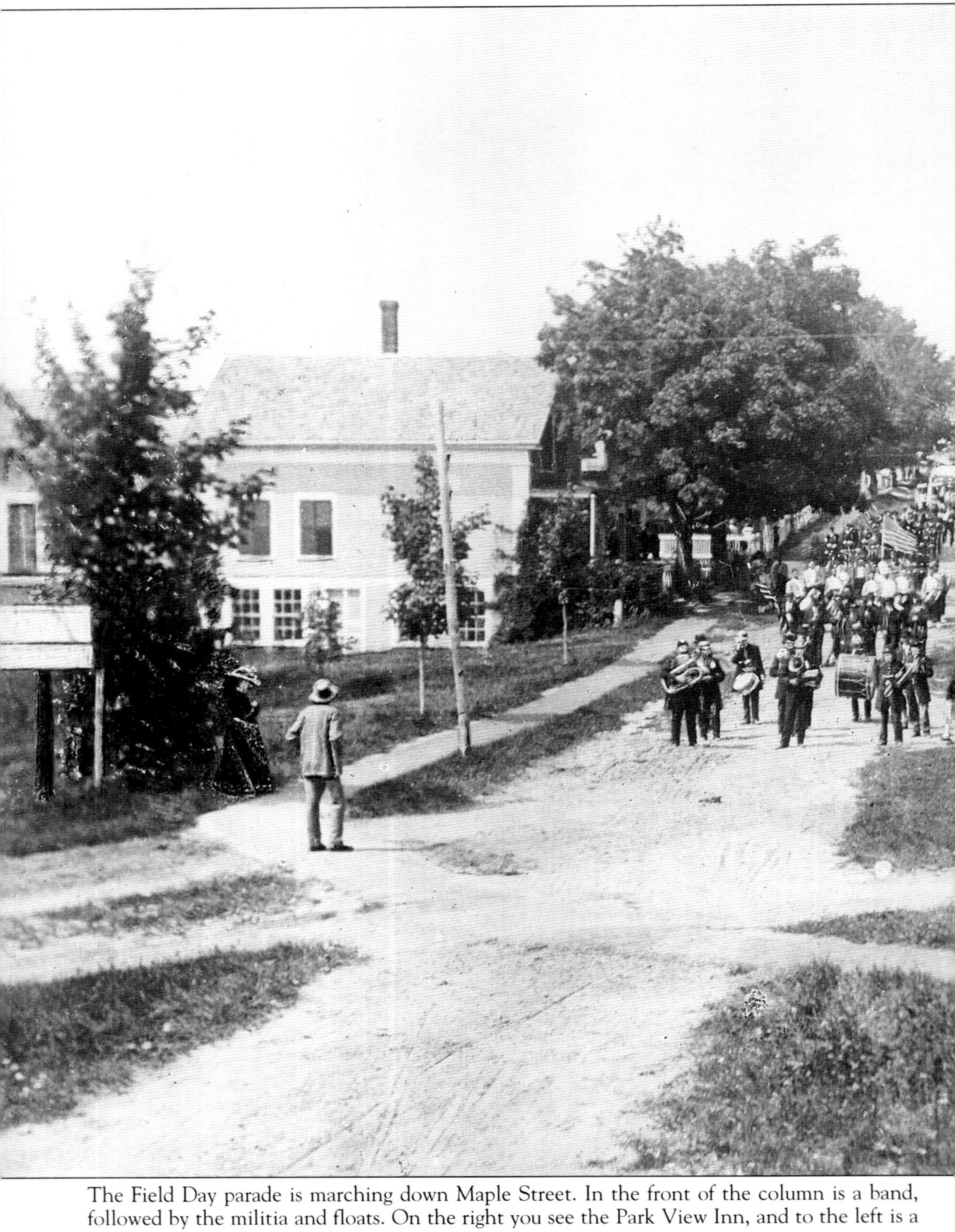

The Field Day parade is marching down Maple Street. In the front of the column is a band, followed by the militia and floats. On the right you see the Park View Inn, and to the left is a

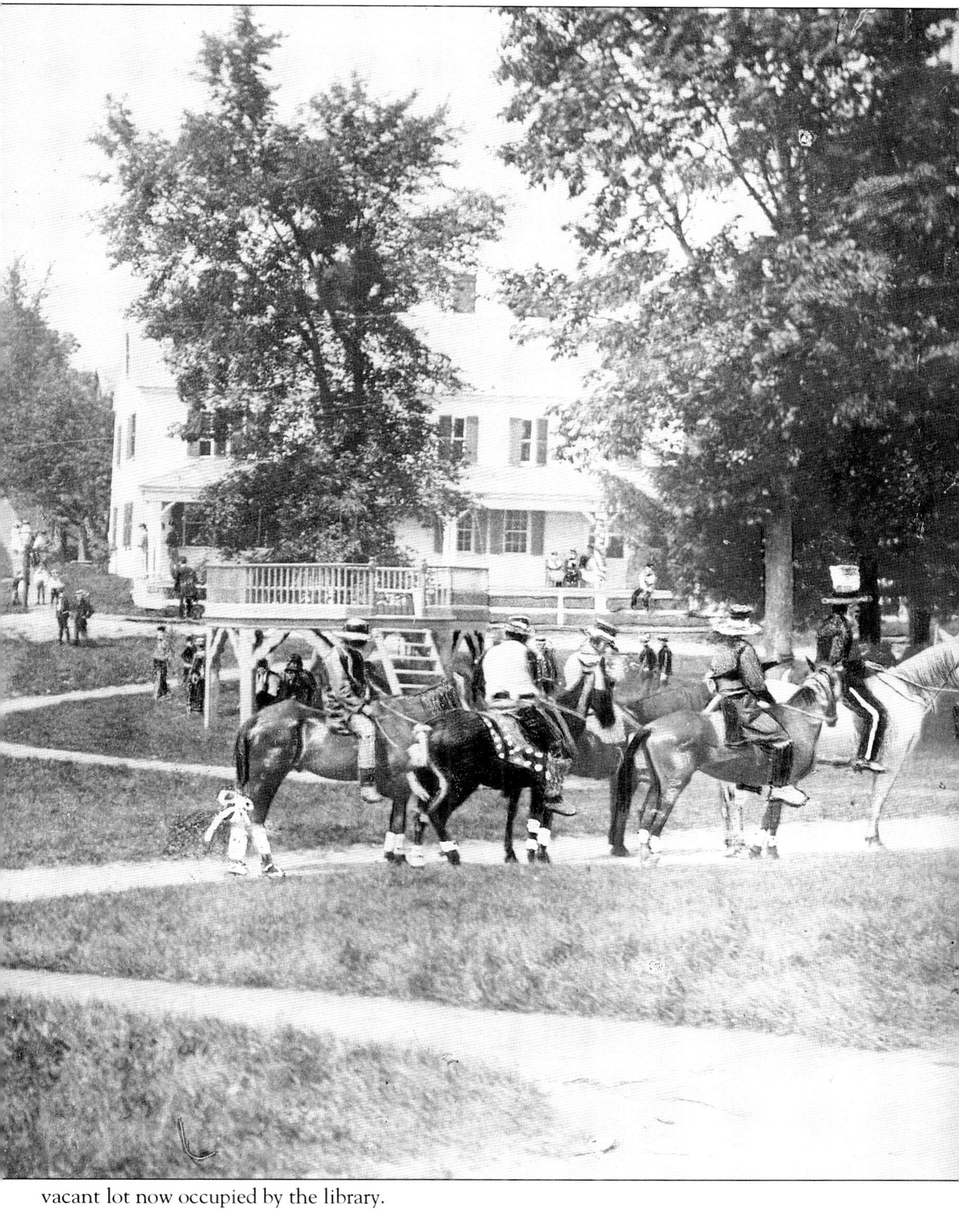

vacant lot now occupied by the library.

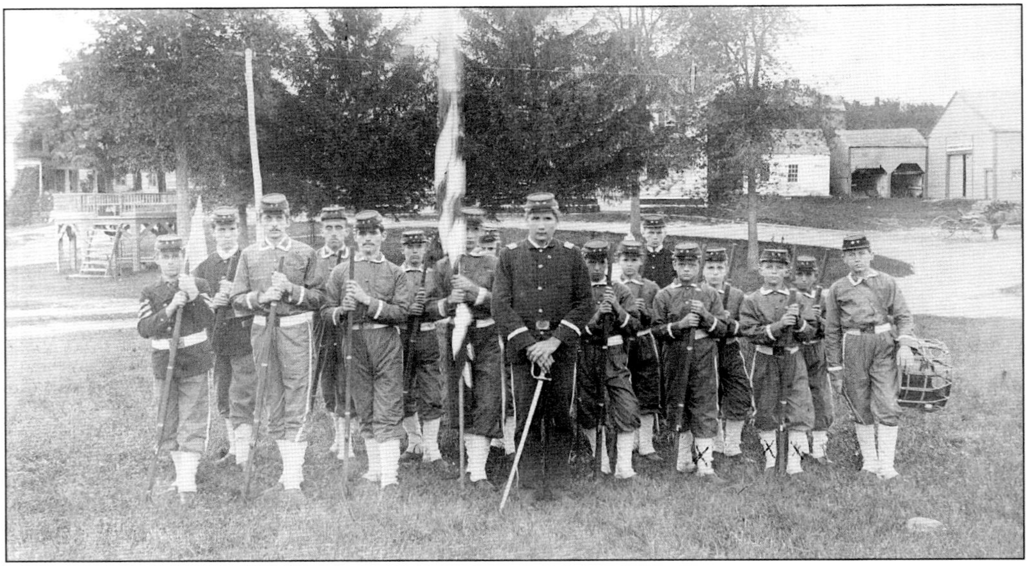

A squad of military cadets poses during their preparations for a Field Day parade.

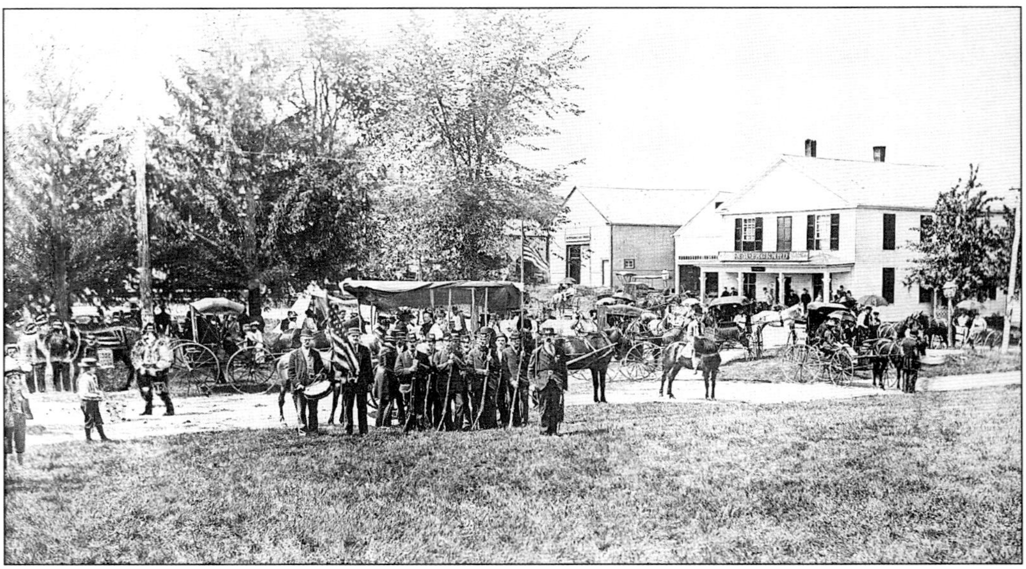

This is a scene from a Field Day celebration. Pictured in the foreground is the militia. Some of the spectators are also shown, along with their carriages in the background. These events attracted hundreds of spectators from Oakham and many of the surrounding towns.

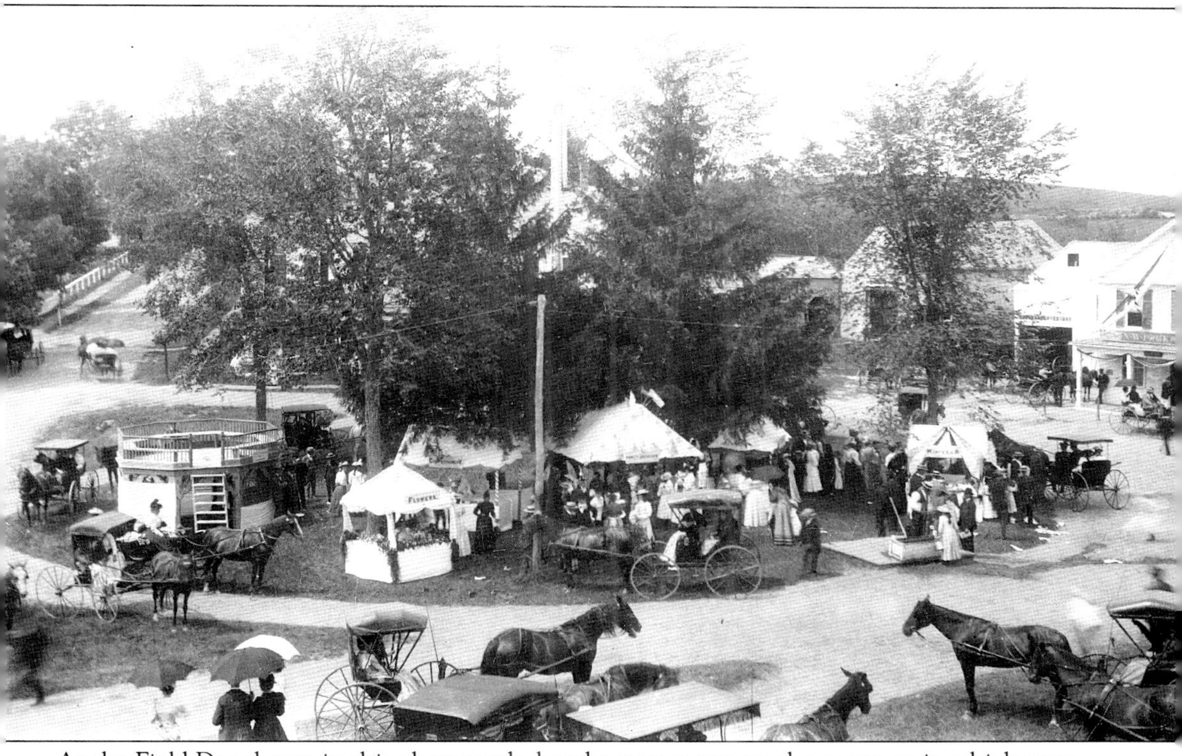

At the Field Day shown in this photograph, booths were set up on the common in which were sold peanuts, candy, fancy articles, mysteries, cake, flowers, light drinks, and ice cream. The proceeds from the sale of these items went to the Oakham Village Improvement Society.

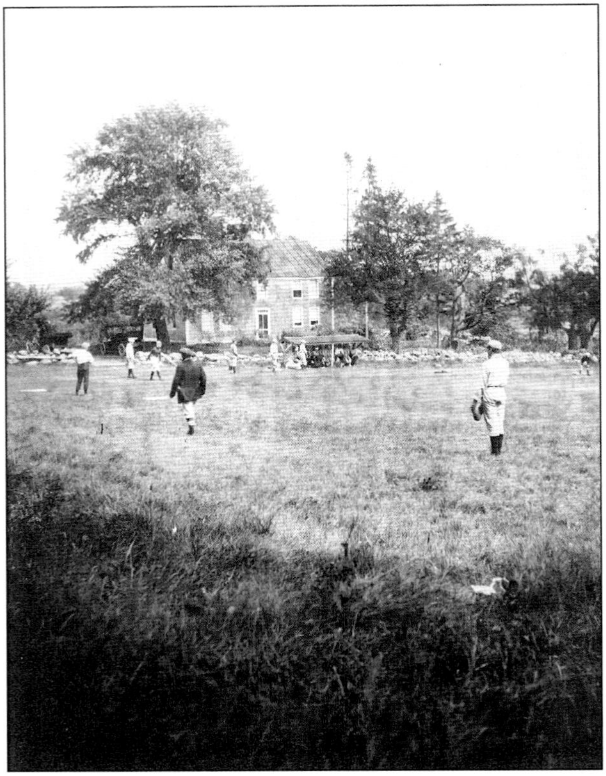

Baseball was a popular game at the time, and many towns had their own teams, including Oakham. The ball field was located in the field just west of the Tomlinson house, which can be seen in the background. Spectators were charged admission, which was shared between the visiting and home teams and used to pay for the team's expenses.

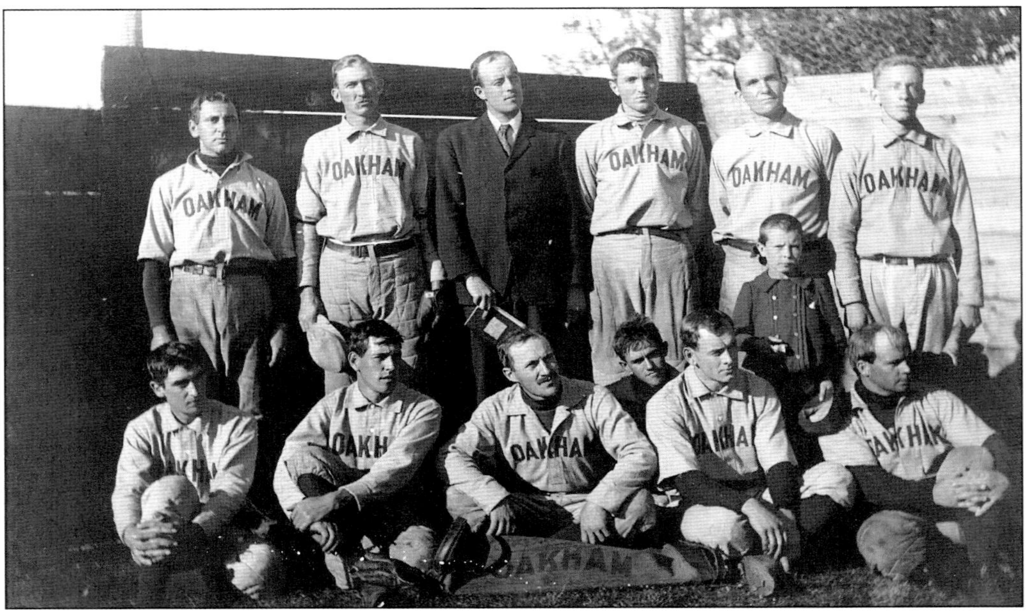

Oakham's baseball team is pictured here around the year 1905, complete with uniforms. From left to right are: (front row) H. Grimes, F Caldwell, A. Angus, C. Grimes, B. Needham, and B. Reed; (back row) ? Geoffrey, W. Woodis, E. Harvey, unknown, H.B. Wright, and B. Malcolm.

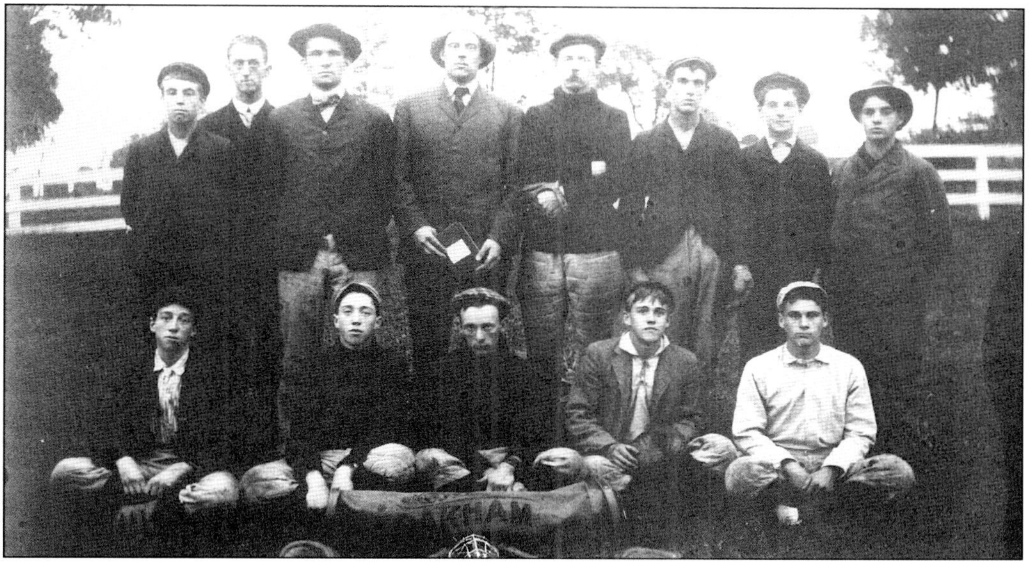
One of Oakham's early baseball teams is pictured here, probably in the late 1890s. It appears the team did not have uniforms yet, although they have some equipment and an equipment bag.

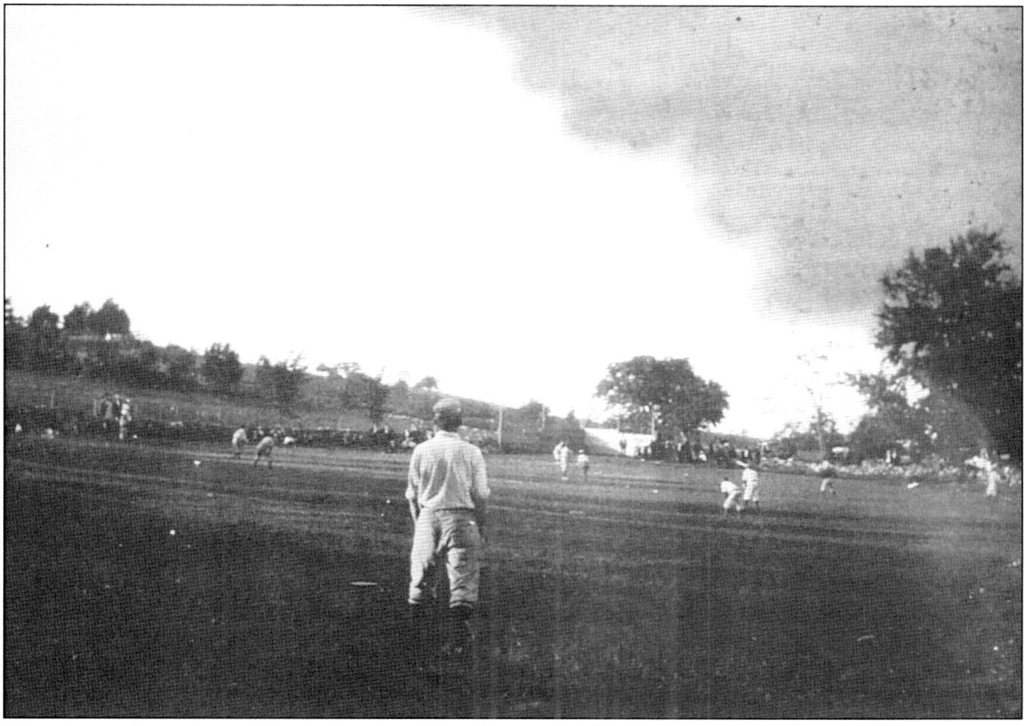
Here is another view of the ballpark at Tomlinson field, looking toward Black's hill.

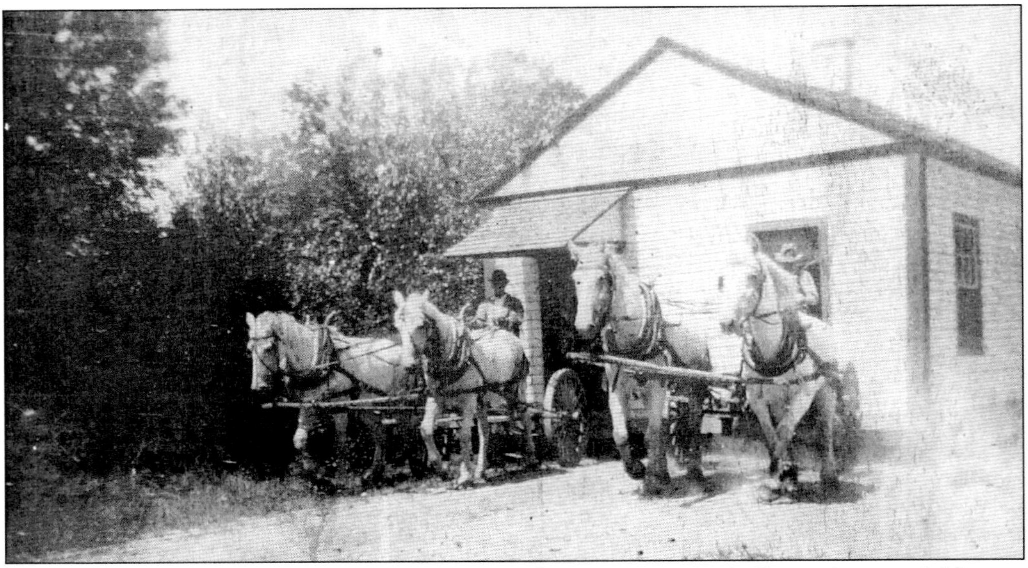

Roy Burt (left) and Charles Clifford are shown here moving the ball team's new clubhouse, formerly a school, down to the ballpark.

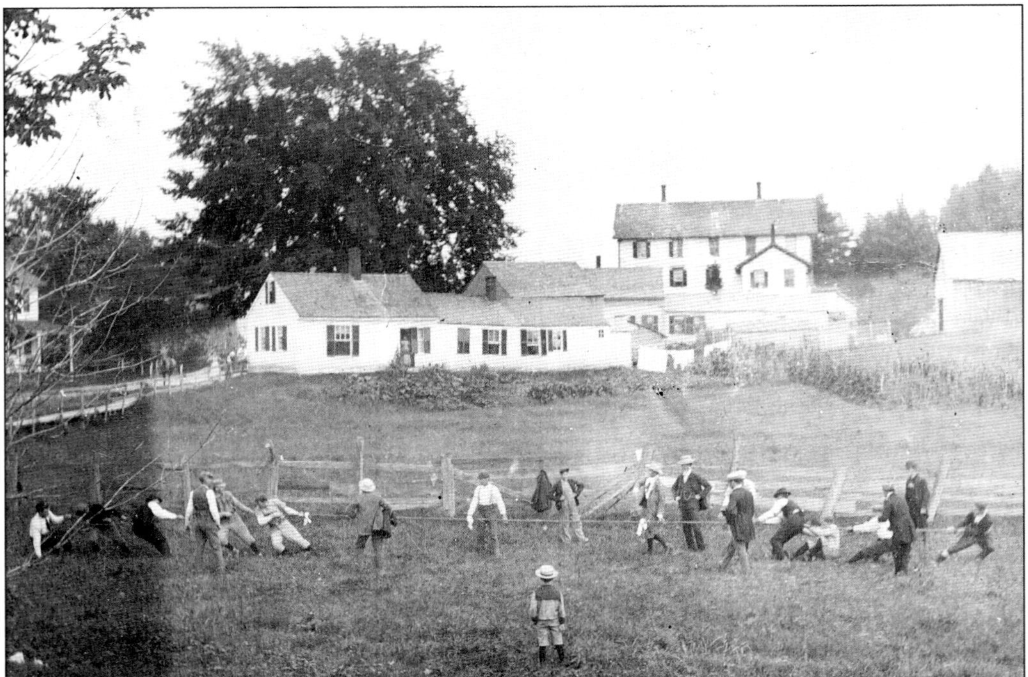

A tug-of-war contest is taking place in Coldbrook. It appears the contest was not spontaneous, as referees are present. On the rise in the background is the Coldbrook House.

Shown here is a playbill from 1891 for the Cantata of "Esther the Beautiful Queen." The director, F.S. Conant, lived on Maple Street.

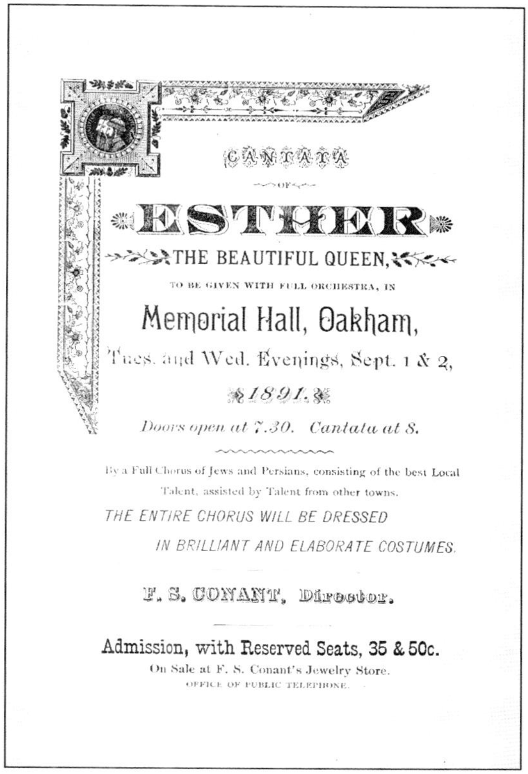

CANTATA

OF

ESTHER

THE BEAUTIFUL QUEEN,

TO BE GIVEN WITH FULL ORCHESTRA, IN

Memorial Hall, Oakham,

Tues. and Wed. Evenings, Sept. 1 & 2,

1891.

Doors open at 7.30. Cantata at 8.

By a Full Chorus of Jews and Persians, consisting of the best Local Talent, assisted by Talent from other towns.

THE ENTIRE CHORUS WILL BE DRESSED IN BRILLIANT AND ELABORATE COSTUMES.

F. S. CONANT, Director.

Admission, with Reserved Seats, 35 & 50c.

On Sale at F. S. Conant's Jewelry Store.

OFFICE OF PUBLIC TELEPHONE.

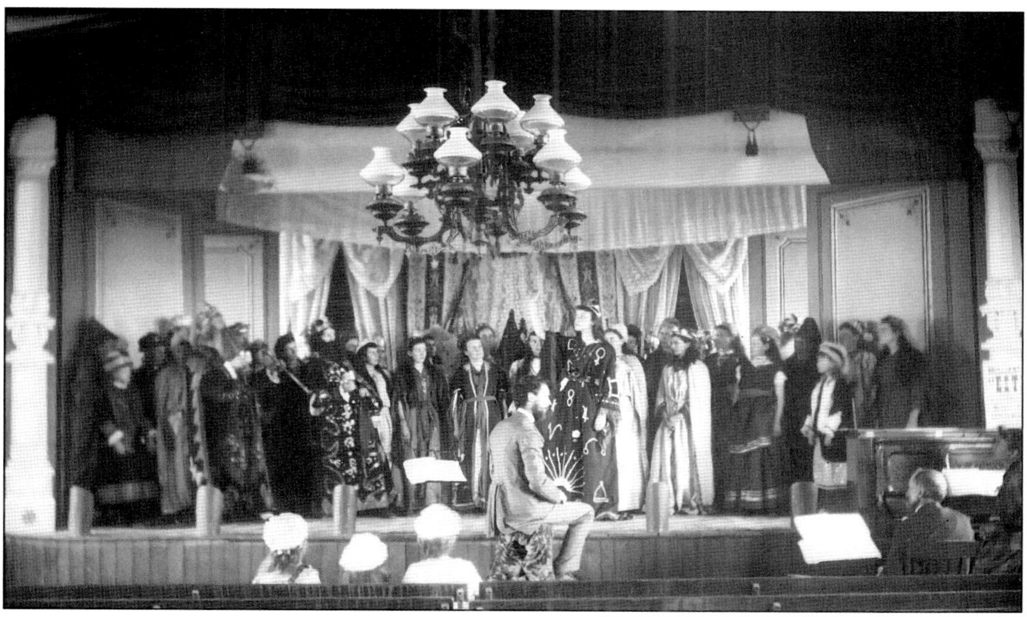

This is a scene from *Esther the Beautiful Queen*. As advertised, the cast is outfitted in very elaborate costumes, as is the stage. This play must have taken considerable effort to put on, and apparently the show only ran for two nights.

DRAMATIC ENTERTAINMENT

AT

Memorial Hall, Oakham,

FIELD-DAY AFTERNOON,

AUGUST 15, 1906.

"MR. BOB"

CAST OF CHARACTERS.

Philip Royson - - - - HERMAN BROWN

Robert Brown, of the law firm of Benson & Benson,
ADDISON C. ANGUS

Jenkins, Miss Rebecca's Butler,
CHARLES H. TROWBRIDGE

Miss Rebecca Luke, a maiden lady, RUTH B. DWELLY

Katherine Rogers, her niece, - FLORINE LINCOLN

Marion Bryant, nick-named "Bob," Katherine's friend,
ALTHEA E. RUSSELL

Patty, Miss Rebecca's maid, - ALICE L. WRIGHT

H. J. Lawrence, The Journal Print, North Brookfield.

In 1906, the afternoon entertainment at Field Day included the play *Mr. Bob*. Some of the names of the cast may be familiar: Dwelly, Lincoln, and Wright.

Memorial Hall, - - Oakham,

TUESDAY & WEDNESDAY EVES, APRIL 20-21, '97.

—— The 5-Act war drama, ——

THE CONFEDERATE SPY.

— Presented by —

The Oakham Dramatic Club.

CAST OF CHARACTERS.

GEORGE WATERMAN, a young Unionist, ... Geo. L. Parker
PHILIP BRADLEY, a daring Confederate Spy under Lee, ... I. W. Mullett
FRED AINSLEY, a Rebel Aid-de-Camp from Jackson's lines, ... Walter Green
MAJOR-GENERAL BANKS, United States Army, ... E. Mullett
COLONEL WILLARD, United States Army, ... W. A. Woodis
OFFICER MULGARRY, one of the Finest when out of danger, ... E. S. Crawford
CLAY, a Gemman of Color what knows whar de chickins roost, ... Geo. L. Perkins
SOCKERY SCHNEIDLEBECKER, the Drafted Dutchman, ... Frank Nye
MRS. WATERMAN, Mother of George and Widow of the late Captain Waterman, ... Miss Susie Gleason
MAUD BRADLEY, a Southern Belle and Sister of Spy, ... Mrs. Grace Keep
NORAH McLEGGIN, down on the "Haythen Chinazers," .... Miss Edna Boyd
Soldiers in blue and gray, villagers, etc.

In 1897 the Civil War was still fresh in many minds, including those of the Oakham Dramatic Club, which presented *The Confederate Spy*.

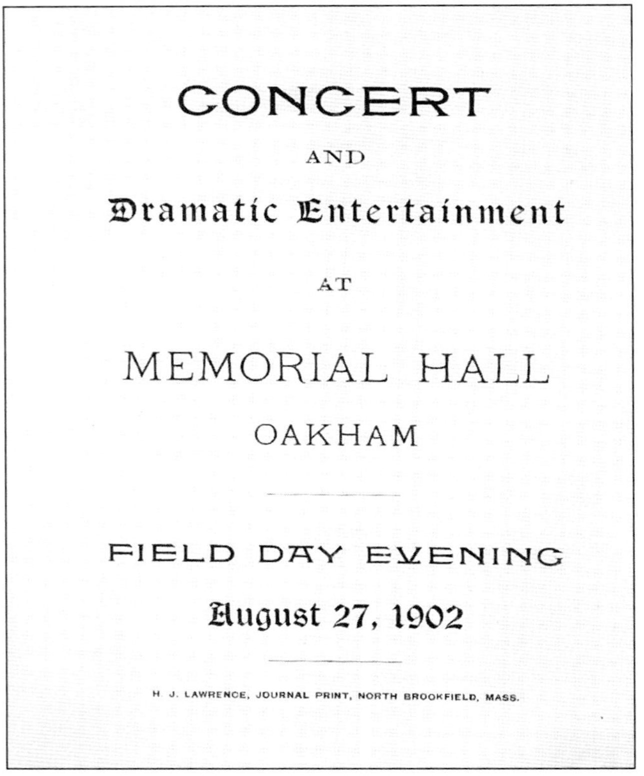

CONCERT

AND

Dramatic Entertainment

AT

MEMORIAL HALL

OAKHAM

FIELD DAY EVENING

August 27, 1902

H. J. LAWRENCE, JOURNAL PRINT, NORTH BROOKFIELD, MASS.

The 1902 Field Day, like many others, had entertainment well into the evening, as shown in this playbill.

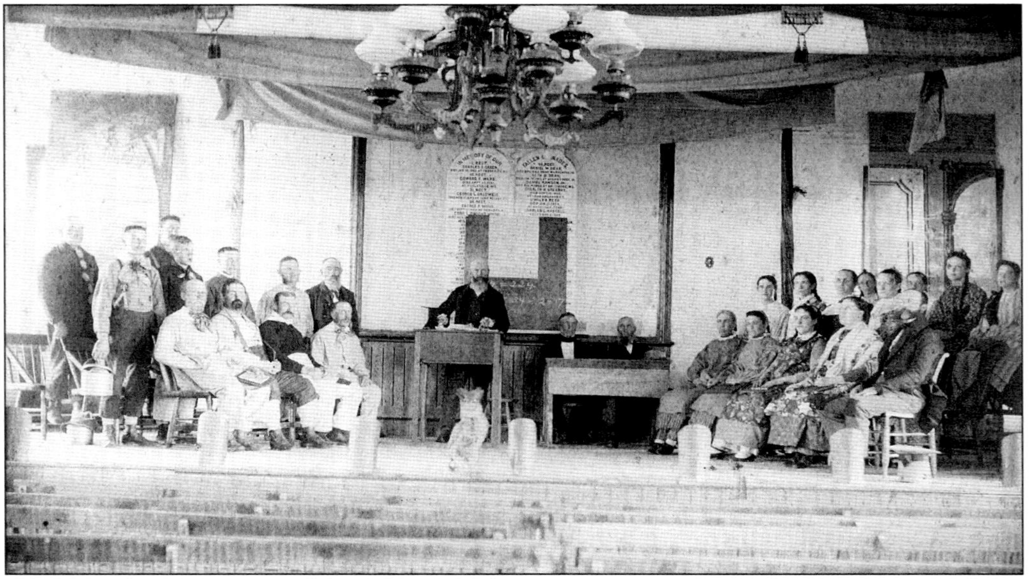

This was a play called *The District School*. The entire cast was made up of Oakham residents. Notice how the stage in the town hall was on the opposite side of the current stage.

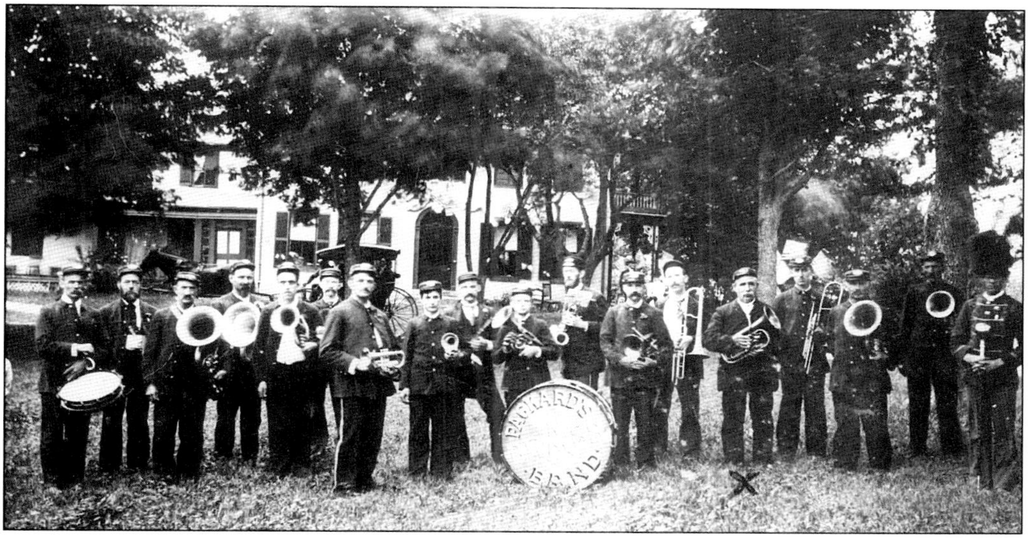

Pictured here is Packard's Brass Band, in uniform and preparing for a parade. In the background is the Fairbank's home.

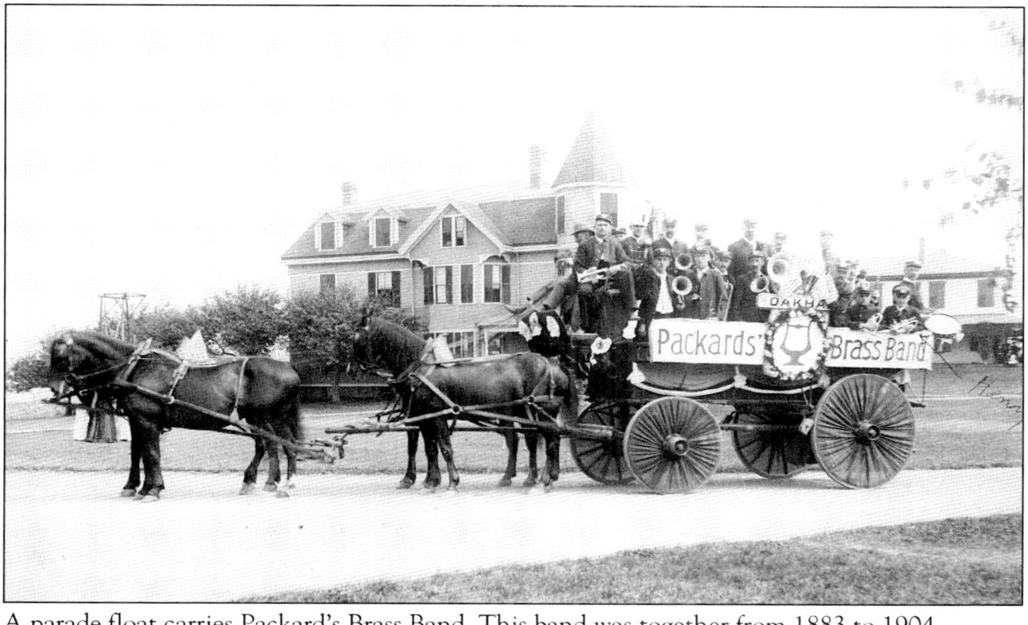

A parade float carries Packard's Brass Band. This band was together from 1883 to 1904.

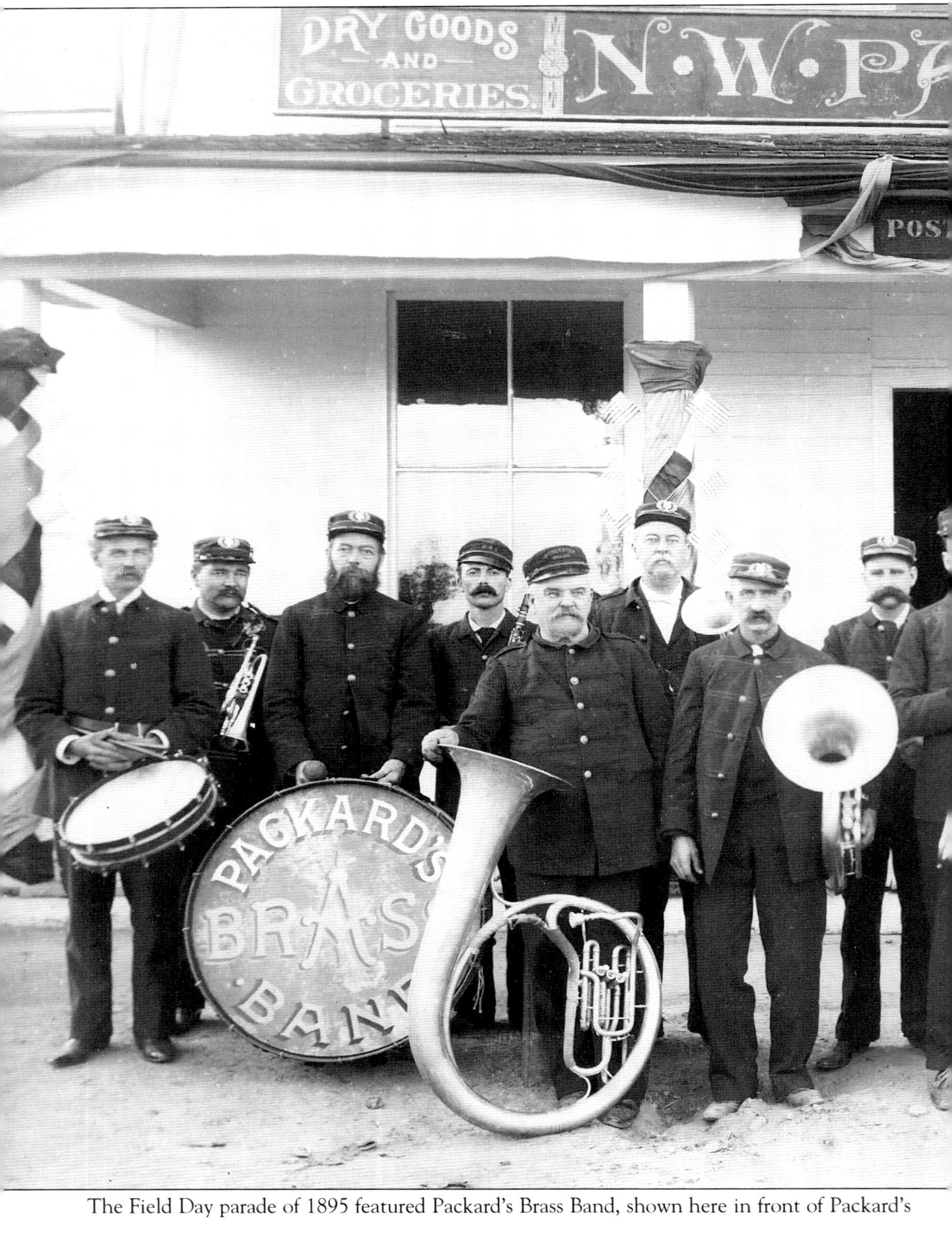

The Field Day parade of 1895 featured Packard's Brass Band, shown here in front of Packard's

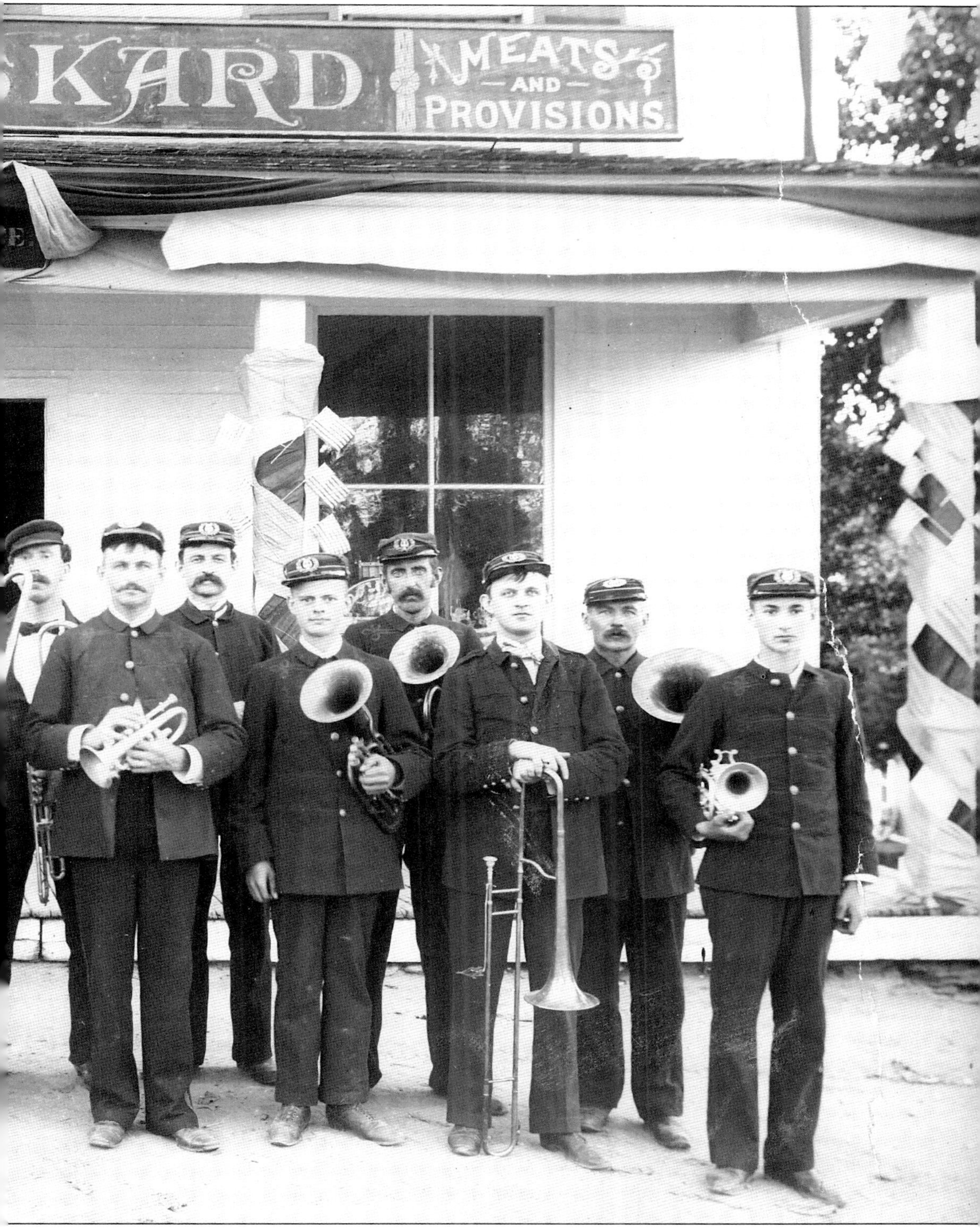

Store off the common.

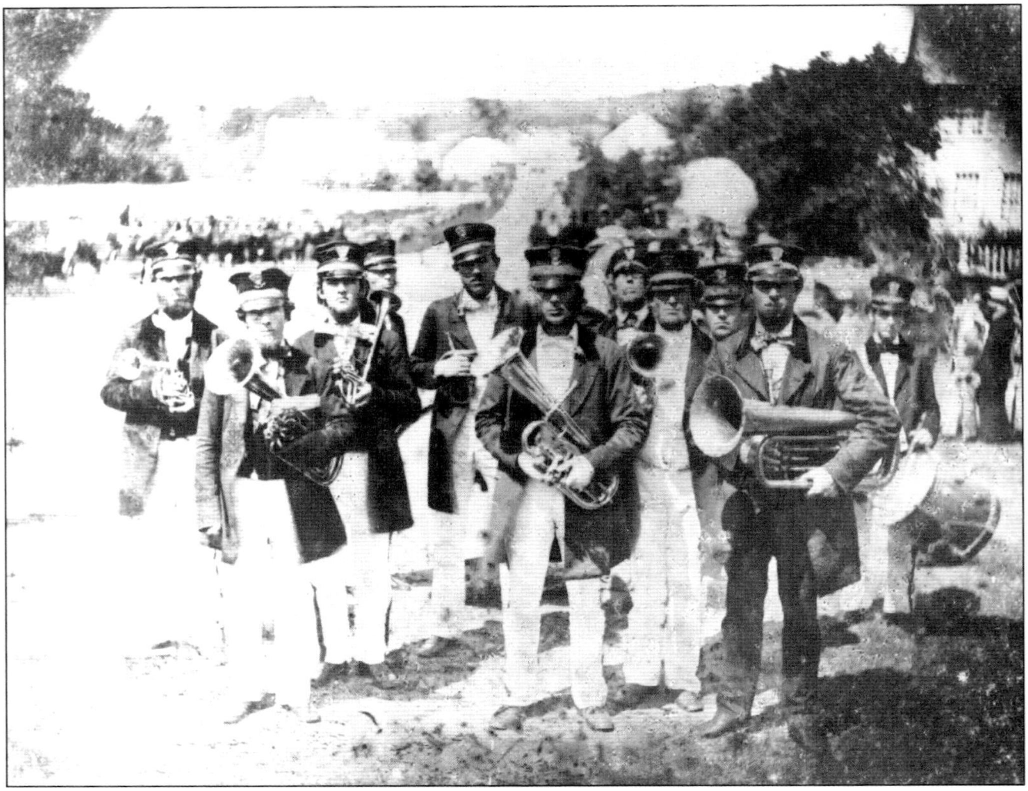

One of the earliest bands was Crawford's Cornet Band. This photo was taken at a Fourth of July picnic in Coldbrook in 1859.

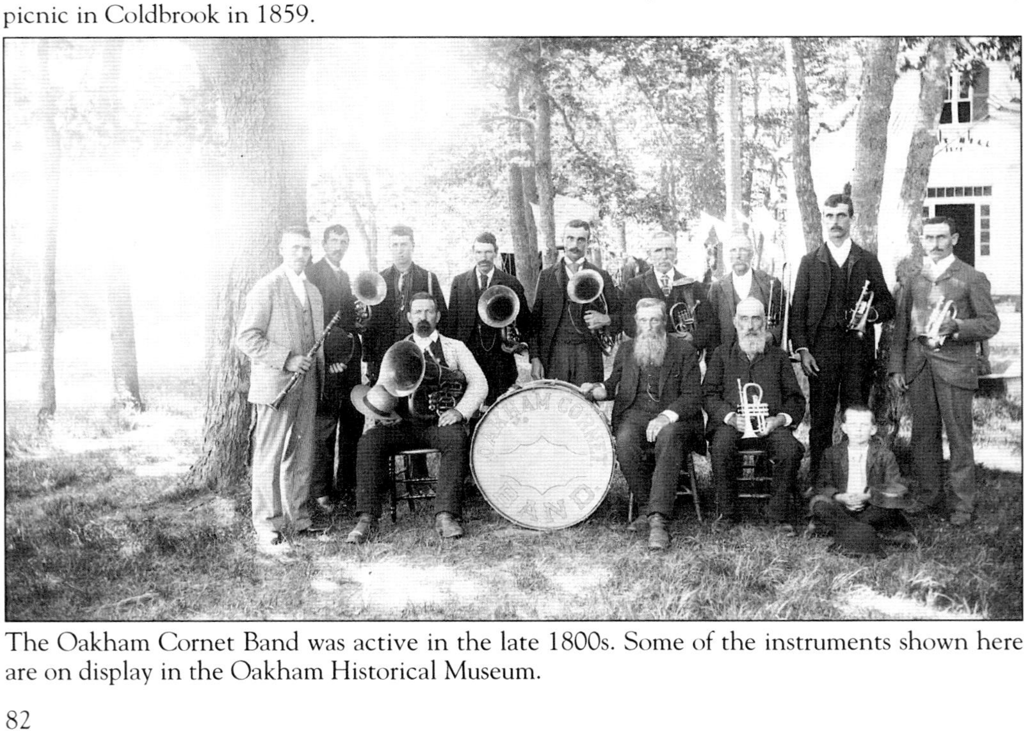

The Oakham Cornet Band was active in the late 1800s. Some of the instruments shown here are on display in the Oakham Historical Museum.

Five

HOUSES

From post and beam, to stone structures, to homes in the Grecian style, early construction styles in Oakham varied as much as the residents who lived in them. Builders like James Bell, Issac Stone, James Packard, and Timothy Nye were responsible for many of the homes. Often times residents, rather than adding on to their homes by conventional methods, would buy parts of other homes and move them, thereby adding to their homes in a quicker and cheaper manner.

Many of the original homes, including some of the ones shown in the following pages, were destroyed by fire and replaced by newer-style homes.

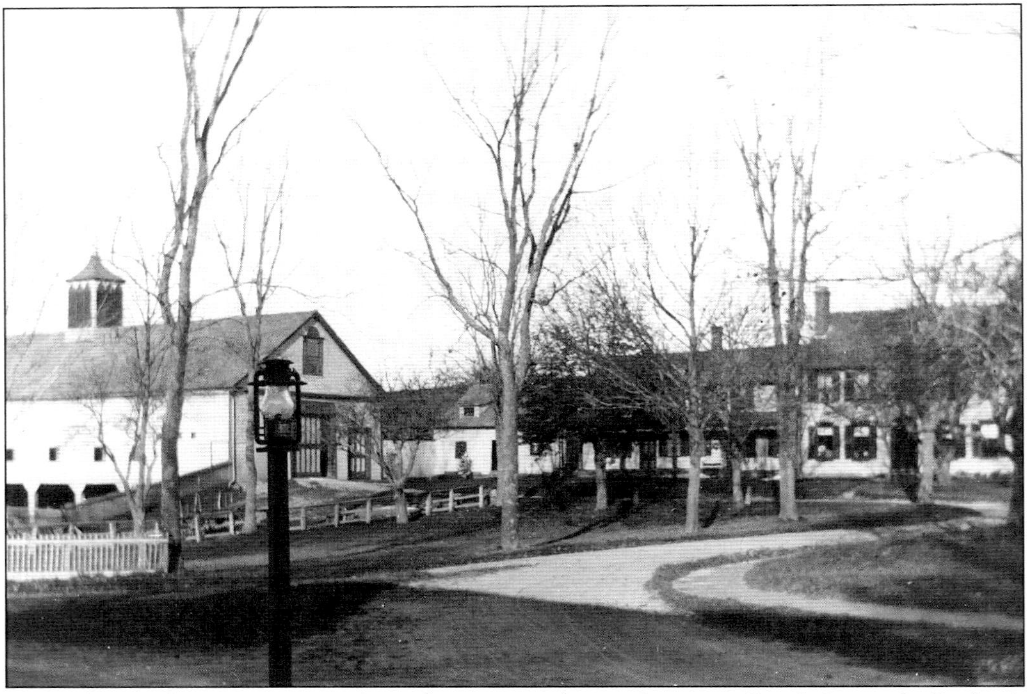

Located near the intersection of Maple Street and New Braintree Road, James C. Fairbank purchased this farm in 1837 from Jonathan Bullard and John Briant.

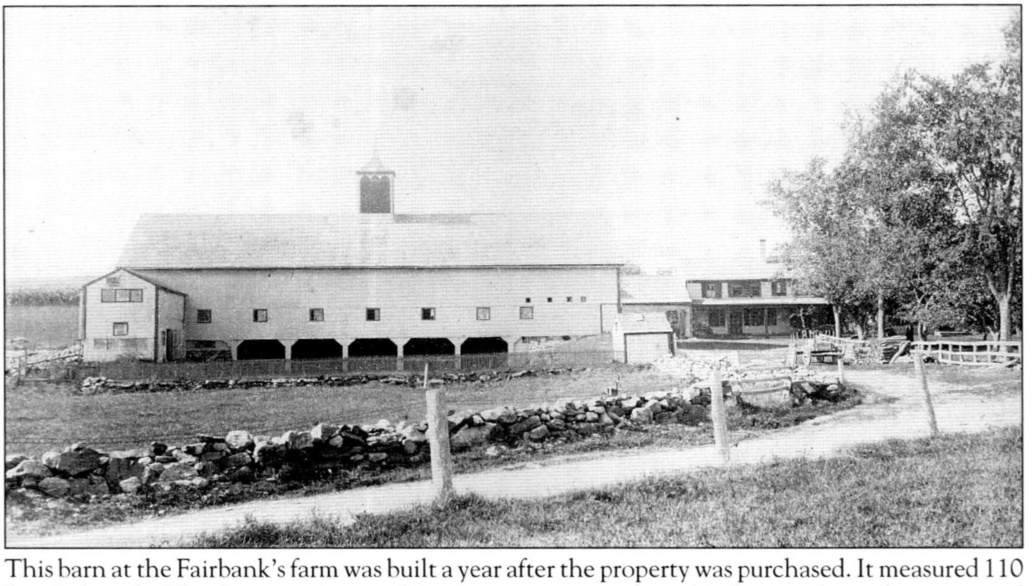

This barn at the Fairbank's farm was built a year after the property was purchased. It measured 110 feet in length. The first mowing machine in town was used on this farm and was demonstrated in 1865. After being hit by lightning in 1908, the barn was destroyed.

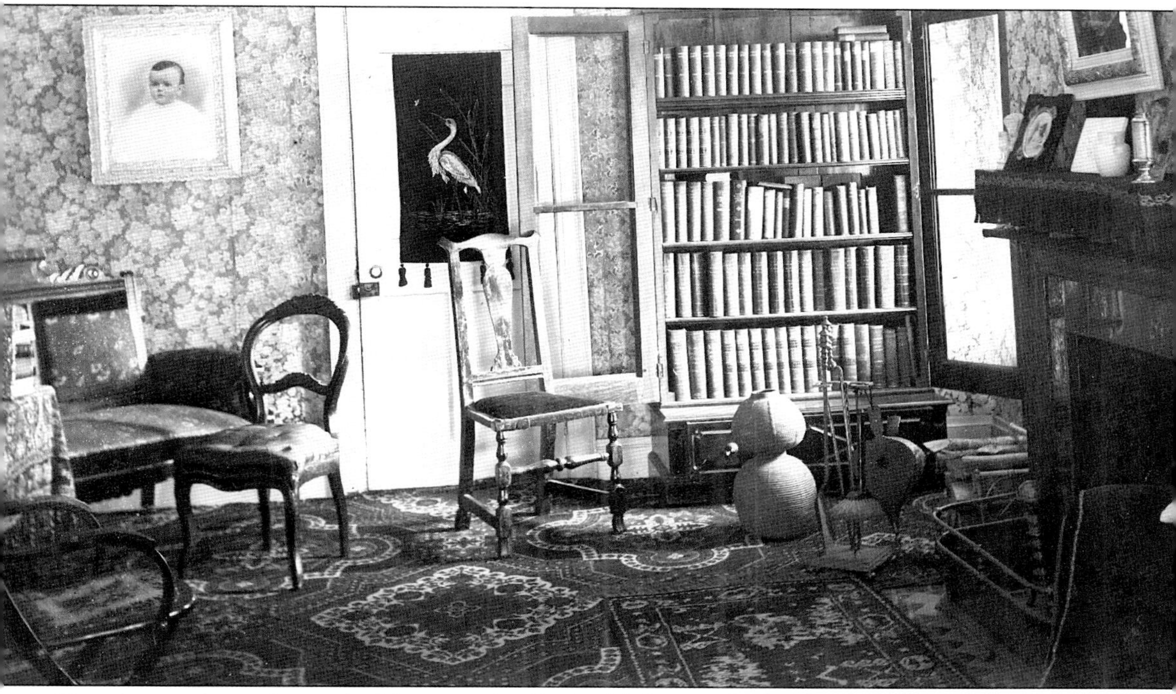

The picture above shows the library in the Fairbank's house. Sadly, this large brick home was also destroyed by fire some 38 years after the barn was lost.

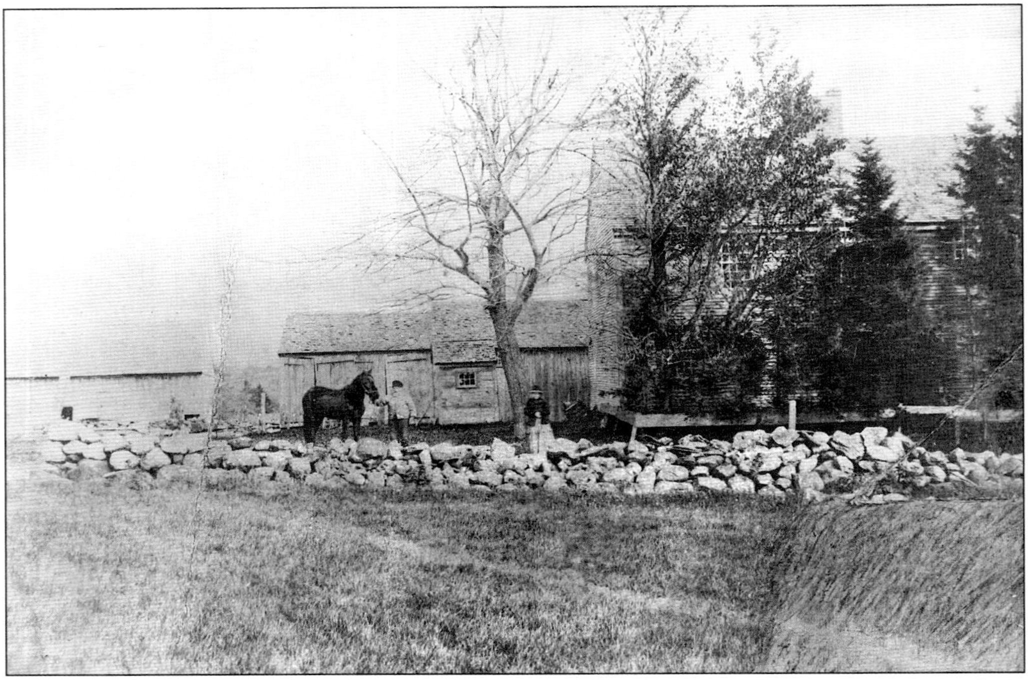

The assessors of the district in 1767 sold all of lot 11 to William Hunter. Nineteen years later this house was built for Reverend Daniel Tomlinson with donations of labor and material from residents. Reverend Tomlinson served the town as minister of the Congregational church from 1780 to 1842. Pictured here are grandchildren of Reverend Tomlinson, Fabian and Marie. This home is located at 29 Tomlinson Road.

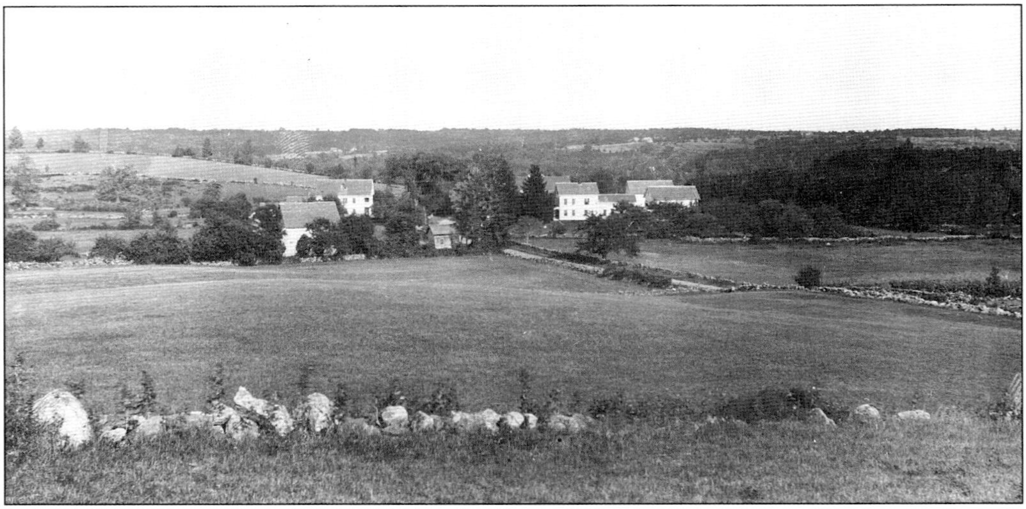

The view from behind Memorial Hall shows the industrious area known as Lincolnville. The residence in the foreground on the left was the home of Stephen Lincoln Jr. Behind it was the home of Albert Burt, who married Lincoln's daughter Elizabeth. The house on the right was built in 1858 by James W. Packard for Moses O. Ayres. Not shown in this picture is the home of Martha E. Burt and Lincoln's Wire Company. All these building are in the area of 113 to 163 Rutland Road.

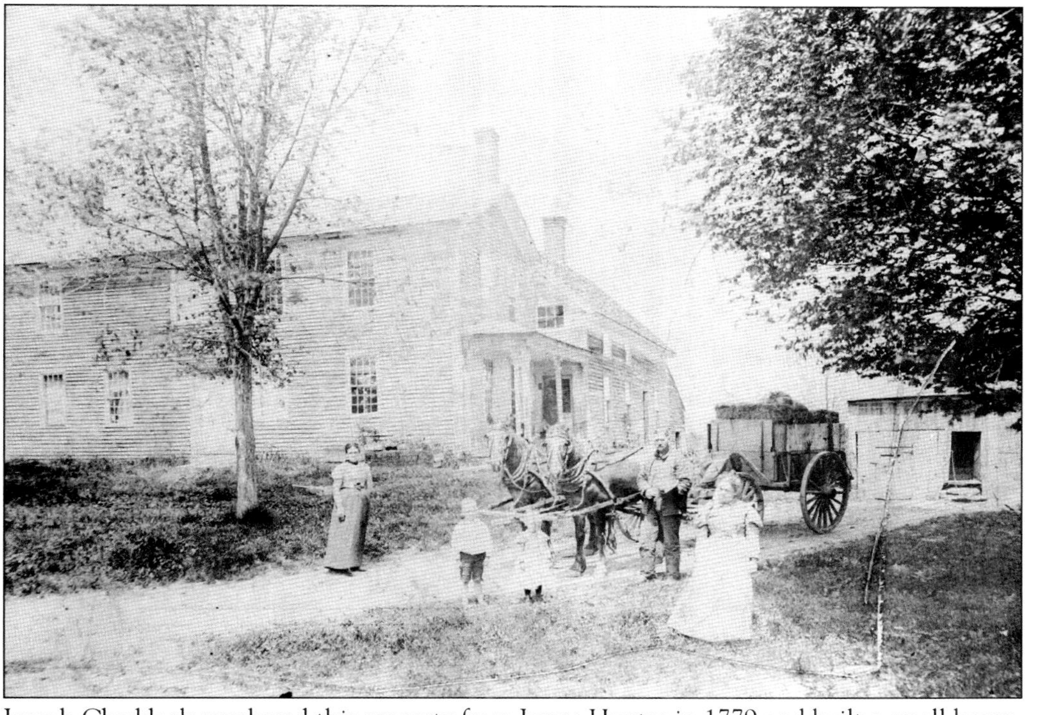

Joseph Chaddock purchased this property from James Hunter in 1779 and built a small house. Seventeen years later it was sold to George Haskell and remained in the Haskell family until 1884. It was during that time that the front portion was added on after it was moved from the Sumner Reed property on Ware Corner Road. Pictured here from left to right are: Florence Sargeant, Henry Clifford, Evelyn Clifford, Charles S. Clifford, and Flora Crawford Clifford.

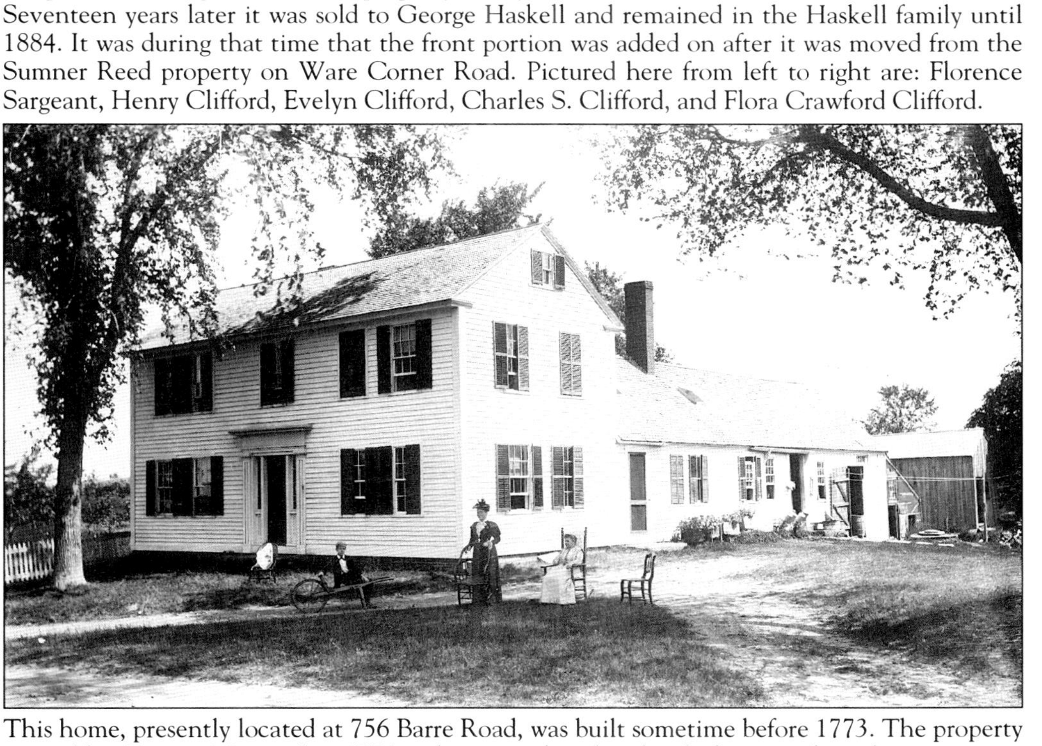

This home, presently located at 756 Barre Road, was built sometime before 1773. The property was sold to Francis Maynard in 1776 and remained in that family for a number of years.

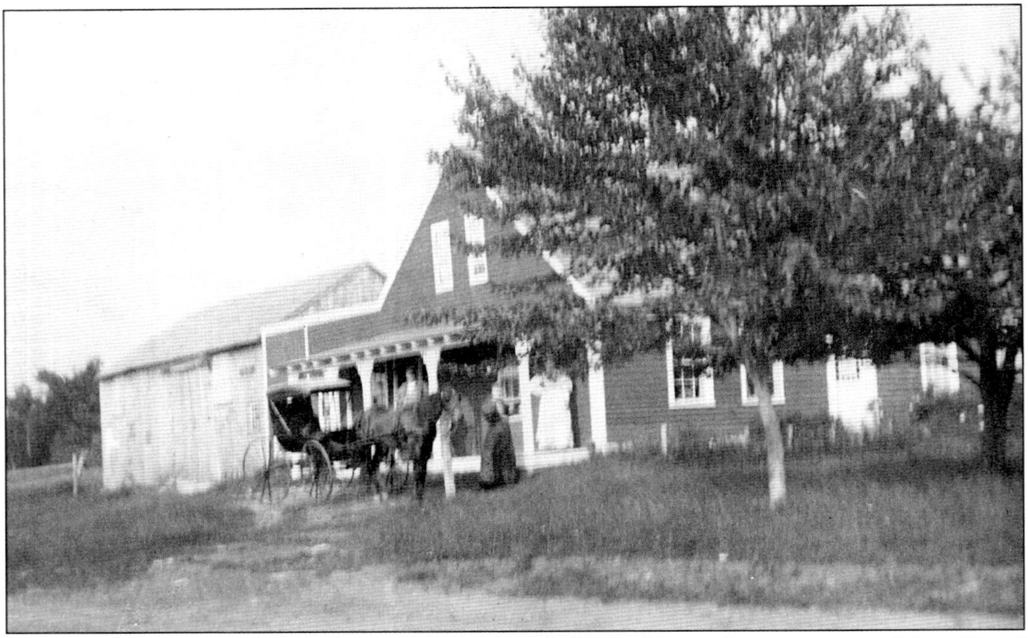

Known as the Sherman house, this property and the buildings thereon were sold to David Goodale in 1817. At one time, a blacksmith shop stood on the property. This home is located at 1019 North Brookfield Road.

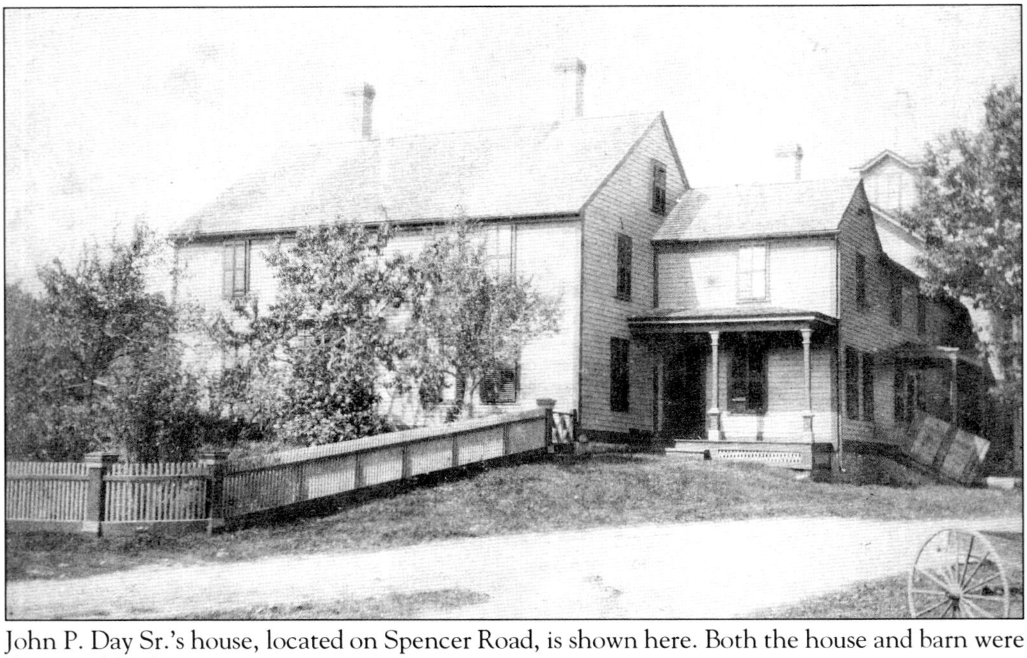

John P. Day Sr.'s house, located on Spencer Road, is shown here. Both the house and barn were destroyed by fire.

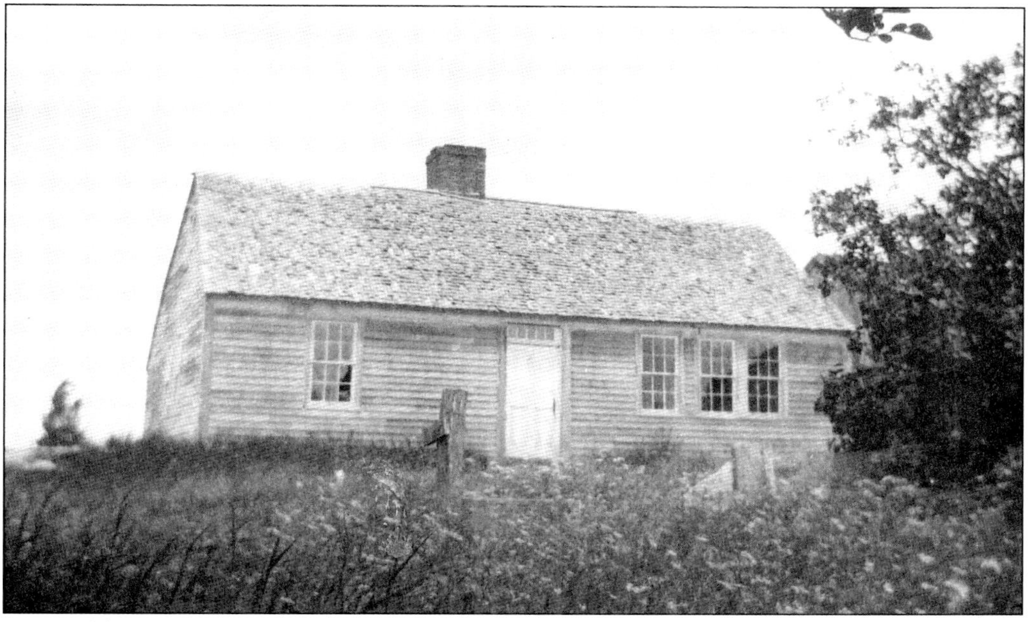

Pictured here is the Presho house, located on Lincoln Road. It was eventually torn down by Charles Trowbridge.

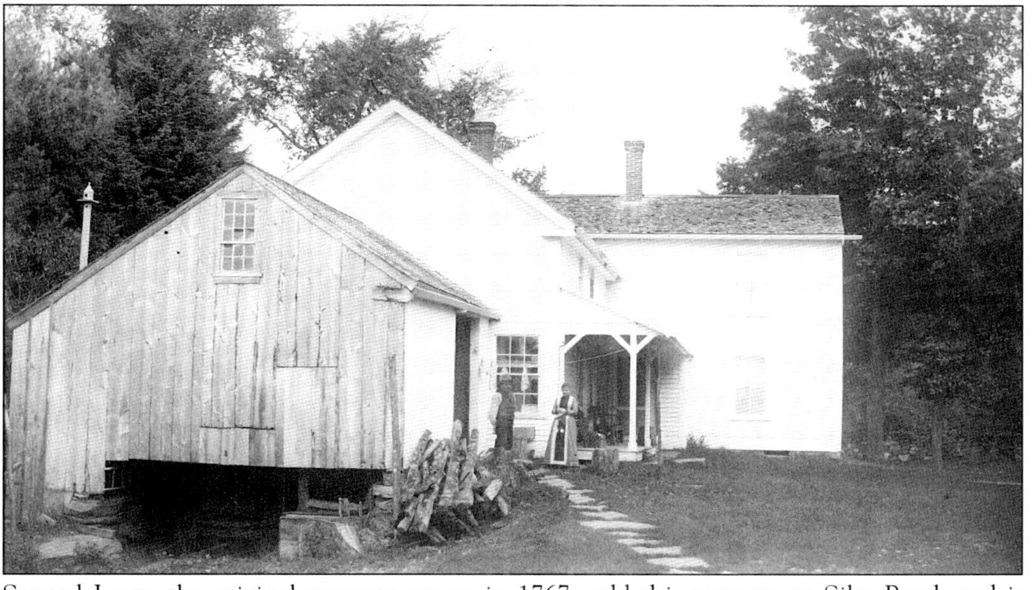

Samuel Jones, the original property owner in 1767, sold this property to Silas Reed, and it was in 1806 that Reed built this home. Although the property changed owners many times, it remained in the Reed family. In 1870, a portion of this house was moved by oxen to become the front part of the Mark Haskell house, located at 231 Rutland Road. Another portion of this same house was moved and became part of the Conant house at 23 Maple Street. Two very interesting facts concerning this house are that the cellar was walled off into separate rooms, and the date it was built is carved into one of the beams of the second floor. The house now stands at 218 Ware Corner Road.

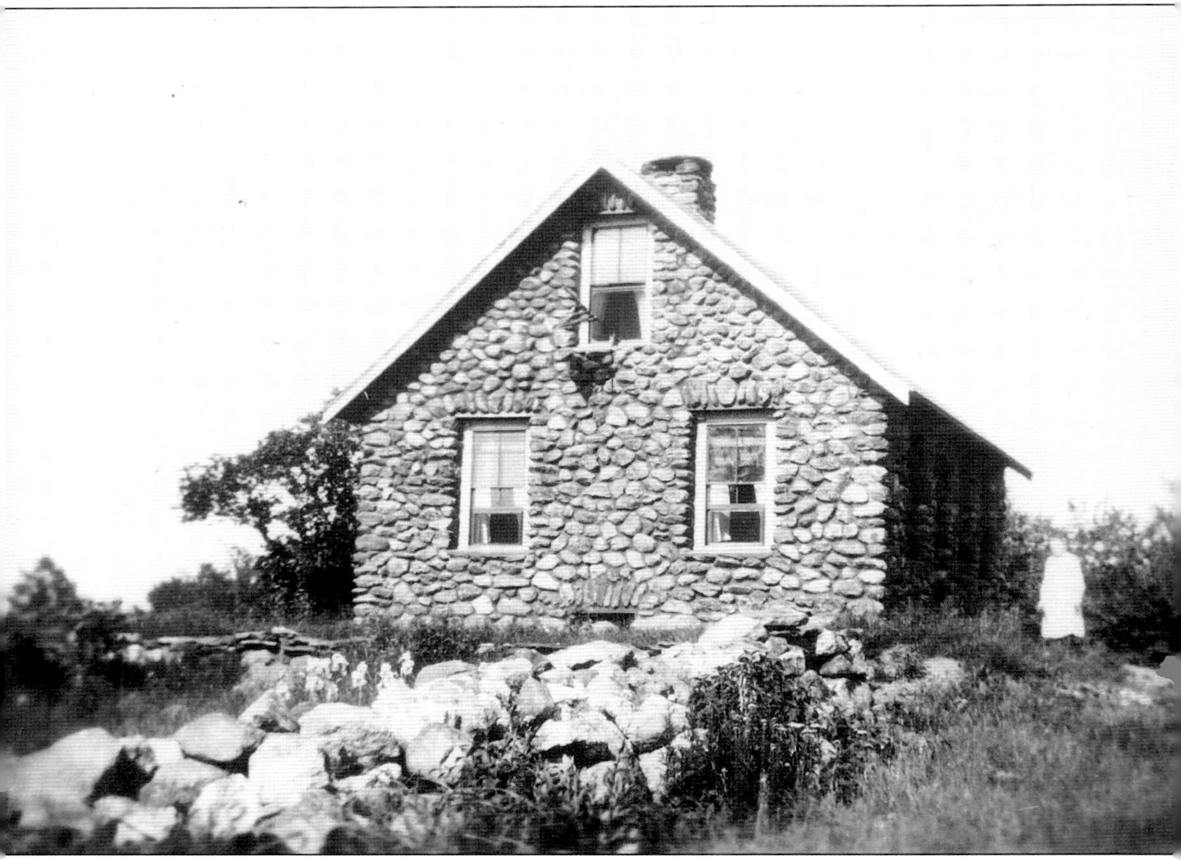

The panoramic view above is of 439 Lincoln Road.

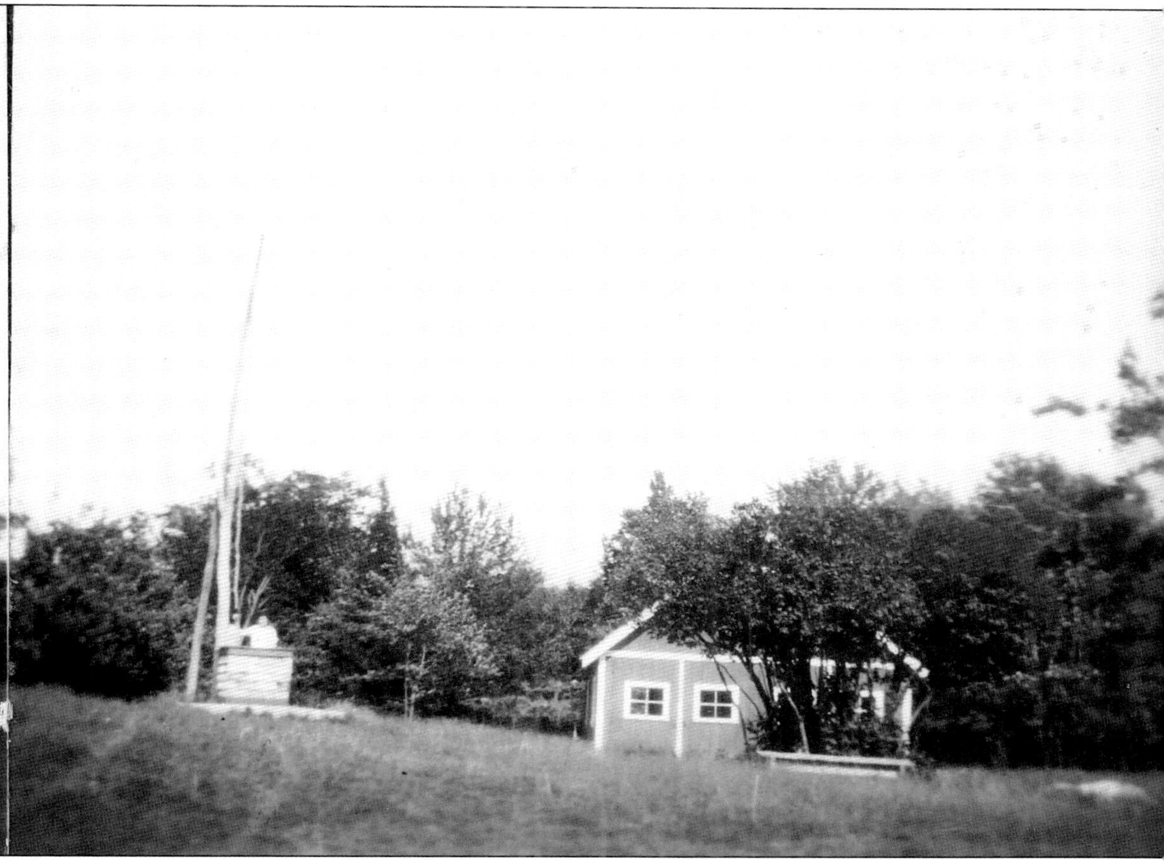

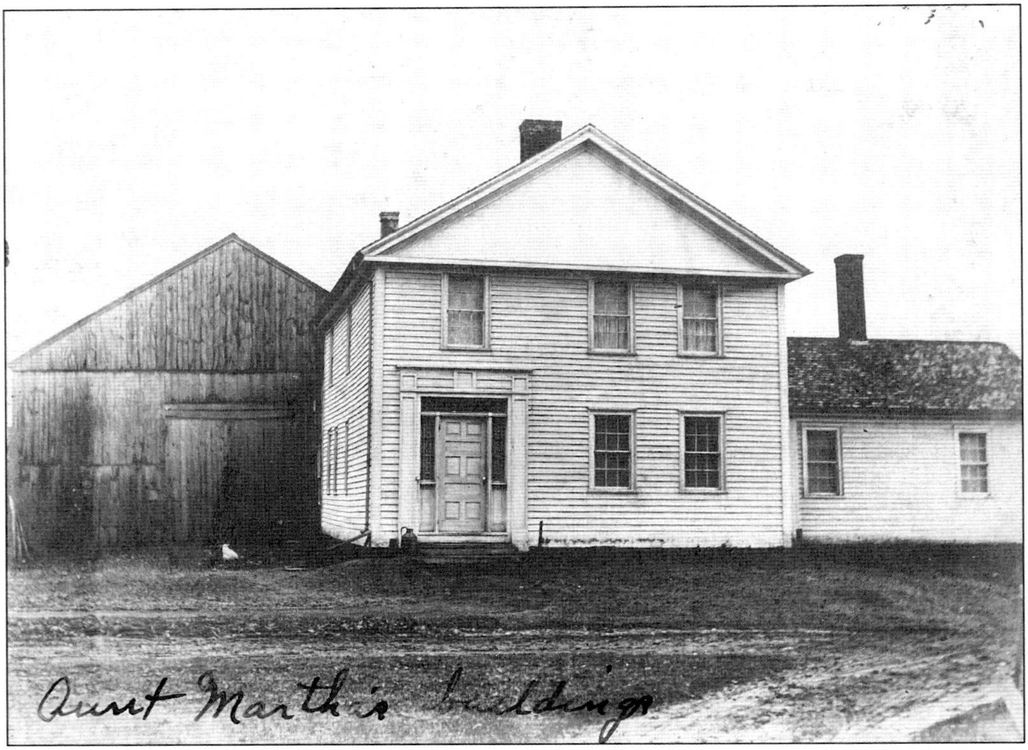

Once part of the Silas Reed property, this home on Sargeant Lane was built in 1834 by Reed's son Lewis. The homestead was sold to James C. Sargeant in 1867.

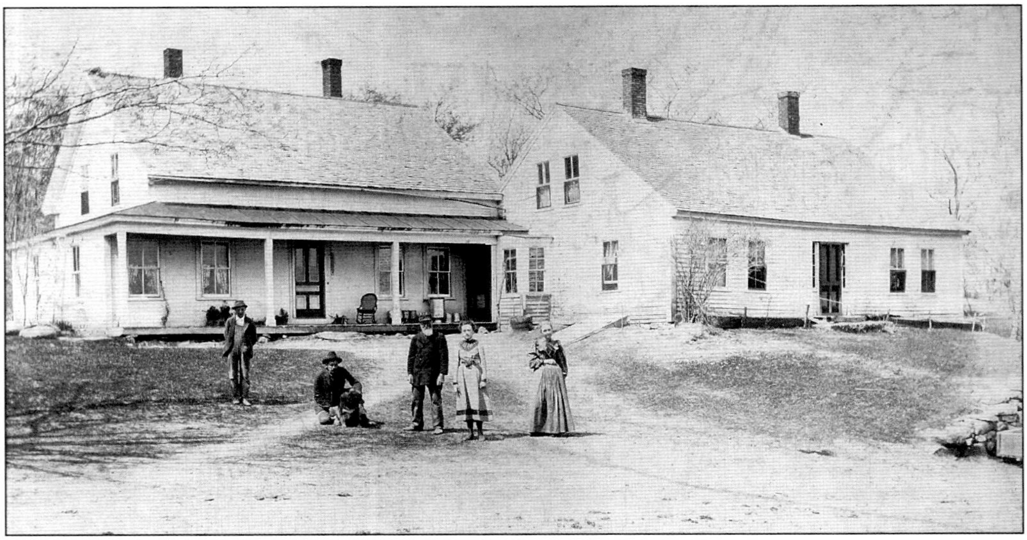

One of Oakham's first settlers, Alexander Crawford, sold this land to his son John in 1758. John built his home across the street from this house located at 687 Lincoln Road. This house was built in two sections, the first in 1825 and the second in 1865, by Samuel Crawford. In 1844, Samuel's widow sold the property to Alonzo Lincoln. Those pictured above are believed to be part of the family of Horace W. Lincoln, son of Alonzo.

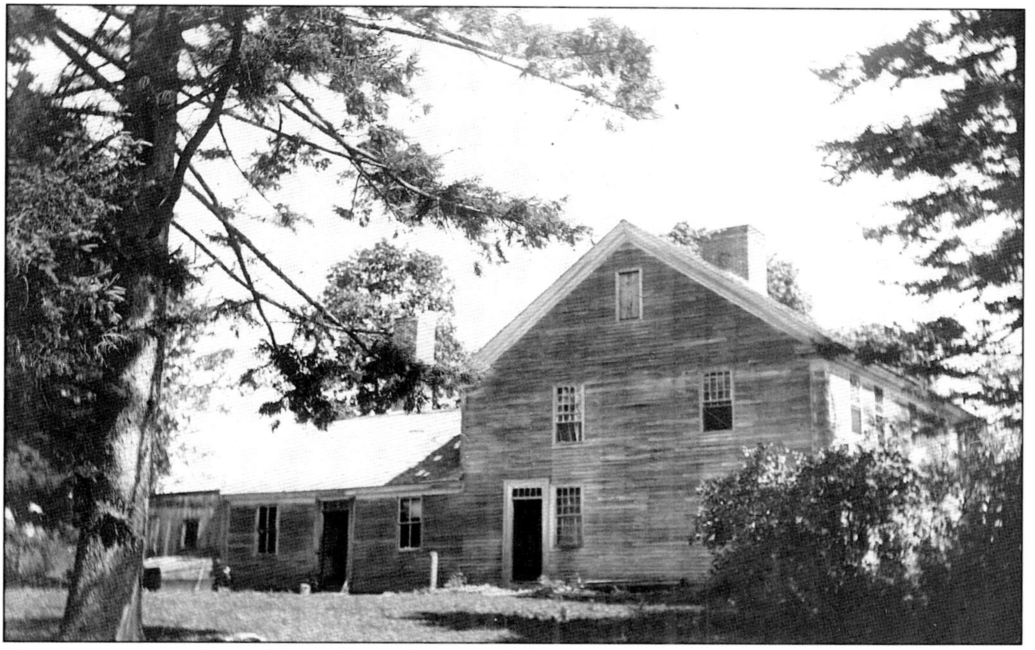

This property was first sold to Alexander Crawford in 1748, and it has remained in the Crawford family ever since—a total of 250 years. The house, built in 1790, was directly across the street from the log home that Alexander Crawford built when he first settled in Oakham. The home is located at 337 Crawford Road, and the current residents are the great-great grandchildren of General William A. Crawford.

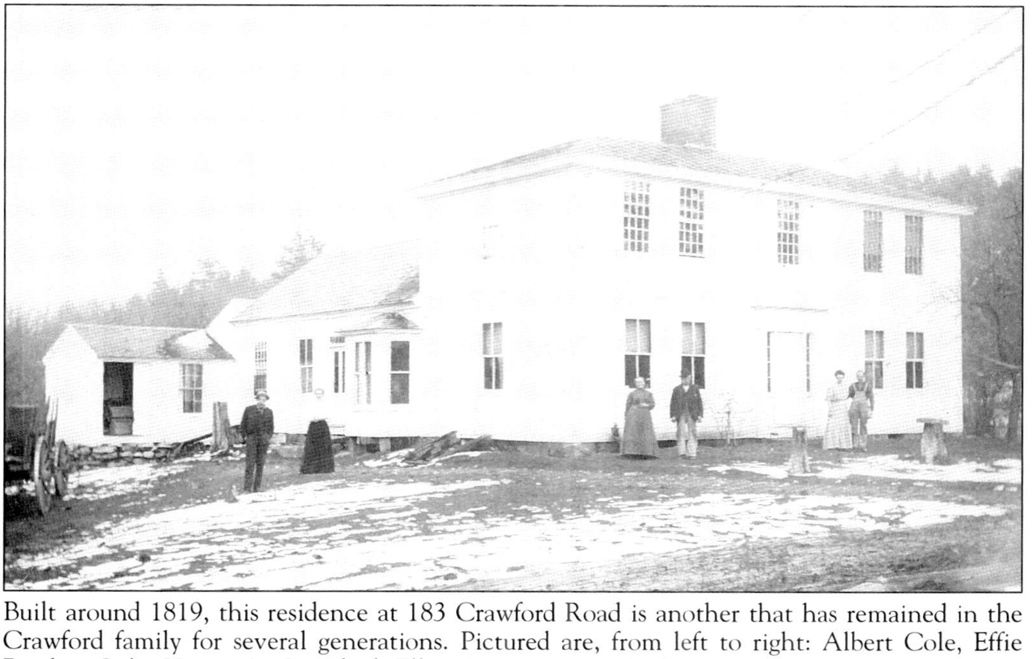

Built around 1819, this residence at 183 Crawford Road is another that has remained in the Crawford family for several generations. Pictured are, from left to right: Albert Cole, Effie Bartlett Cole, Henry A. Crawford, Ellen Sargeant Crawford, Henry U. Crawford, and Edith Bartlett Crawford.

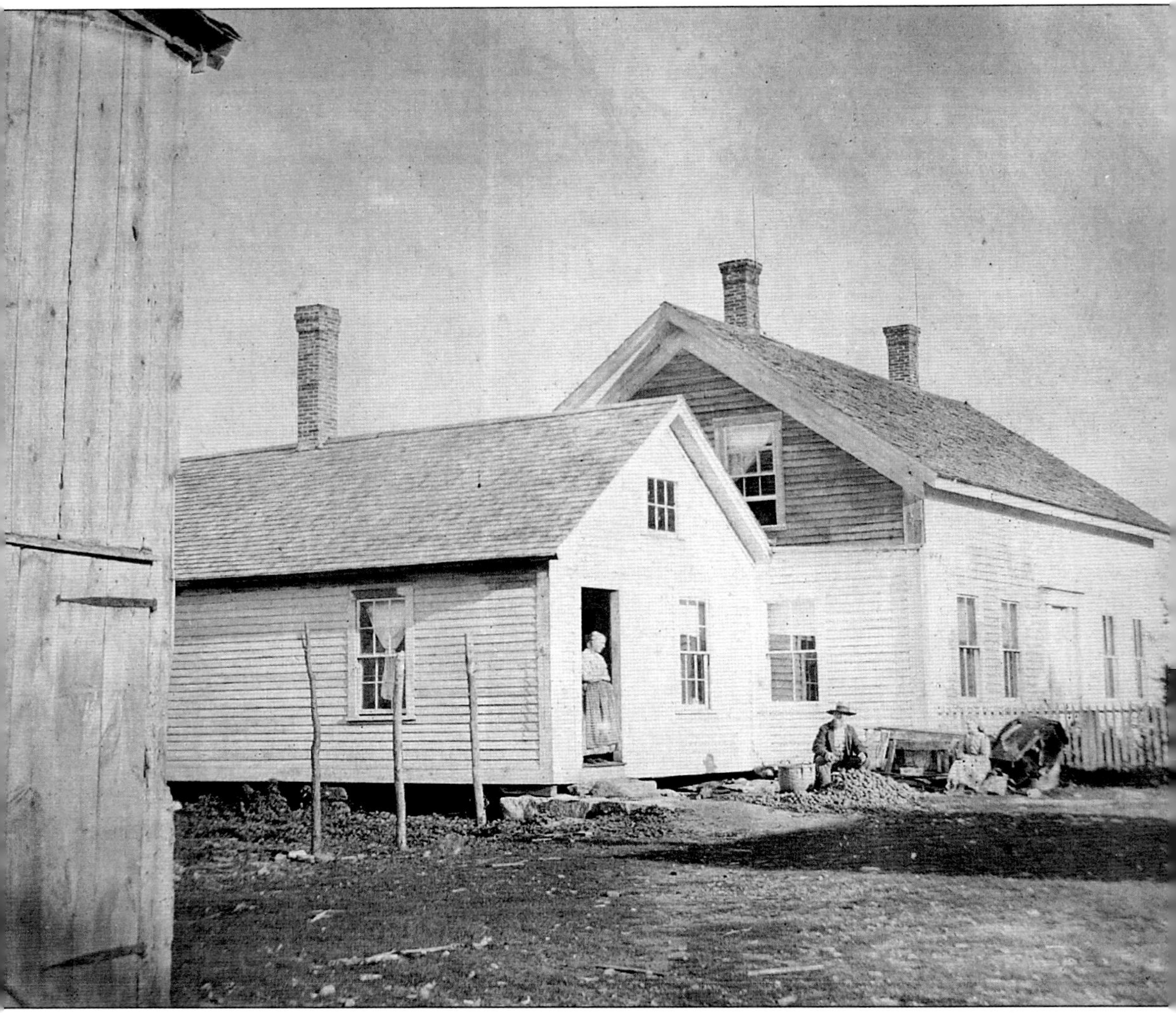

This property at 322 South Road had six owners before being sold to William P. Dwelly in 1856. At one time, a blacksmith shop stood a little southwest of the house. Pictured in the center is Edward "Hub" Dwelly, his wife, Emma Robinson Dwelly, is on the right, and an unidentified friend stands in the doorway. This photo, showing "Hub" preparing seed potatoes for planting, was taken in the spring of 1891.

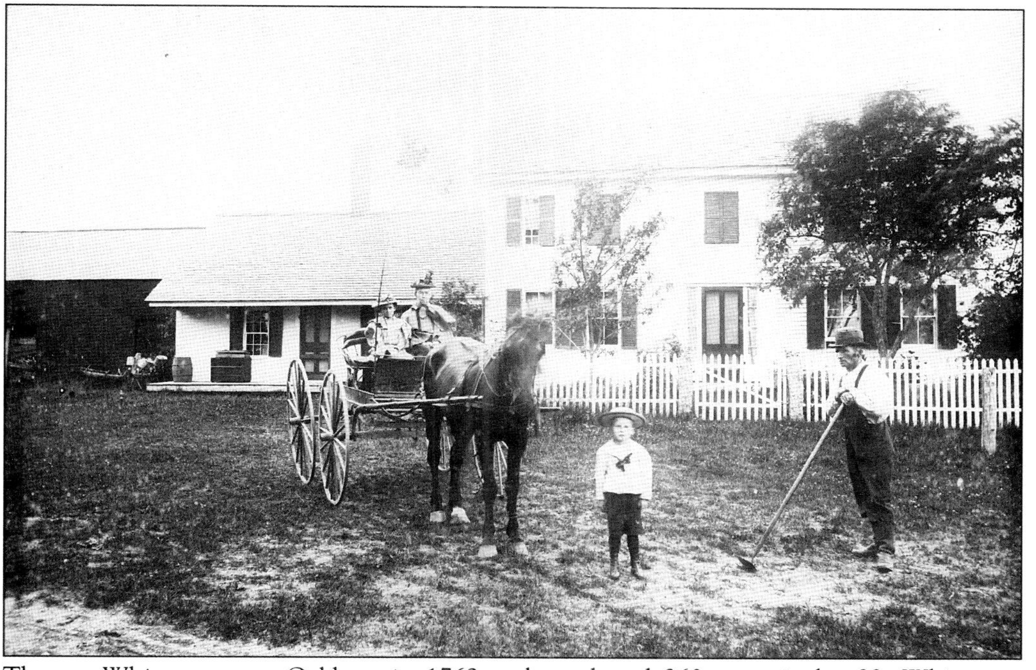

Thomas White came to Oakham in 1762 and purchased 360 acres in lot 33. White was Oakham's first representative to the General Court in 1775. Located at 114 Dennis Whitney Road, the McClanathan family resided here for many years. Pictured are Sarah E. Stevens McClanathan and her daughter Sadie in the wagon, and standing is Walter and his father, Charles P. McClanathan.

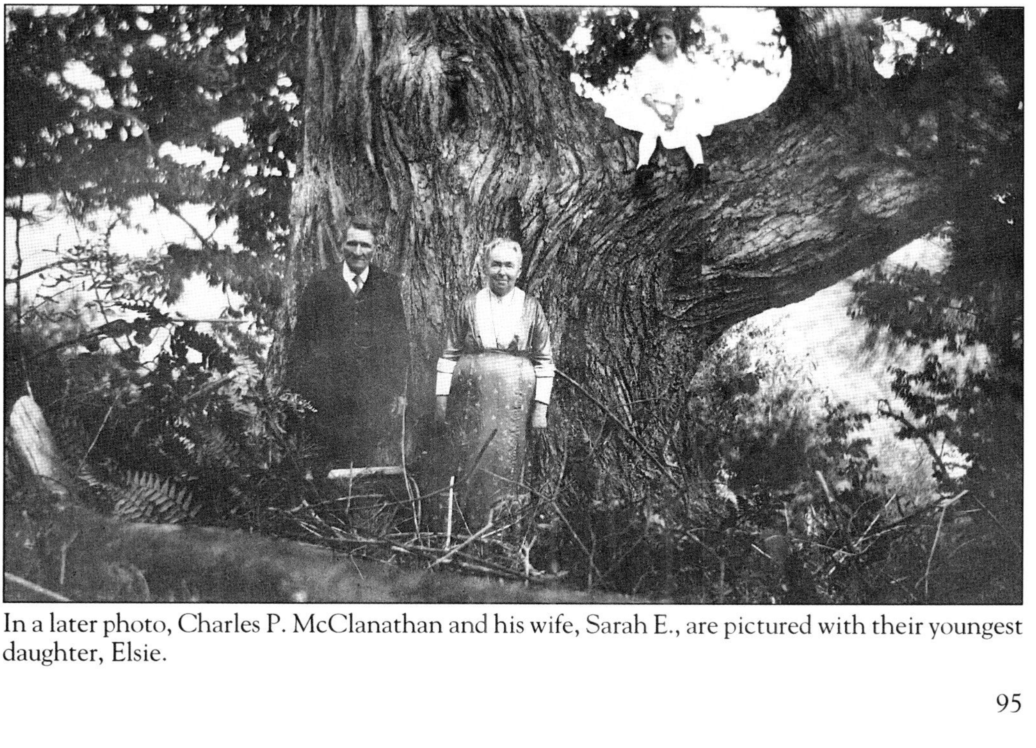

In a later photo, Charles P. McClanathan and his wife, Sarah E., are pictured with their youngest daughter, Elsie.

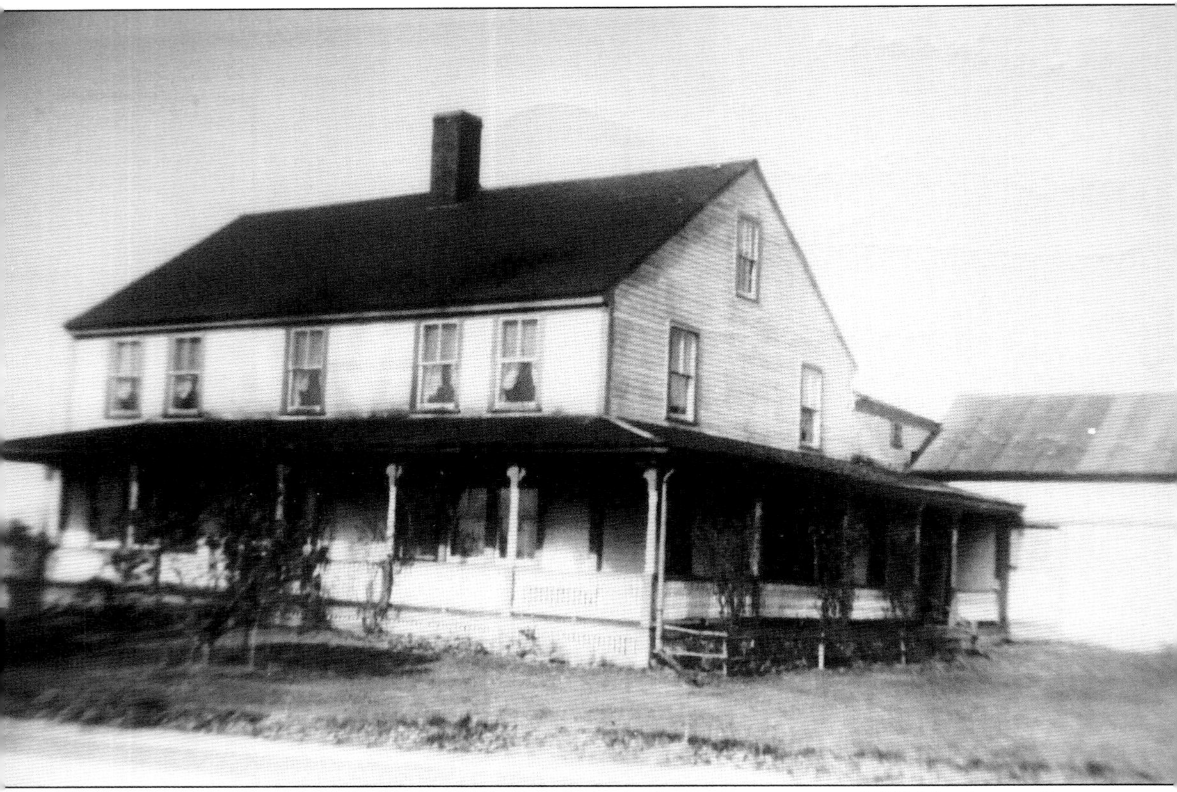

This residence at 1148 Old Turnpike Road was built sometime around 1790 by James Conant. Conant was a merchant and innkeeper for many years. The horses used by the stage coach line were changed here and kept in his barn across the street.

Six

People and Scenery

We may think of traveling by horse and carriage as a quiet, sedate manner of transportation and a lovely way to view the scenery. But it too had its problems. Driving too quickly did not begin with the automobile. There are reports of horse and carriage collisions and accounts of people being thrown from carriages. The *Oakham Herald* of April 1, 1891, tells us, "Daniel Holden's horse became frightened and took a pleasure trip about town and finally brought up in Mrs. L.P. Lovell's kitchen."

In addition to Flint Rock, shown in the following pages, there are other rocks and caves of note in Oakham. Missionary Rock, located off East Hill Road, sheltered a family for the better part of a year. Albert Parkman, who did extensive research on early Oakham, wrote of "some rock ledges which form a rough cavelike appearance, and is called Indian Cave. Legend has it that an Indian traveling through the territory broke his leg and took refuge in the cave." There is a similar rock grouping called Rocky Hill off Old Turnpike Road.

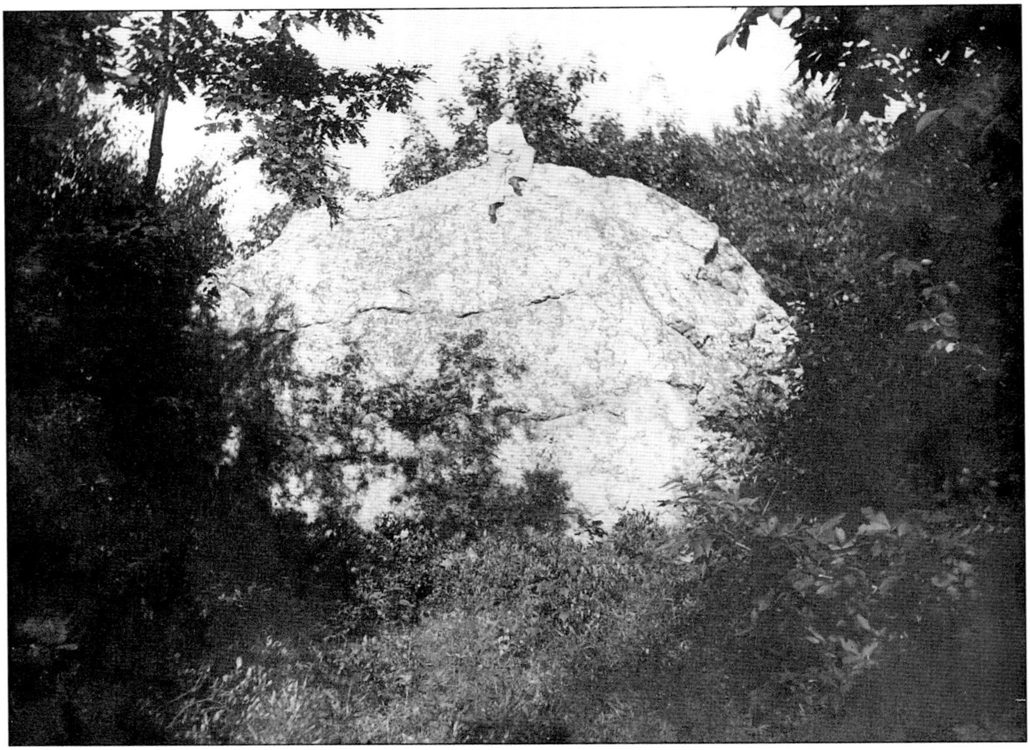

Believed to have been left by glacial activity thousands of years ago, Flint rock is one of the "natural wonders" found in the woods off Spencer Road. Seated atop the rock is William S. Crawford.

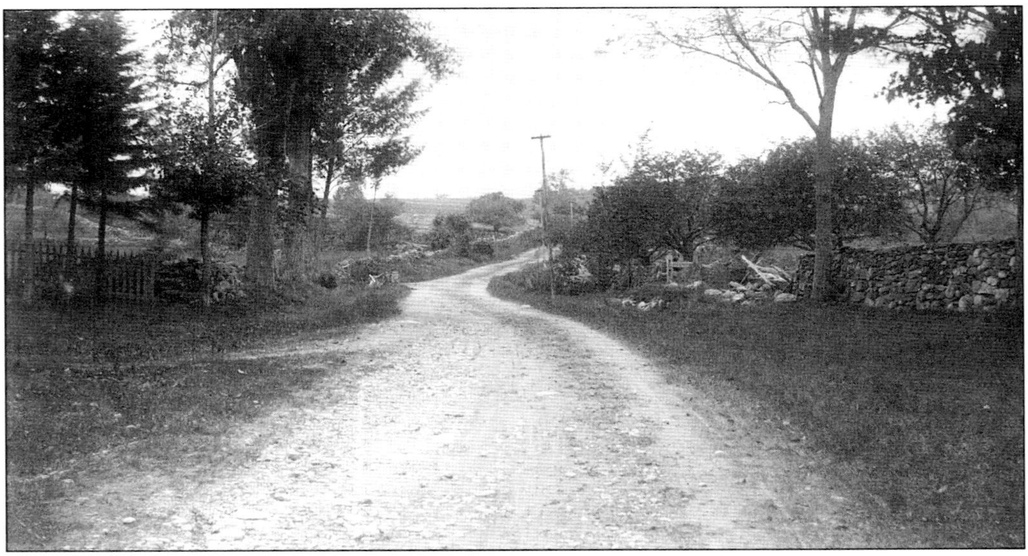

Archibald Ware came to Oakham prior to 1797. He was elected selectman eight times and represented the town in the General Court for two terms. Seven of his grandsons were Union soldiers. Looking towards the center, this new road in 1835 extends from Davis (Hapgood) Road to the center. Ware Corner Road is named for Archibald Ware and his family.

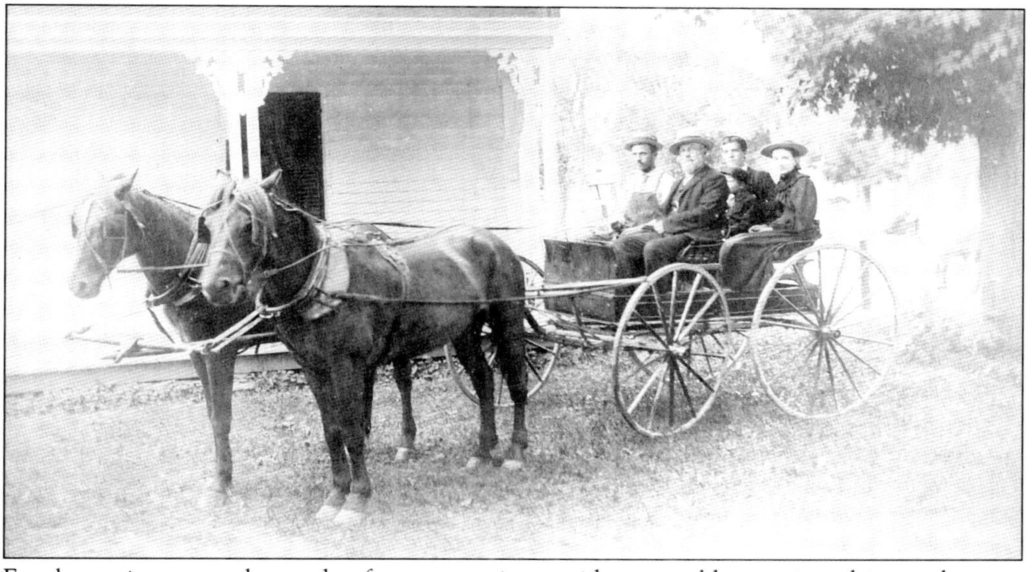

Fast becoming a popular mode of transportation, residents would sometimes hire, or borrow, a neighbor's carriage for excursions to nearby towns. One can only imagine that Daniel and Armory J. Holden, seated in the front, are taking Henry, Ellsworth, and Alice Wright to meet the train in Coldbrook Springs, as the Wrights were summer residents. This photo was taken next to the porch at the Holden residence on Maple Street.

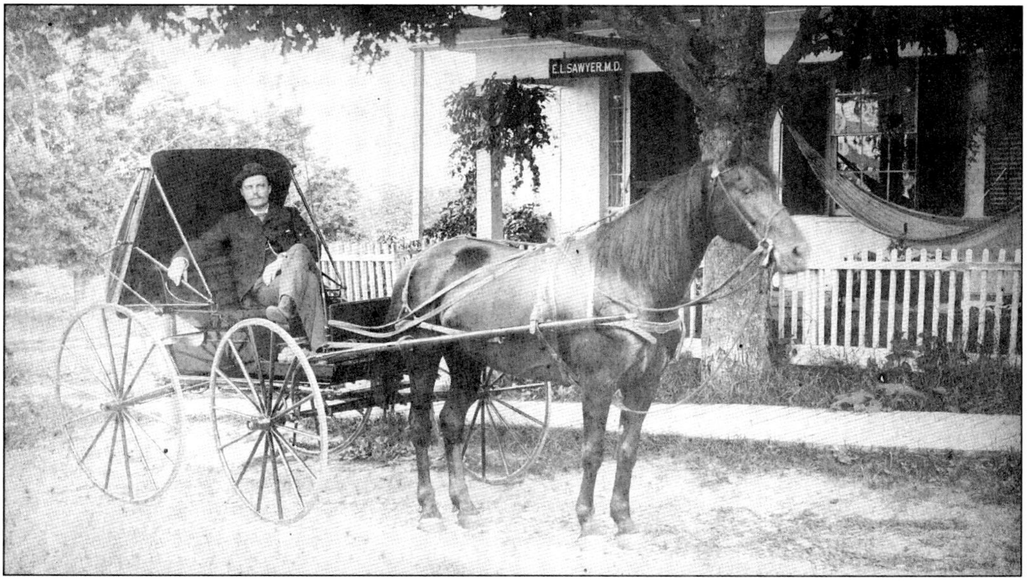

Dr. Elishu L. Sawyer shows off his favored means of transportation. He is pictured in front of his office at 17 Maple Street, also known as the Tottingham house.

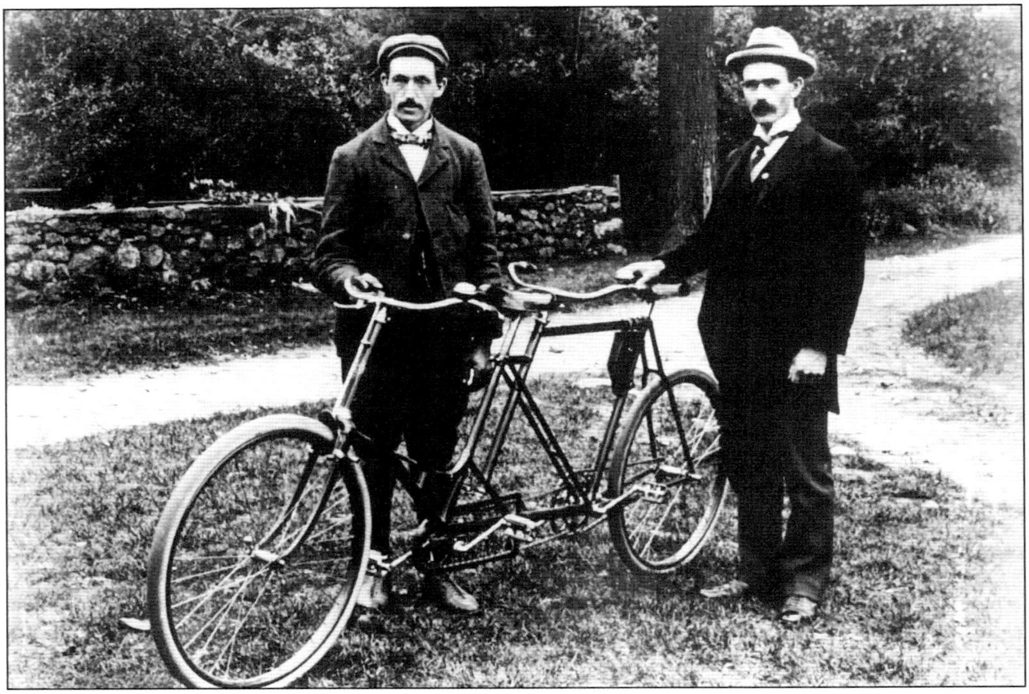

Bicycling was another means of transportation around the countryside. Here Henry A. and Edward J. Crawford take a break to show off their new bicycle to the photographer. Some residents have been known to travel by bicycle to Worcester and back in the same day.

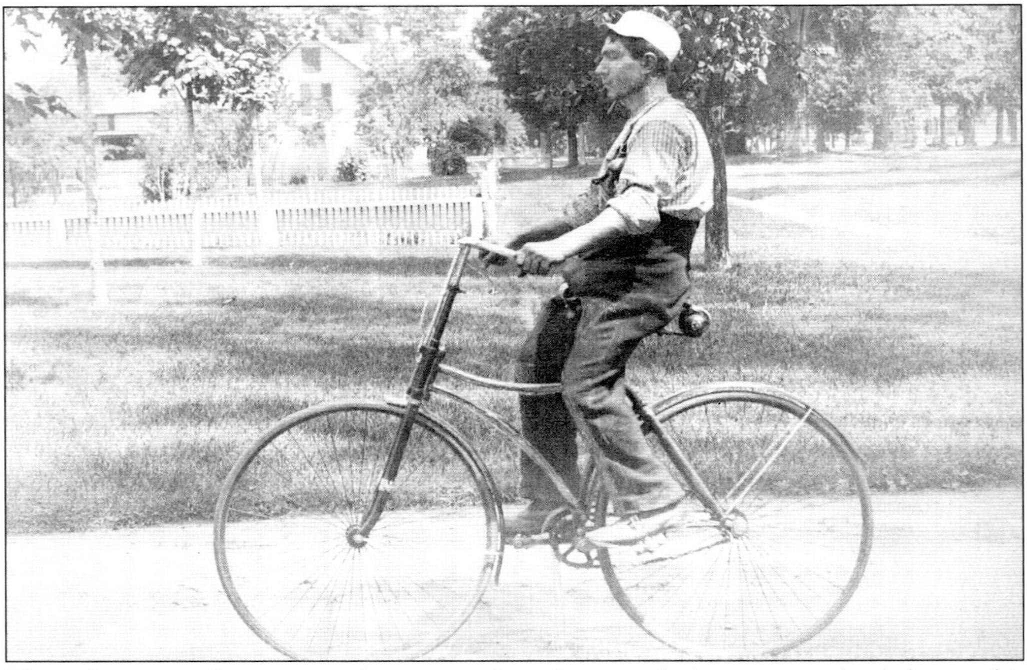

This unknown resident seems to be enjoying his ride, or maybe he is just good at balancing his bicycle without moving.

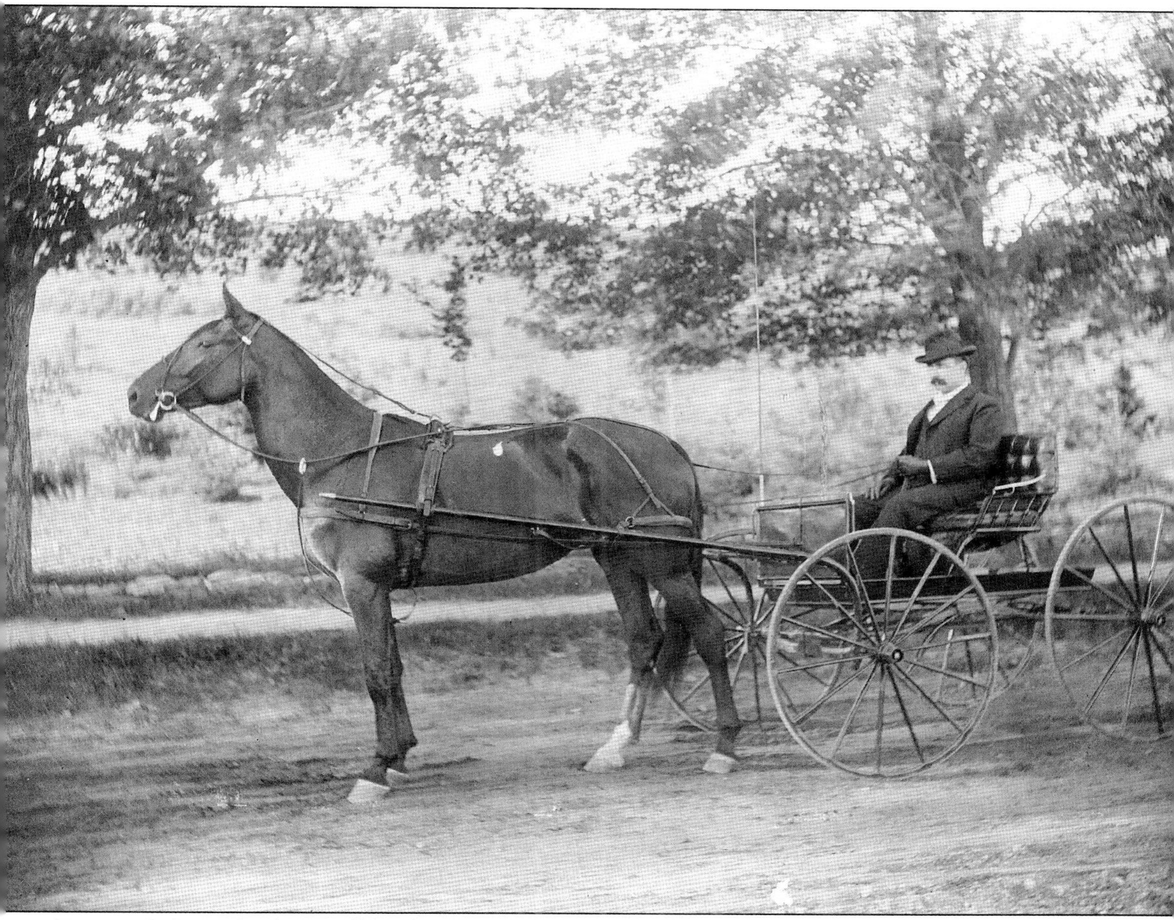

Eugene A. Lincoln shows off his fine steed as he goes about his errands. Lincoln graduated from the University of Pennsylvania Dental School in 1898, and after serving as an instructor at his own dental school for many years, he continued his practice in Ireland.

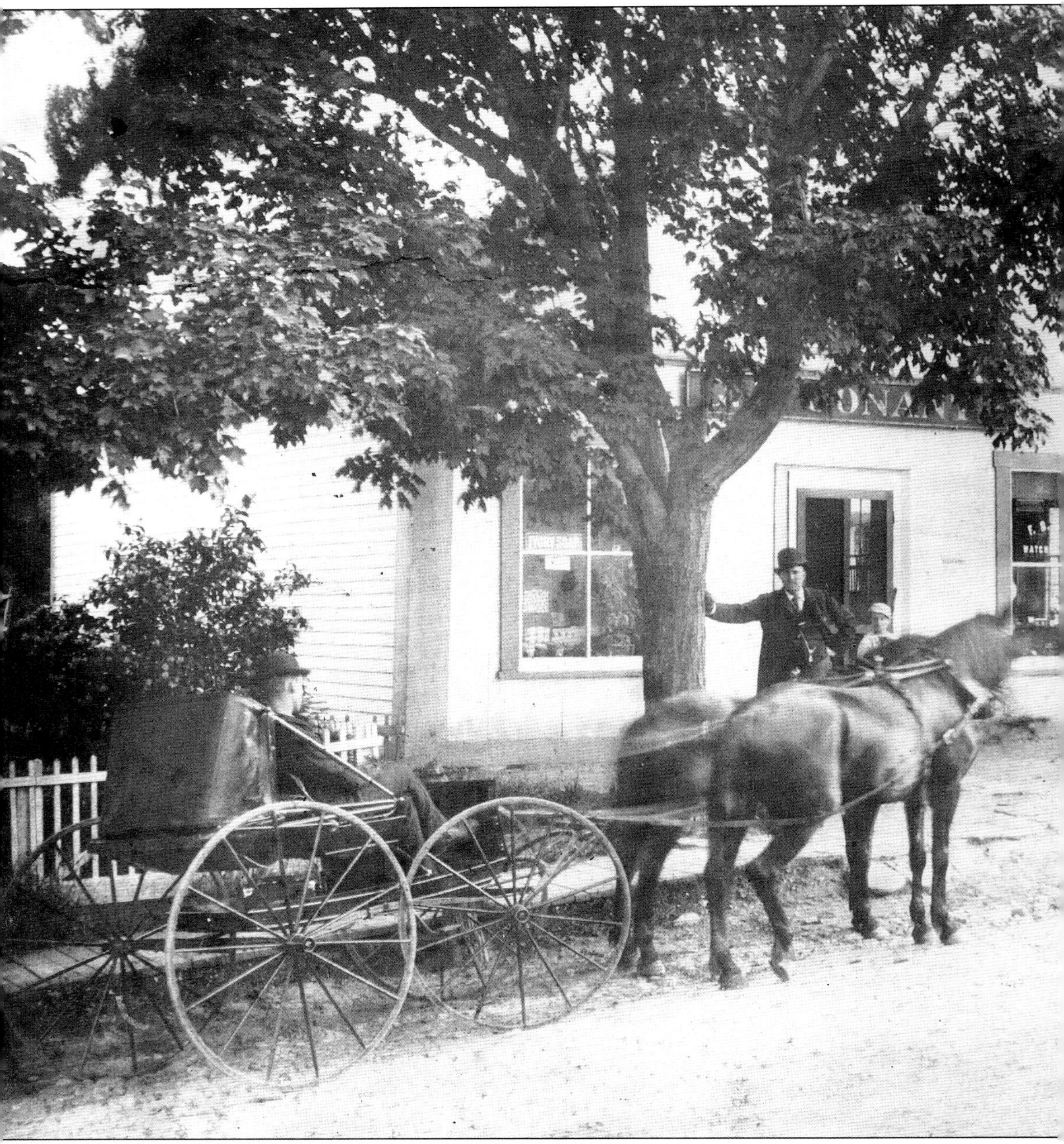

It seems that everyone near the Conant Store stops what they are doing to admire Dr. E.L. Sawyer's team and carriage, or are they inquiring as to the doctor's destination on his errand of

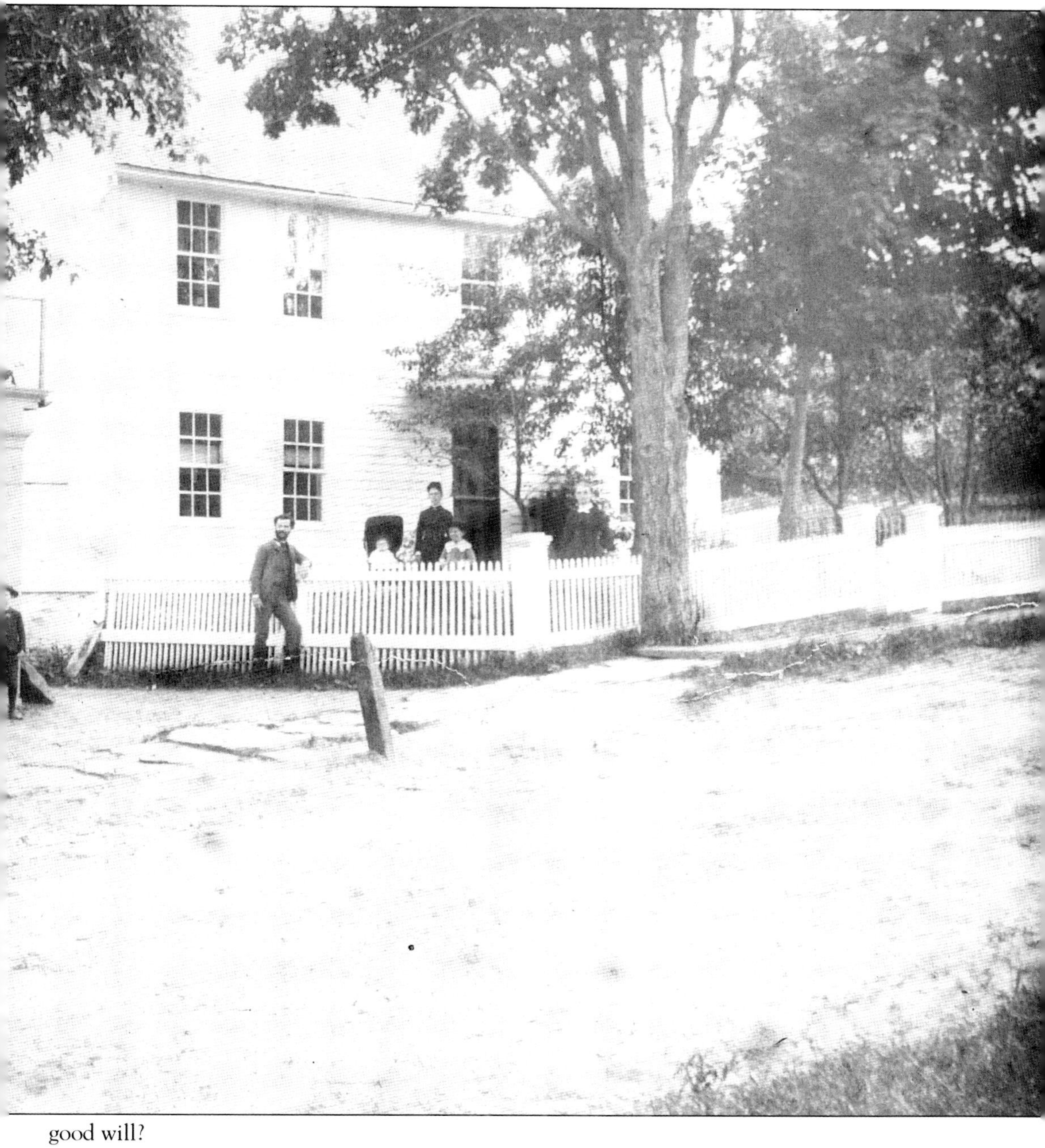

good will?

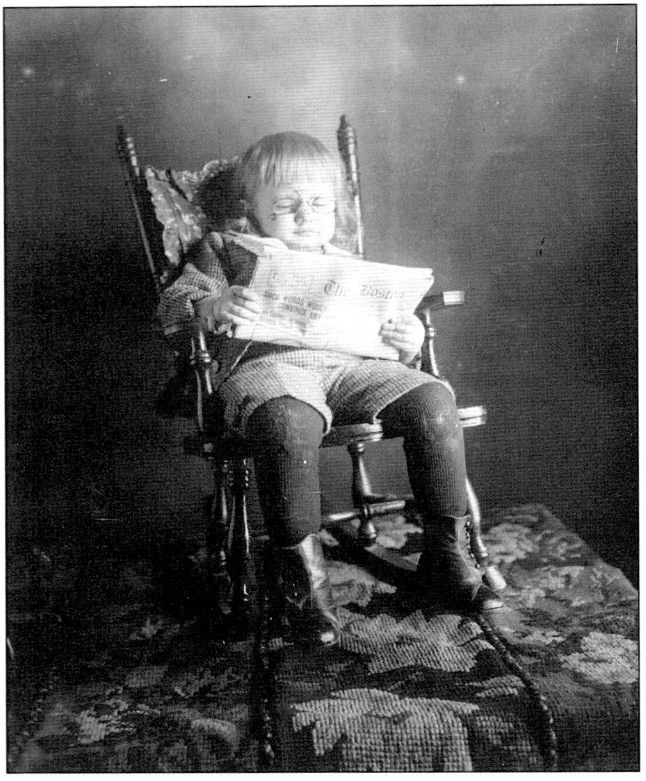

It seems that little Earle Parker is quite bored with this issue of a Boston newspaper, or is he studying the business news knowing that one day he would take over his father's (Clarence L. Parker) store in Coldbrook Springs?

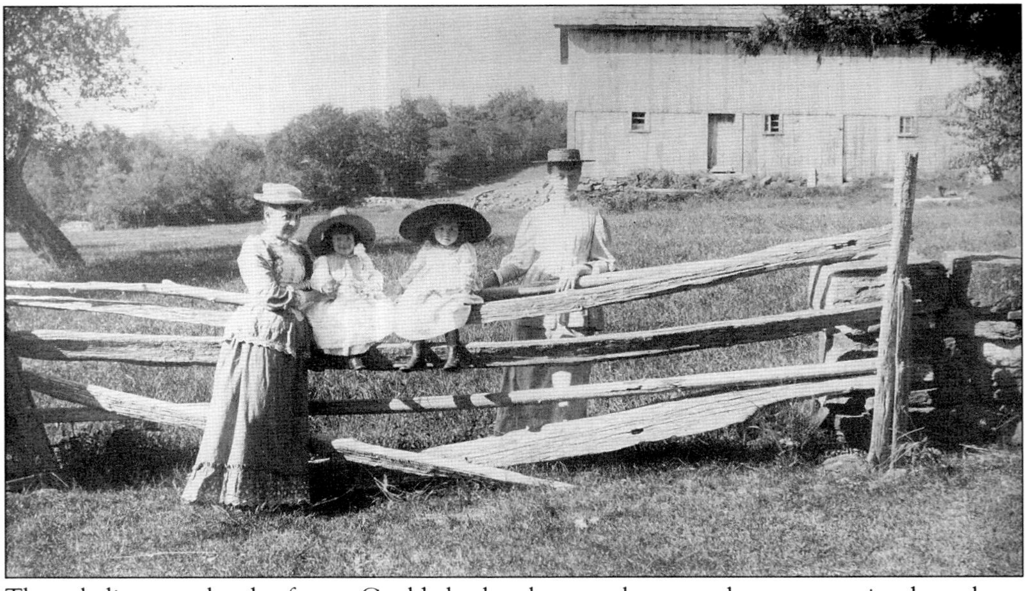

These ladies pose by the fence. Could the lovely straw bonnets they are wearing have been made at what once was the Center School building in the center?

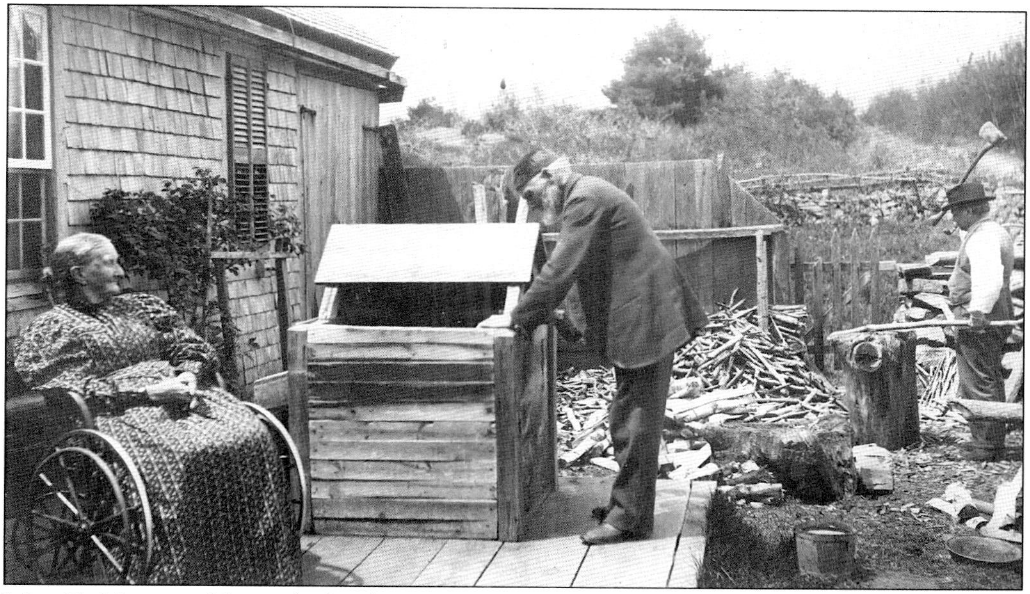

John N. Morse and his wife, Sarah, are pictured here with an unidentified gentleman on the right. Morse was a cabinet maker, and from 1840 to 1842 served as the town's undertaker. This photo was taken while the Morse family lived on East Hill Road.

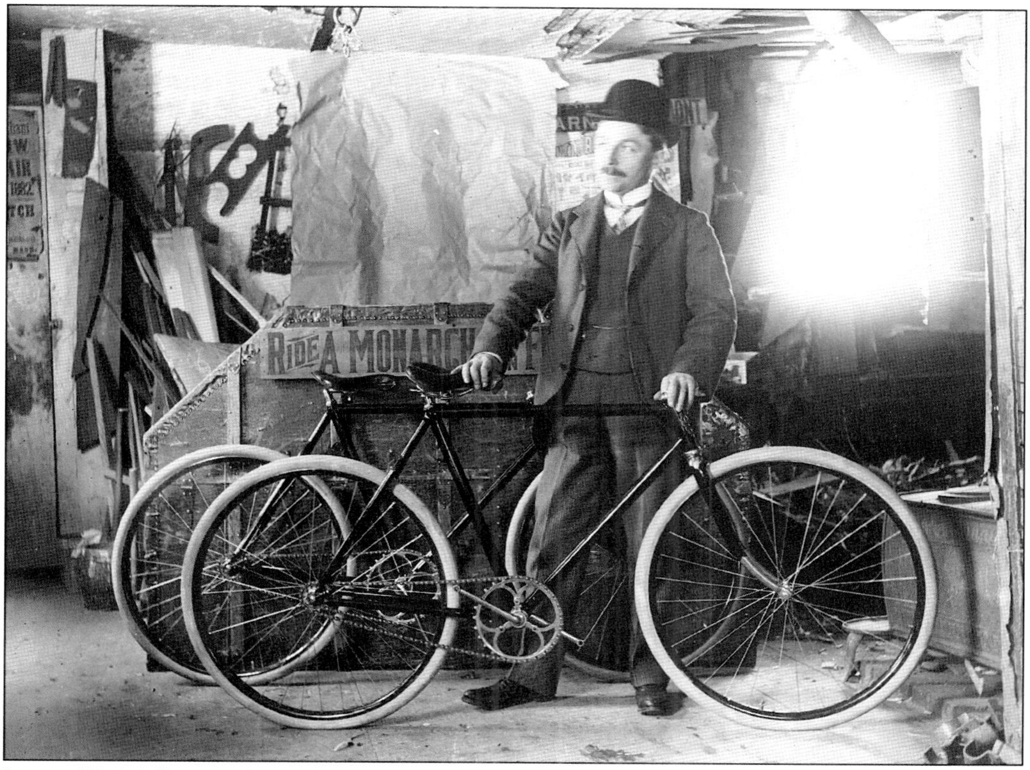

Irving W. Mullett is shown here with a bicycle in Crawford's Carriage Shop near the center of town.

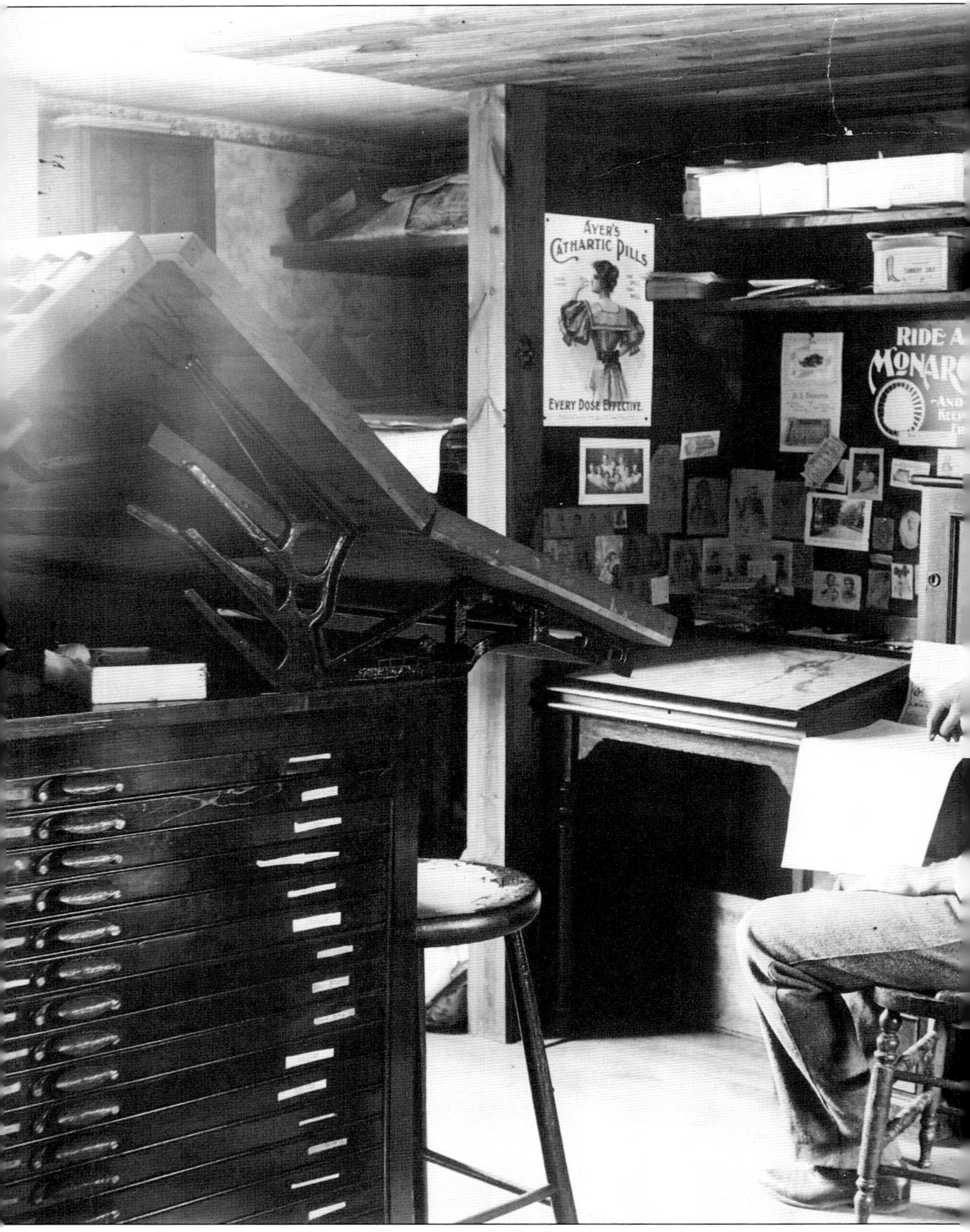
AYER'S
CATHARTIC PILLS
EVERY DOSE EFFECTIVE.
RIDE A

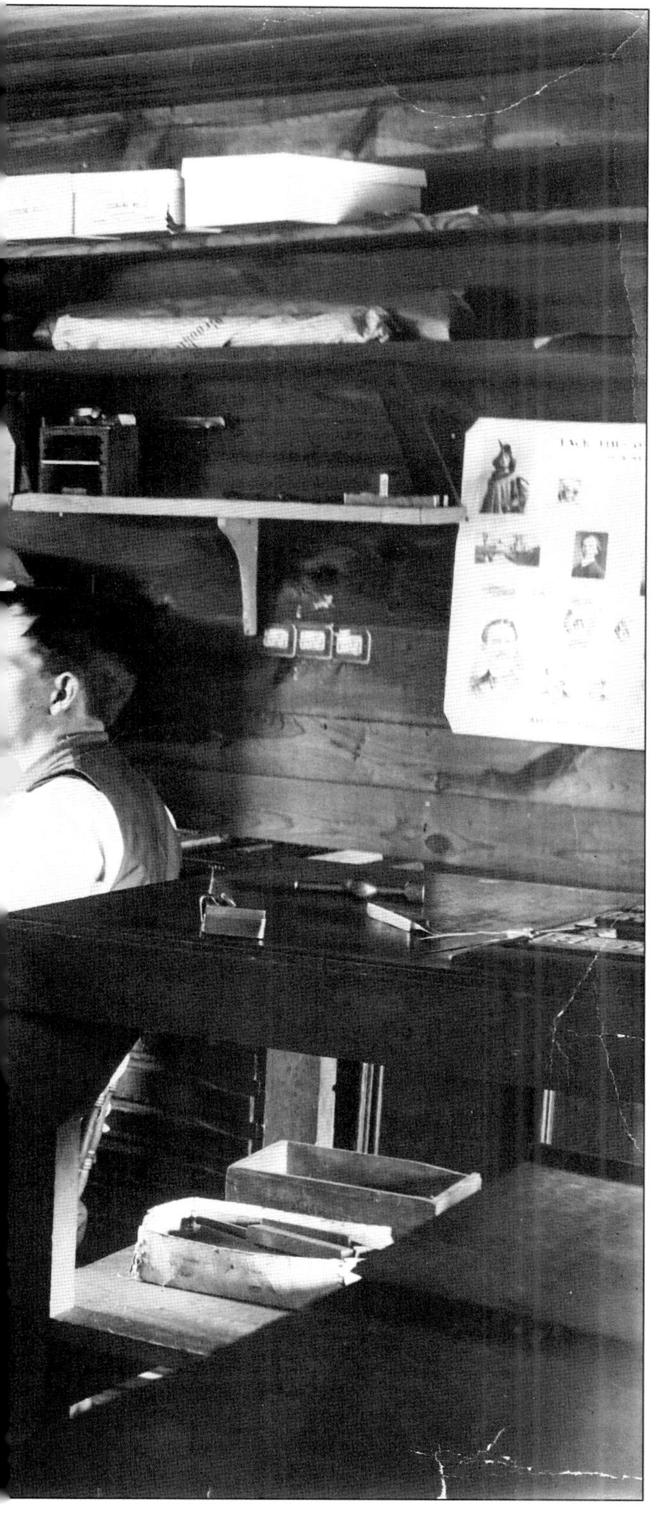

Publisher Irving W. Mullett is seen here contemplating the next issue of the *Oakham Herald*. The weekly newspaper was printed from 1890 to 1902. During 1900 there were four hundred issues of the *Herald* printed each week. The print shop of the *Herald* also took orders for letterheads, name cards, stationery, and bill heads. Several other newspapers were distributed in town at various times, including the *Young People's Enterprise*, the *Oakham Express*, the *Literary Magazine*, and the *Tuesday Evening Journal*. Many of these newspapers were short lived and were published under the auspices of the Oakham Library Association.

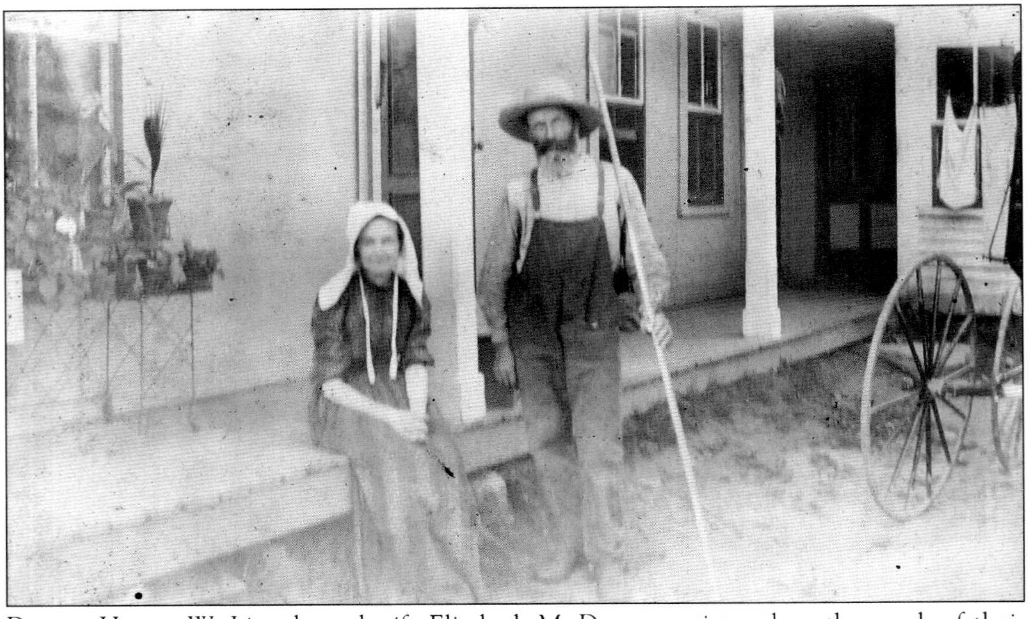

Deacon Horace W. Lincoln and wife Elizabeth M. Dean are pictured on the porch of their home at 687 Lincoln Road. Lincoln was elected as a deacon of the Congregational church in 1870, served on the school committee from 1862 to 1869, and was an auditor of accounts from 1874 to 1900.

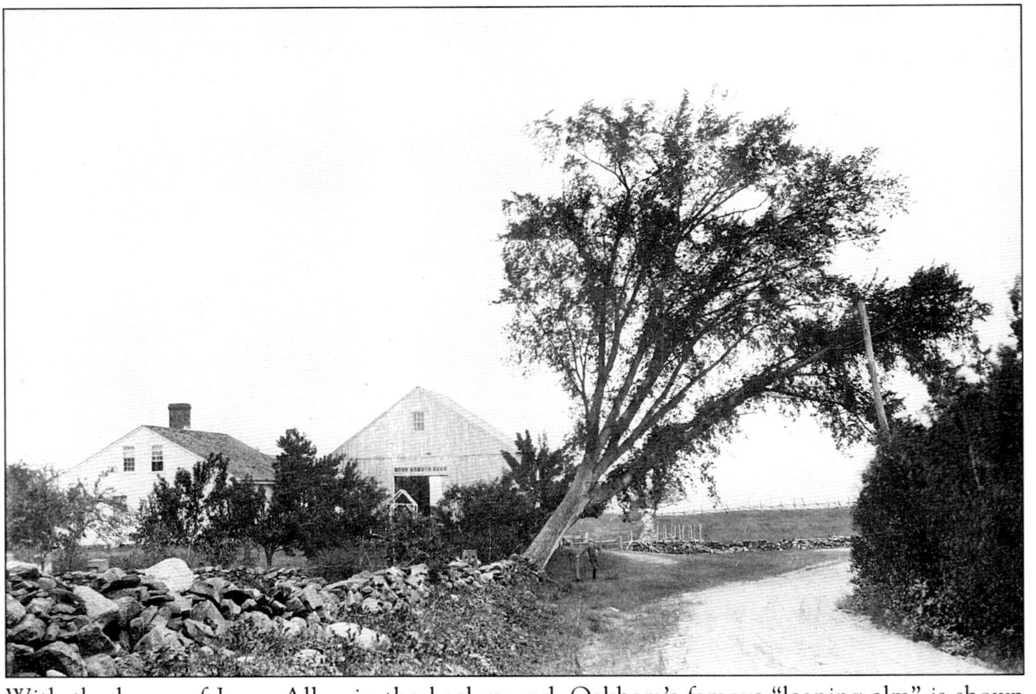

With the home of Jason Allen in the background, Oakham's famous "leaning elm" is shown here. The tree was blown over in a hurricane in 1873, and was removed with some controversy in December 1962.

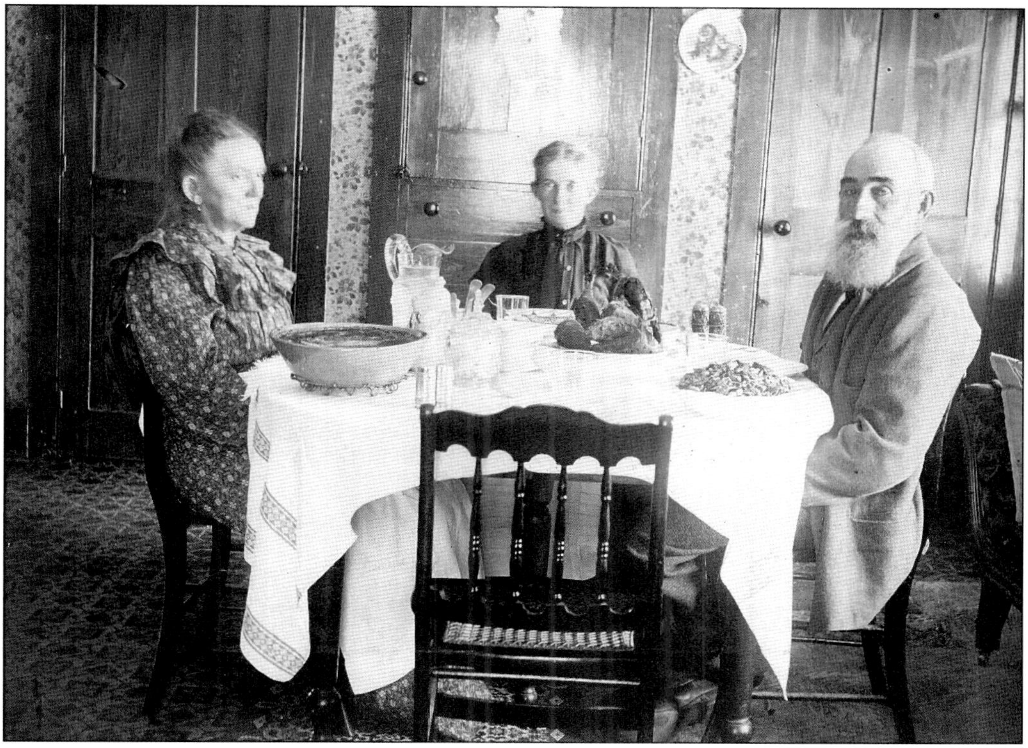

In the parlor of their home, William Sanford Crawford and his wife, Eunice Dean, entertain her sister Emily K. Dean, pictured in the center of the photograph.

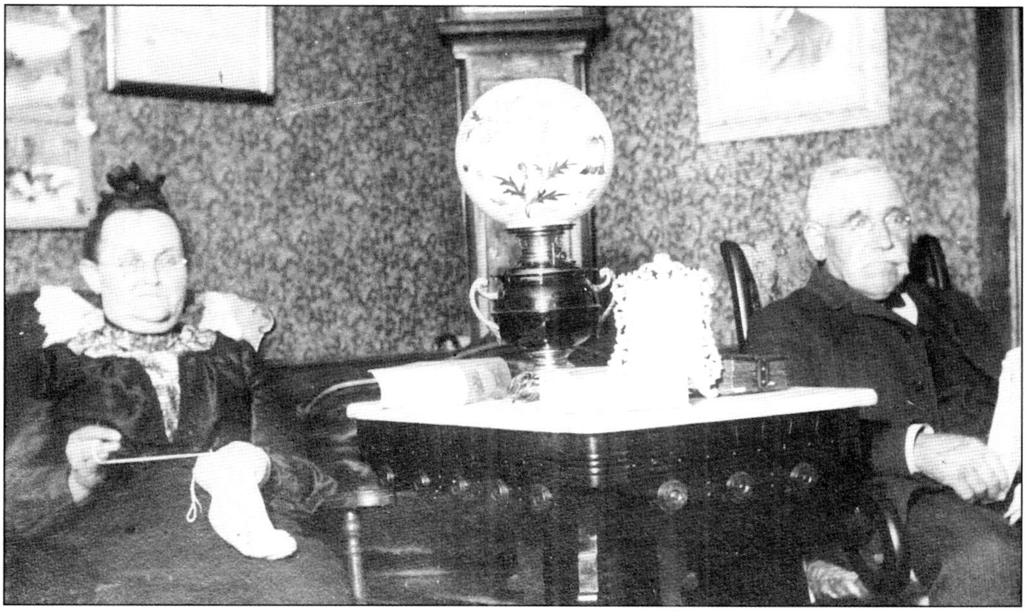

Pictured in their parlor are Henry A. Crawford and his wife, Ellen Sargeant Crawford. The clock in the background was made by Henry's grandfather, William Crawford. The picture on the wall is believed to be Hiram Allen Crawford.

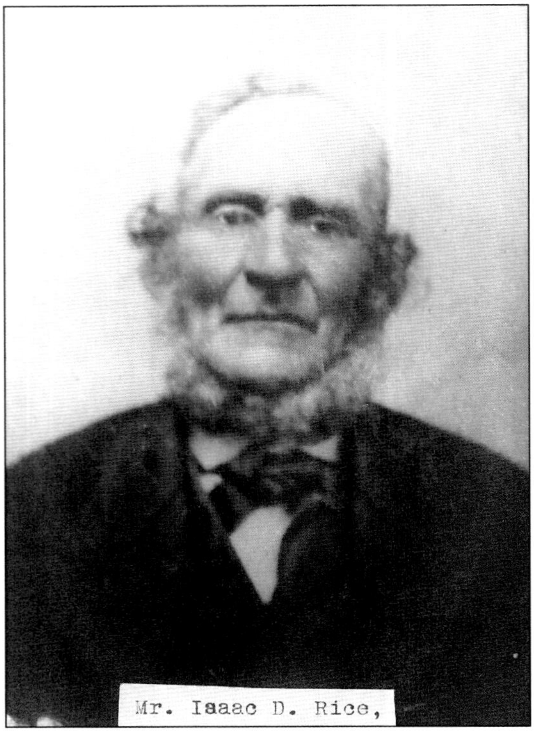

In 1840, a Baptist church stood 1 mile north of Coldbrook Springs. Isaac D. Rice and Captain James Conant purchased the building, had it torn down, and rebuilt on Coldbrook Road. The building was dedicated as a Methodist church in 1843. Rice was the only Oakham resident that served in the United States Army during the Seminole War (1835–1842).

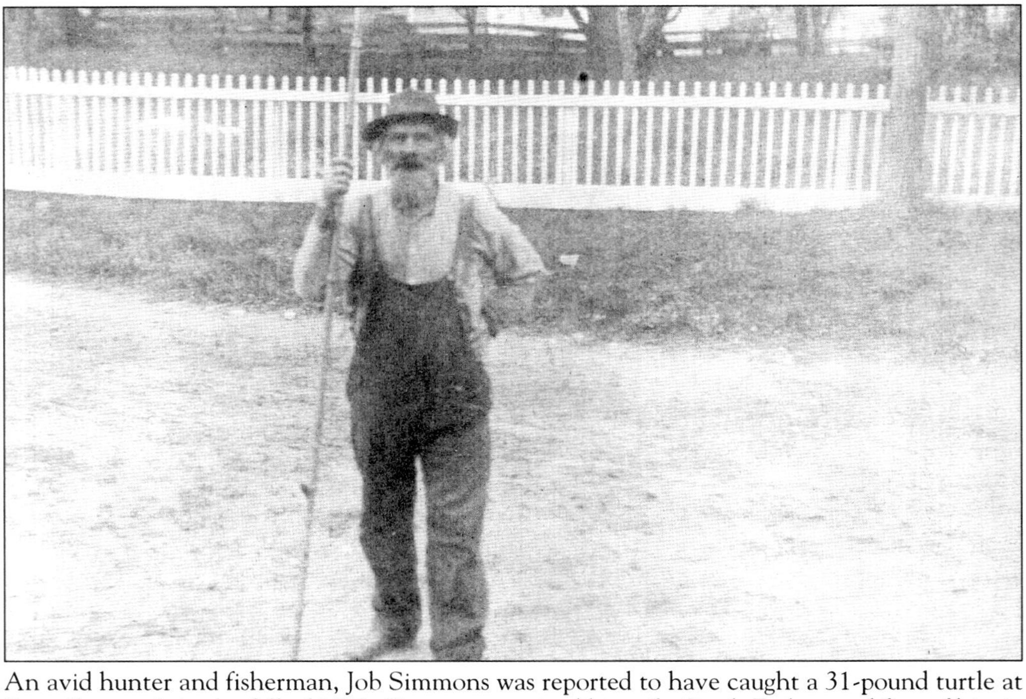

An avid hunter and fisherman, Job Simmons was reported to have caught a 31-pound turtle at Dean Reservoir in the fall of 1891. Simmons survived his wife, Sarah Forbes, and five of his six children, spending his last 42 years doing what he loved to do.

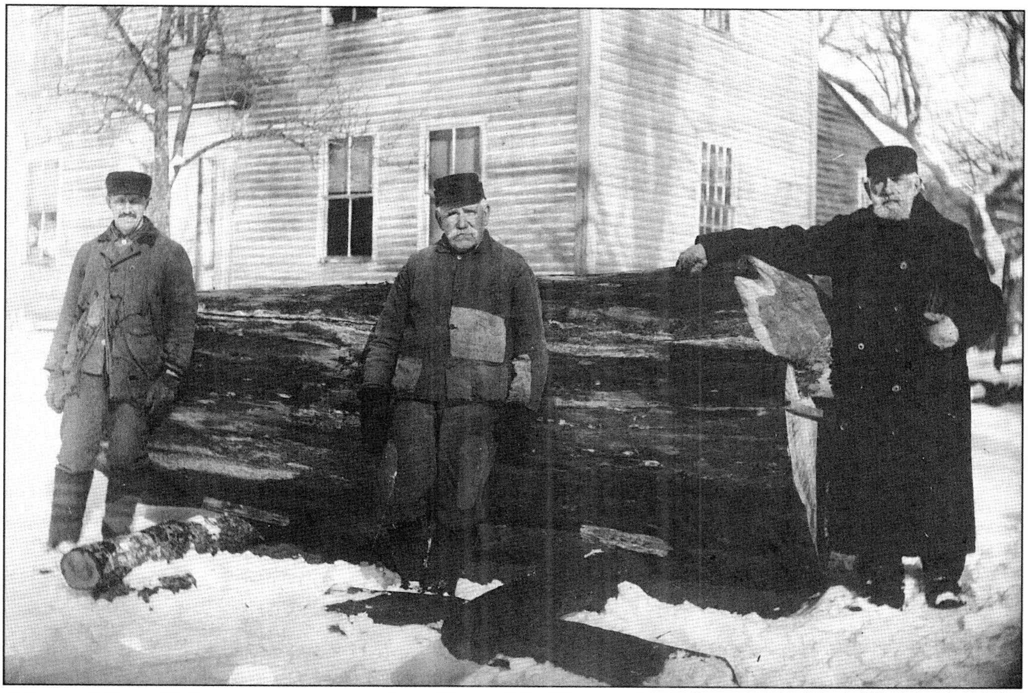

After a job well done on a wintry day, Henry U., Henry A., and William E. Crawford take a well-deserved break.

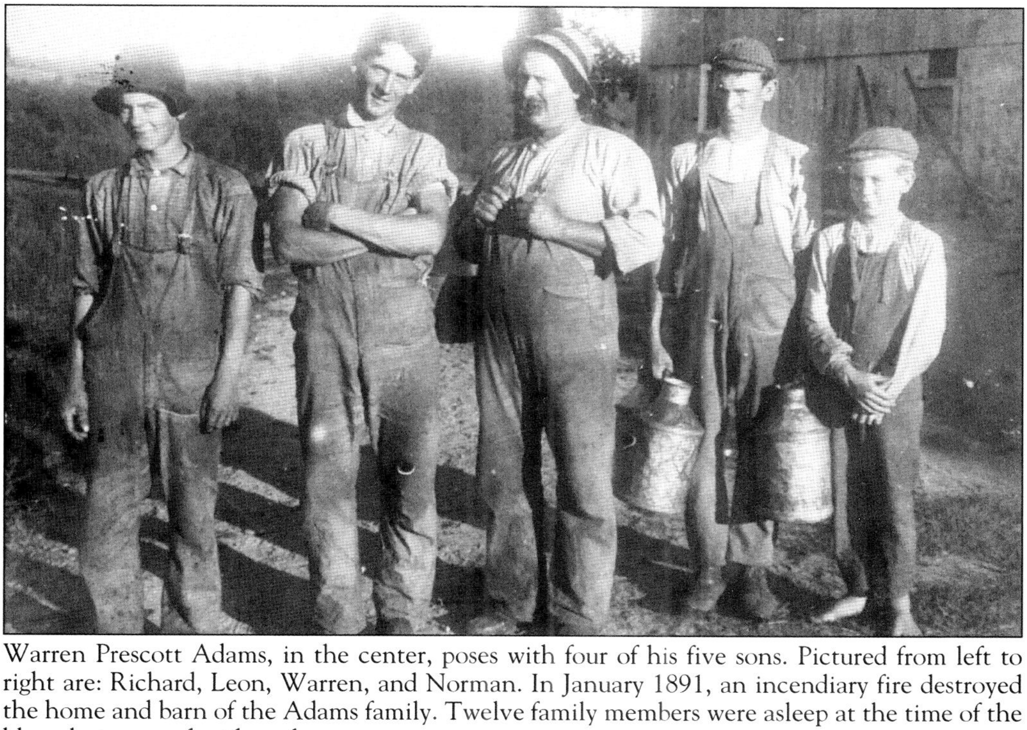

Warren Prescott Adams, in the center, poses with four of his five sons. Pictured from left to right are: Richard, Leon, Warren, and Norman. In January 1891, an incendiary fire destroyed the home and barn of the Adams family. Twelve family members were asleep at the time of the blaze, but escaped without harm.

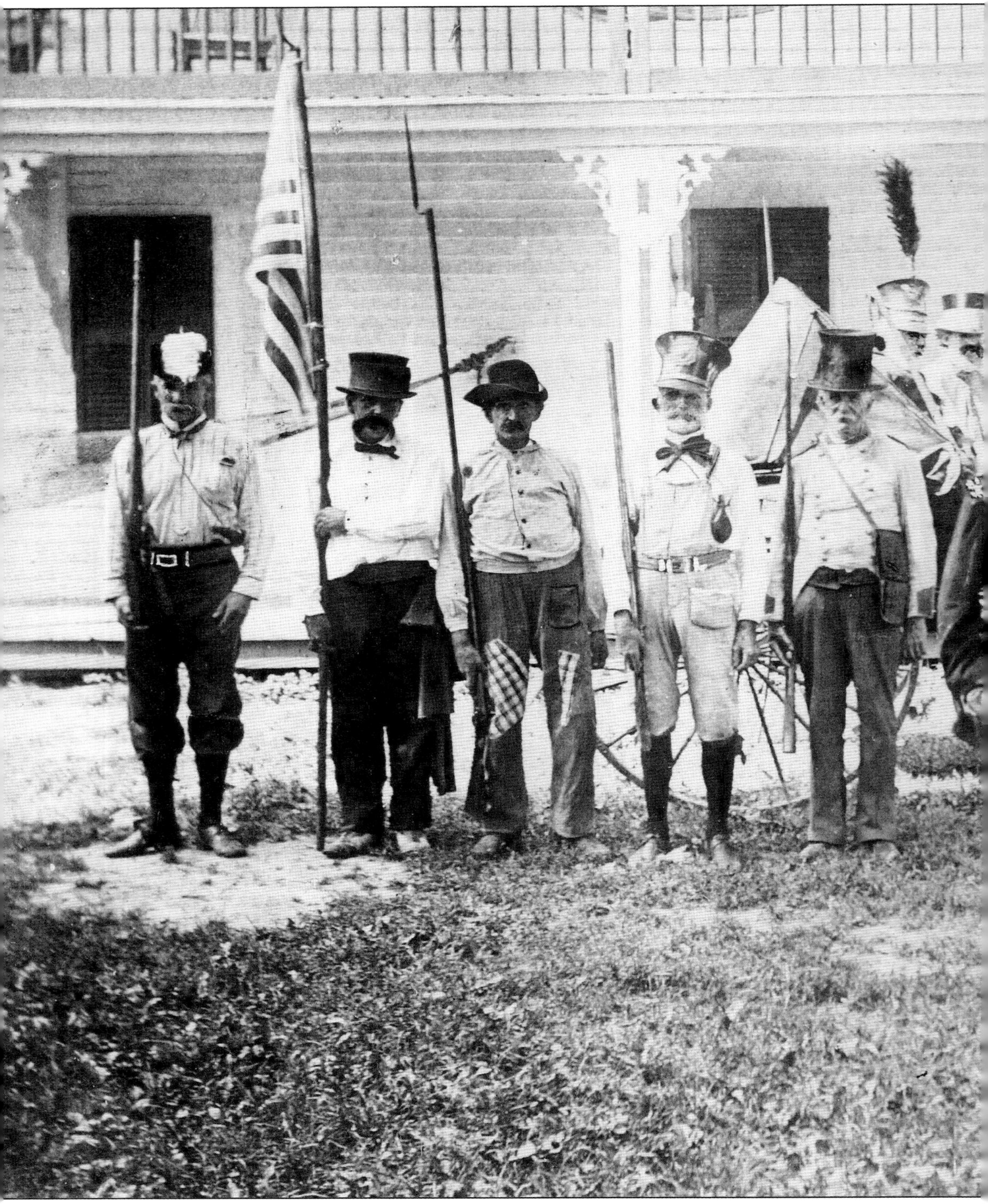

Standing at attention and awaiting the annual Field Day festivities are the "Oakham Minutemen." Pictured from left to right are: W. Bushnell, F. Burt, W. Burt, J. Packard, C. Reed,

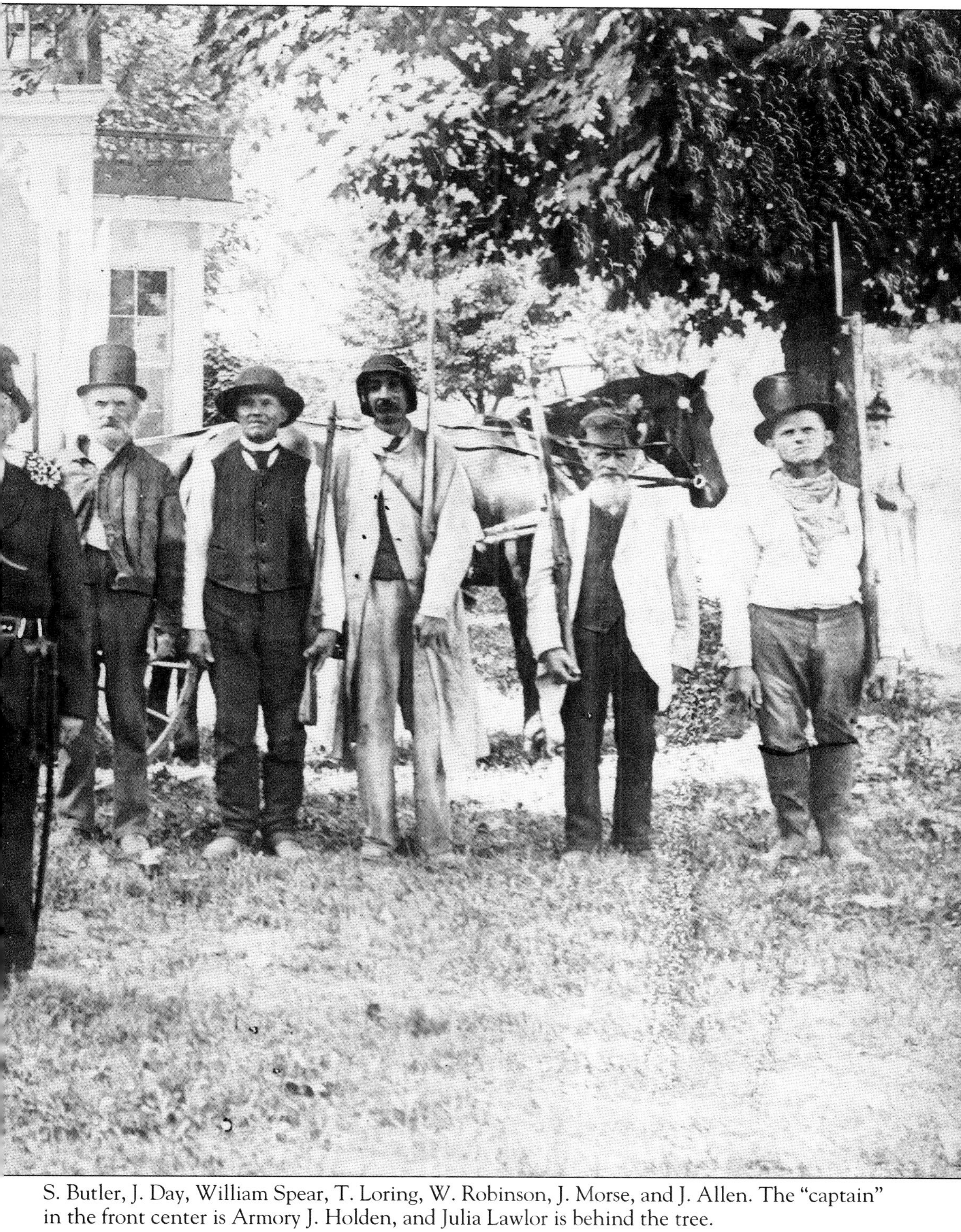

S. Butler, J. Day, William Spear, T. Loring, W. Robinson, J. Morse, and J. Allen. The "captain" in the front center is Armory J. Holden, and Julia Lawlor is behind the tree.

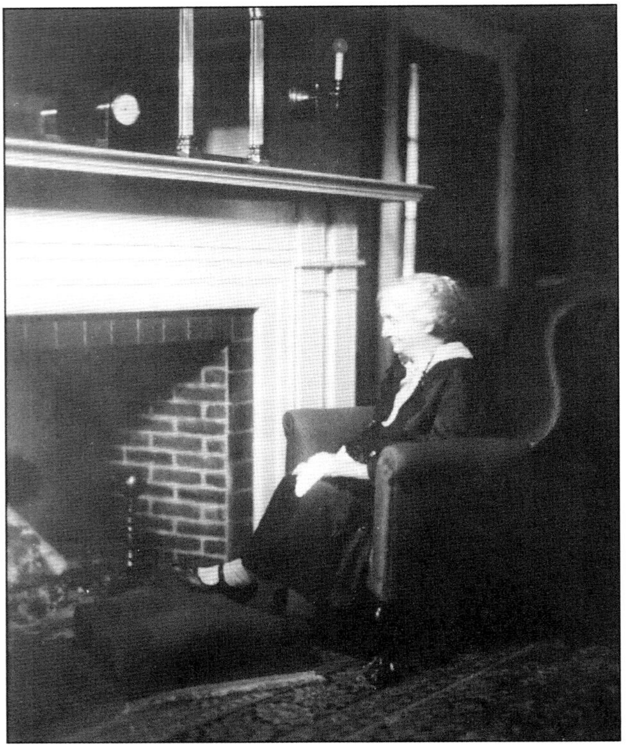

Born October 4, 1844, Amelia Esther Tomlinson was the great-granddaughter of Reverend Daniel Tomlinson. Warren Prescott Adams, son of Cheney and Roxana, was born October 15, 1843. Amelia and Warren were married June 14, 1866. The marriage certificate is signed by James Allen, town clerk of Oakham. The couple was married in Worcester, even though they were Oakham residents.

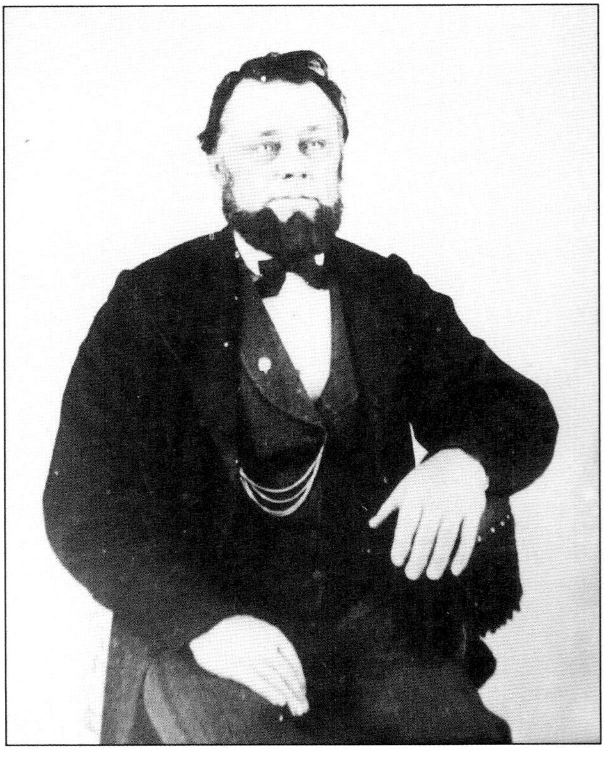

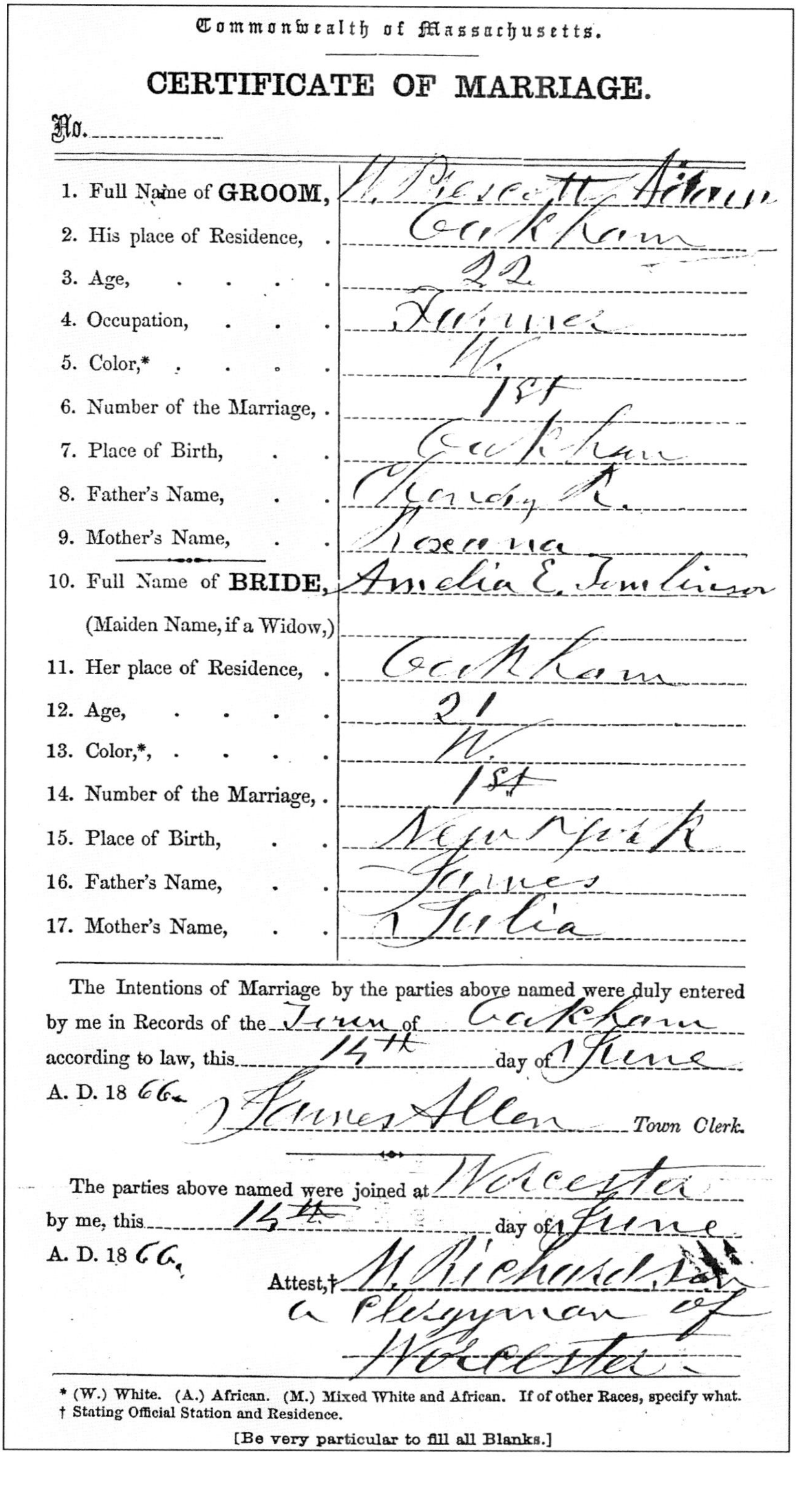

Commonwealth of Massachusetts.

CERTIFICATE OF MARRIAGE.

No. ....

1. Full Name of **GROOM**,	W. Prescott Aiken
2. His place of Residence, .	Oakham
3. Age, ...	22
4. Occupation, . . .	Farmer
5. Color,*	W.
6. Number of the Marriage, .	1st
7. Place of Birth, . .	Oakham
8. Father's Name, . .	Hardy R.
9. Mother's Name, . .	Roxanna
10. Full Name of **BRIDE**,	Amelia E. Tomlinson
(Maiden Name, if a Widow,)	
11. Her place of Residence, .	Oakham
12. Age, ...	21
13. Color,*, ...	W.
14. Number of the Marriage, .	1st
15. Place of Birth, . .	New York
16. Father's Name, . .	James
17. Mother's Name, . .	Julia

The Intentions of Marriage by the parties above named were duly entered by me in Records of the Town of Oakham according to law, this 14th day of June A. D. 1866.

James Allen Town Clerk.

The parties above named were joined at Worcester by me, this 14th day of June A. D. 1866.

Attest,† M. Richardson a Clergyman of Worcester.

* (W.) White. (A.) African. (M.) Mixed White and African. If of other Races, specify what.
† Stating Official Station and Residence.

[Be very particular to fill all Blanks.]

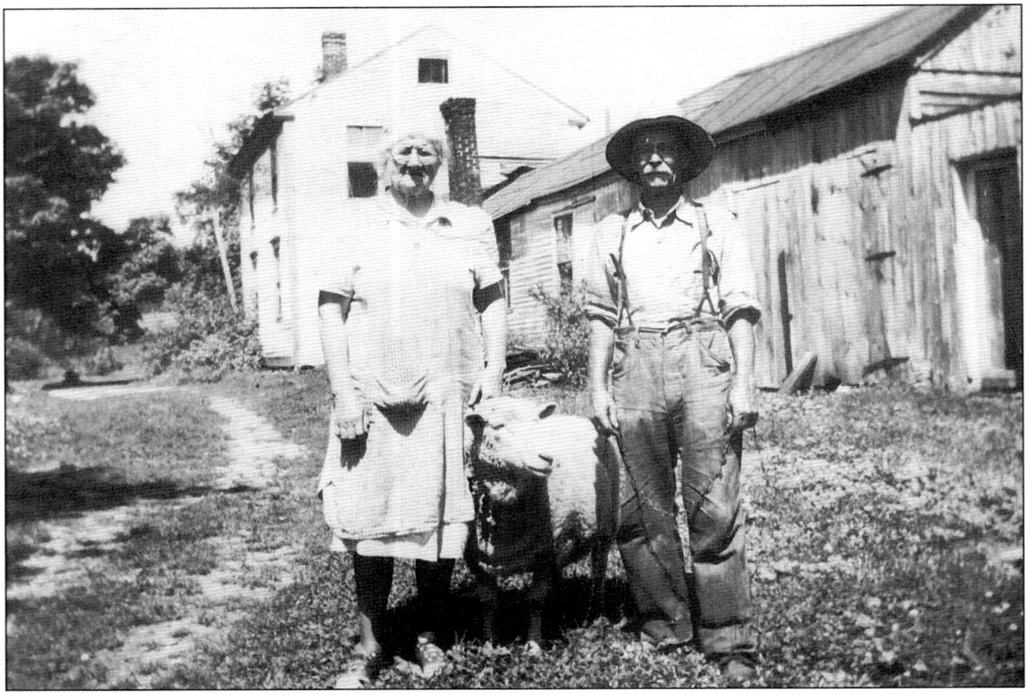

One of Oakham's highest tax payers in 1873 was George N. Briggs, paying $153.27 for 153 acres, one house, four barns, 14 cows, and other animals.

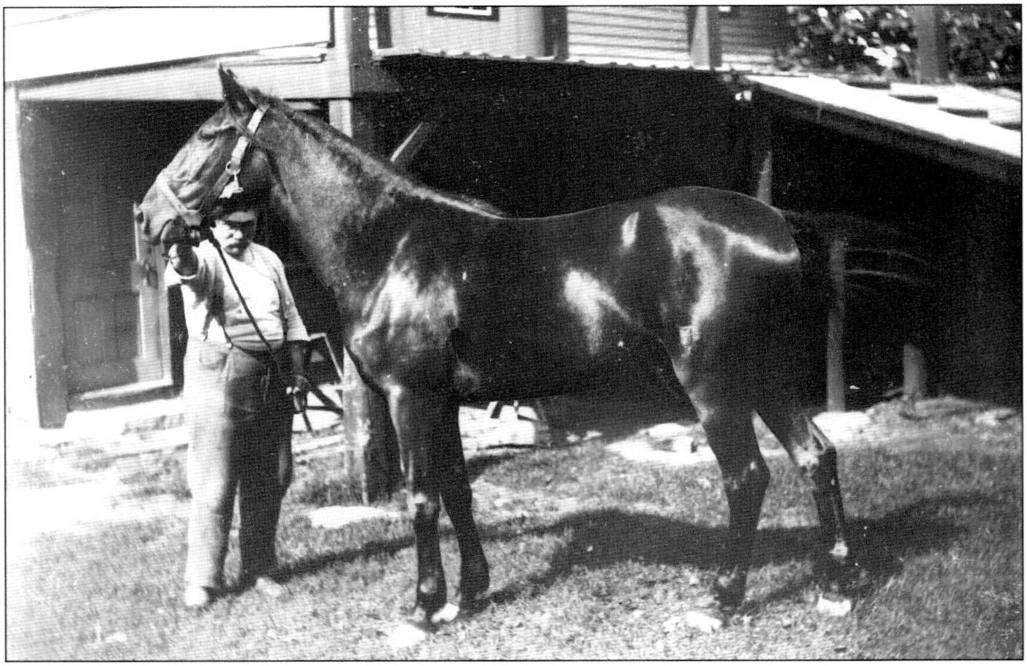

Being shown off in front of the Crawford carriage shop is N.W. Packard's race horse, Brightwood. Packard traveled to fairs in the area to race his horse. An *Oakham Herald* article in 1891 reported that the horse won $150 within a ten-day period.

Isadore and Laura Snay are shown here on their wedding day. Isadore built the house located at 252 East Hill Road. It is said that friends would bring rocks as a sort of house-warming present. The house built of those rocks has exterior walls 22 inches thick.

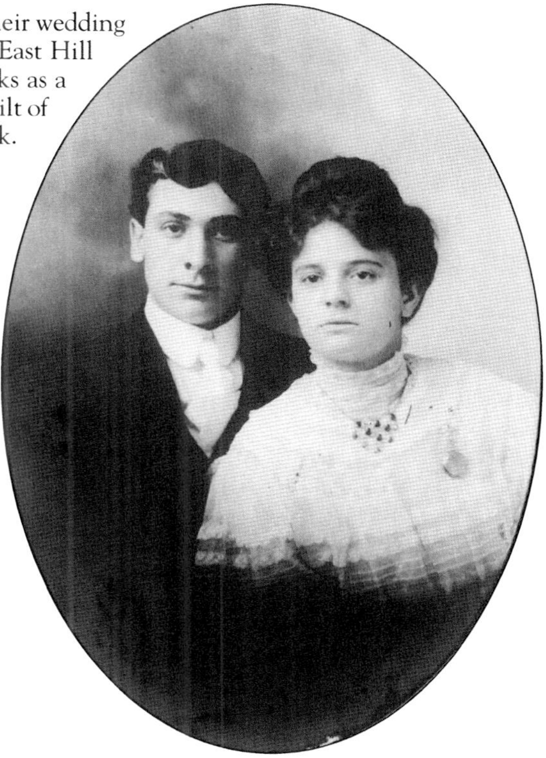

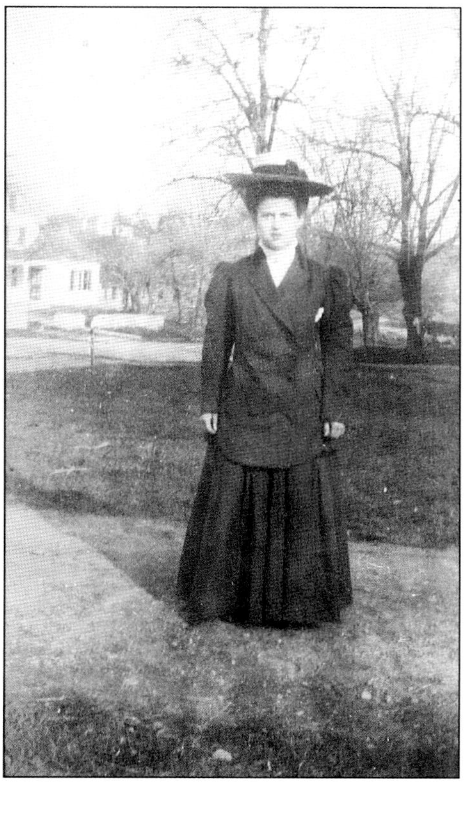

Mildred L. Burt was the daughter of Frank E. and Lillie May Robinson Burt. The Burt family lived at 163 Rutland Road.

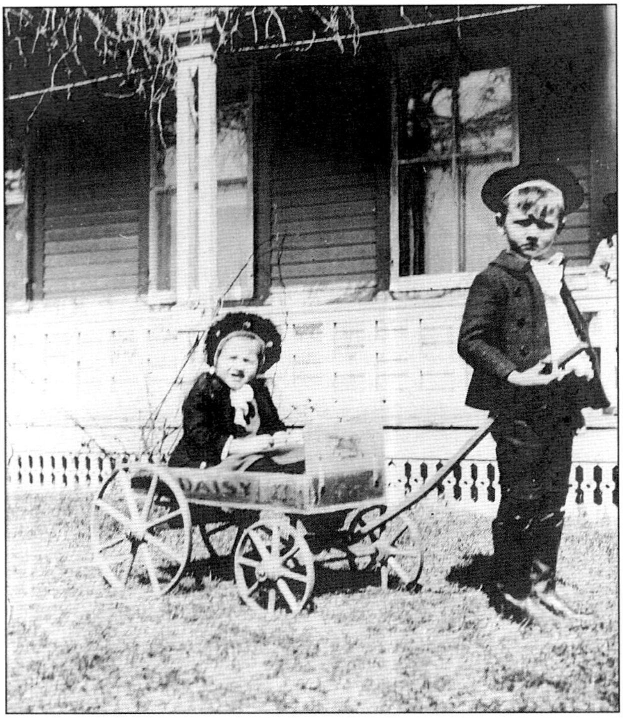

These unidentified youngsters take a few minutes out of their play time to pose for the photographer.

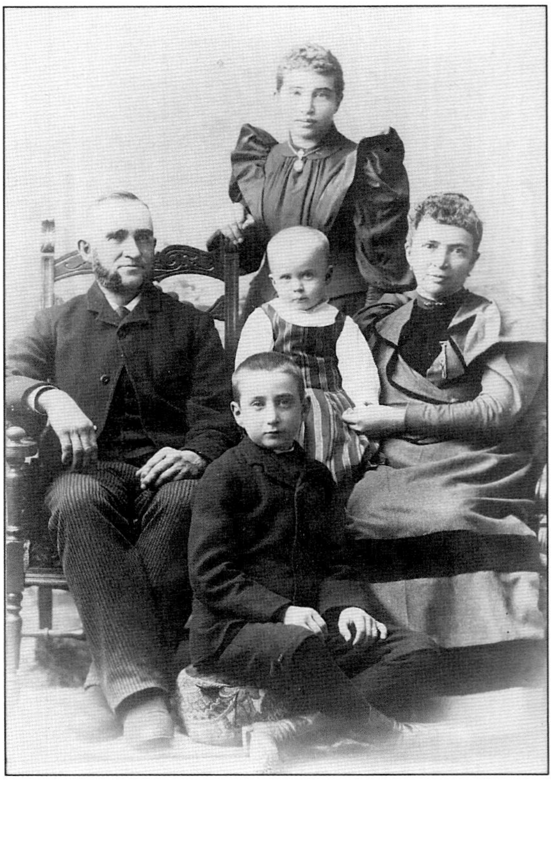

James and Adeline Dean Robinson and their children Fannie, David, and Oscar have their family portrait taken. The Robinson family lived at 426 Ware Corner Road.

Henry P. Wright taught at the East Center School during the winter term of 1860–1861. He went on to become a professor and later Dean of Yale College. In his later years he began writing the history of Oakham. After his death in 1918, his son Henry B. took over the project.

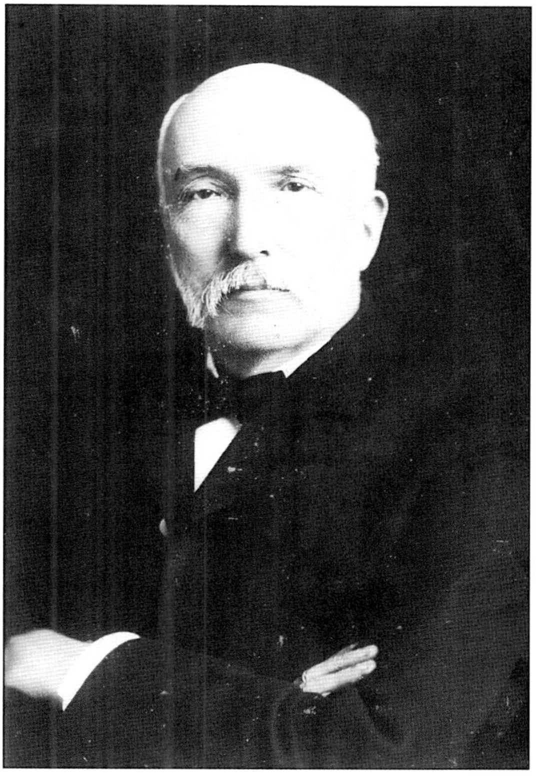

The young man in this photo is believed to be Stephen Lincoln, who in later years operated the S and W Lincoln Company, which manufactured wire goods.

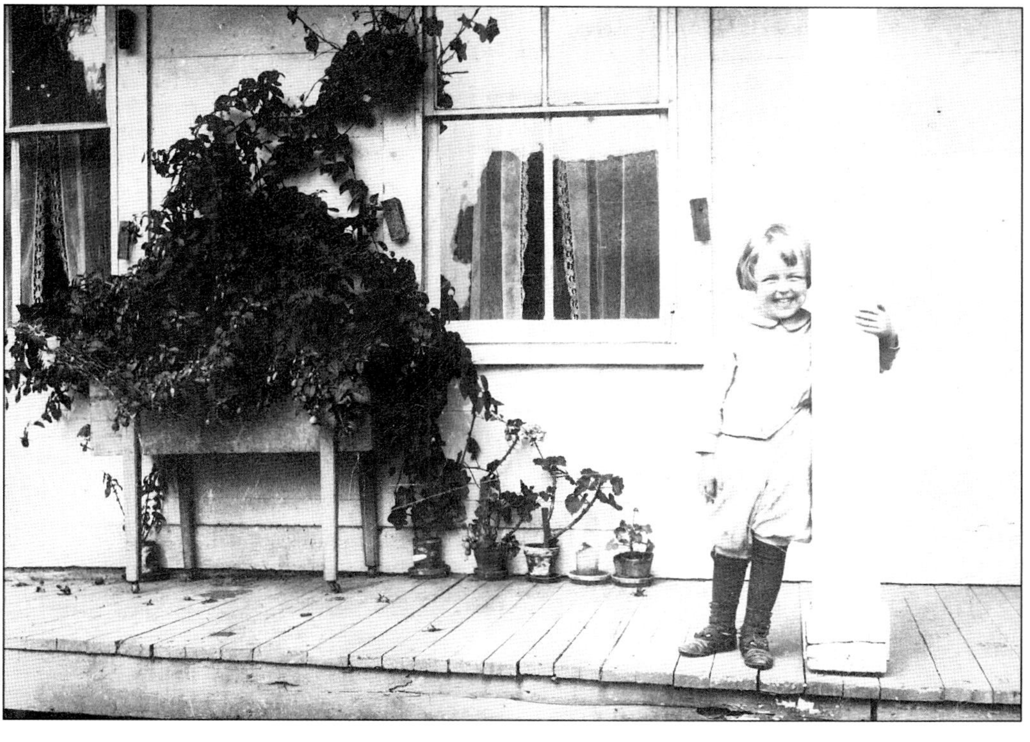

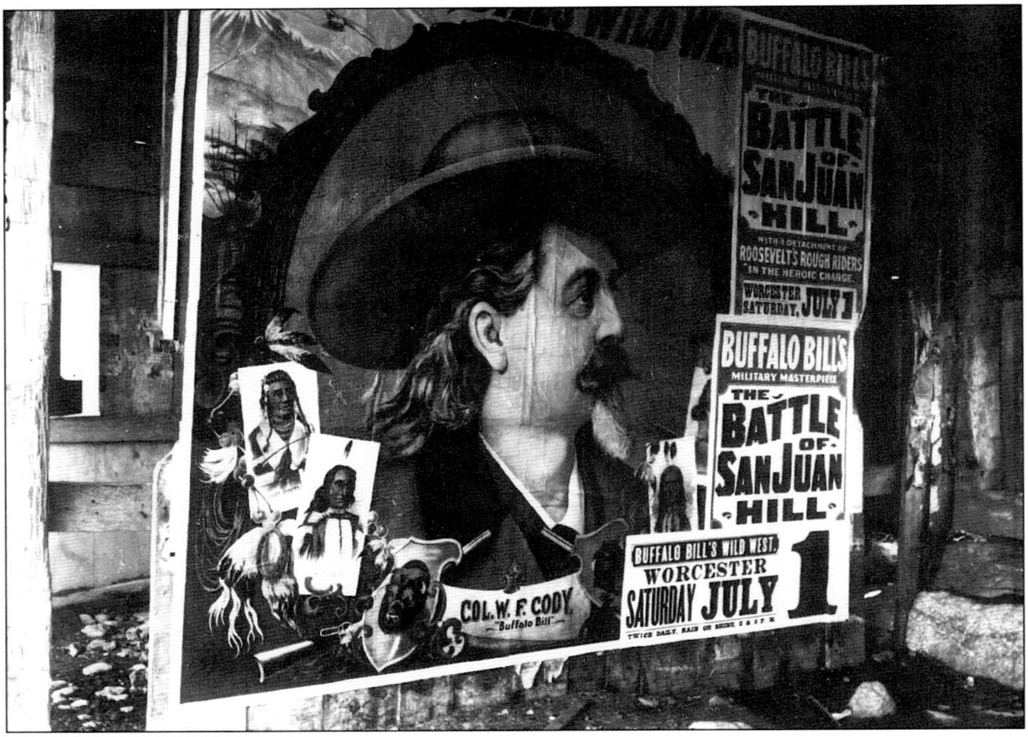

This billboard advertising Buffalo Bill's Wild West Show was attached to the side of William Sanford Crawford's barn. Crawford would often take the old signs and use them to repair his dilapidated barn.

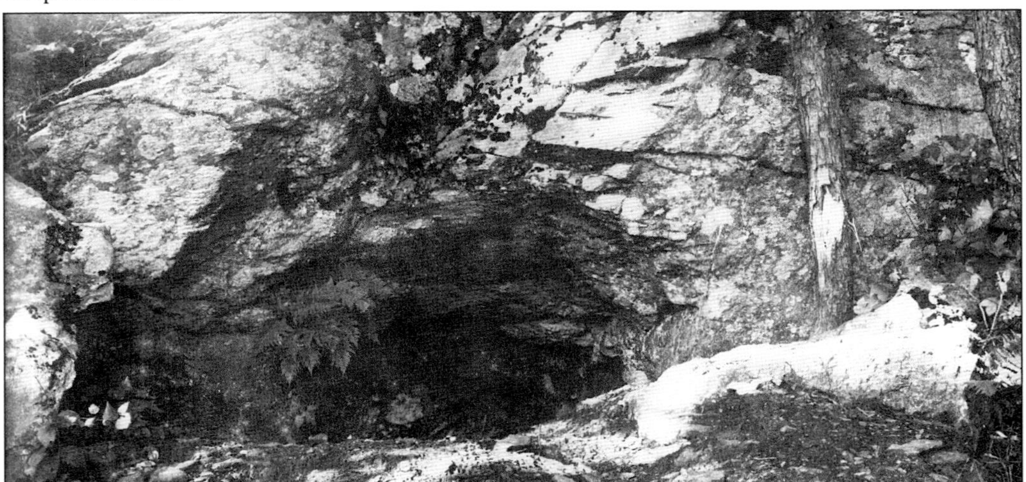

Located off Deacon Allen Drive, "Rattlesnake Den" was once home to hundreds of rattlesnakes. Newspaper accounts report that James Mulholland "with characteristic lack of fear . . . he resolutely began to attack (the snakes) and was soon busily employed. When he was treacherously assailed . . . a rattler of enormous size fixed his fangs in the calf of Mulholland's leg. No evil consequences being felt from the attack." Also, according to an *Oakham Herald* article in 1898, an Indian hatchet was found on this location.

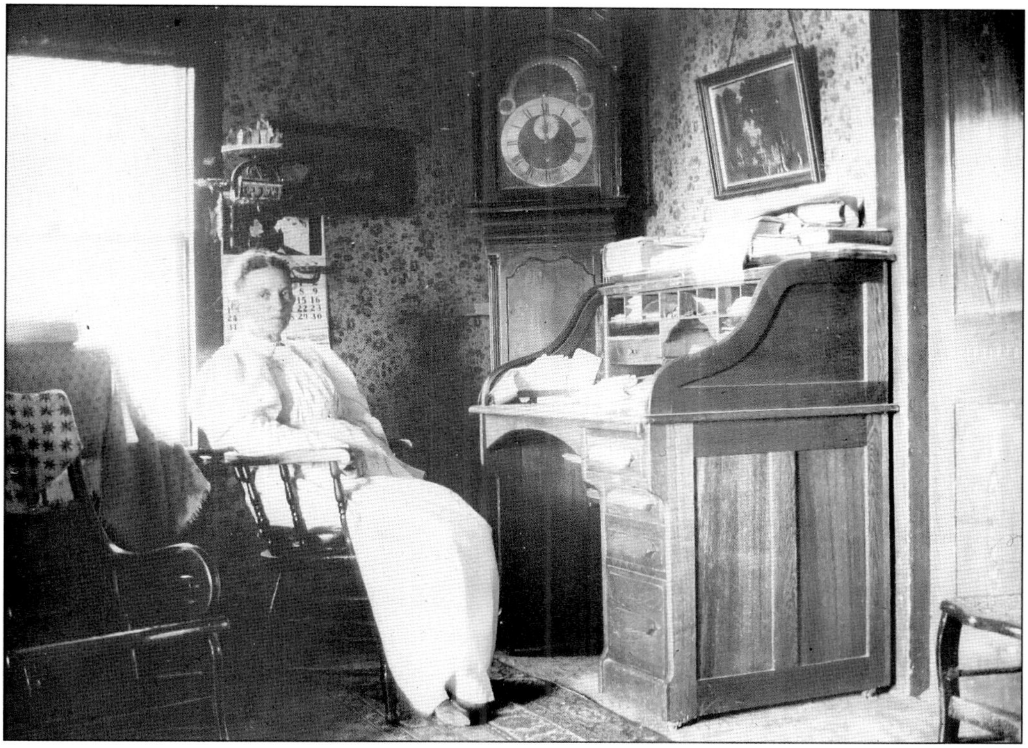

Edward S. Crawford was a popular artist who was responsible for photographing many scenes around town. His sketches helped him obtain a position as an artist with a Boston firm. The clock in the corner of the room was built by Edward's ancestor, William Crawford.

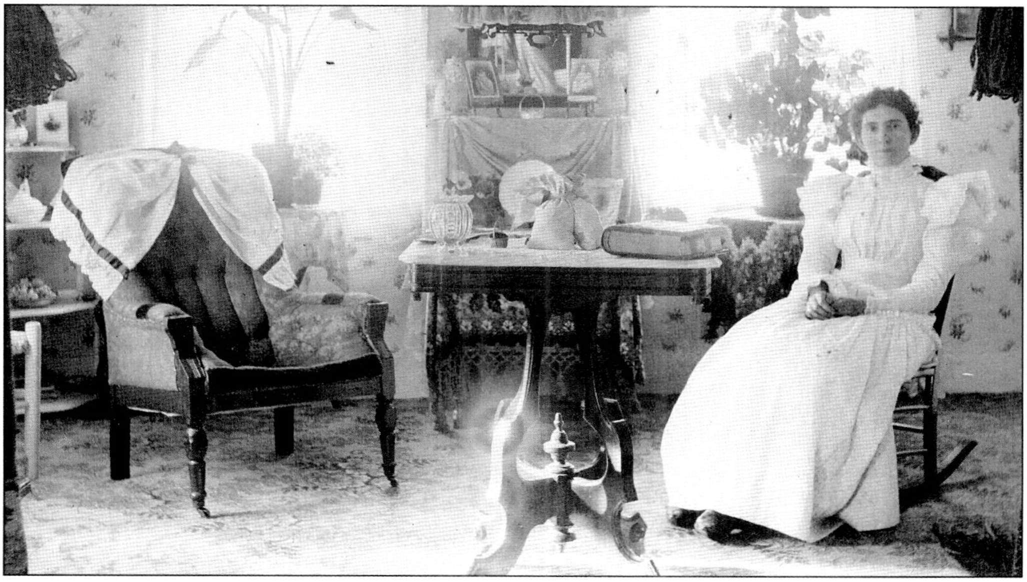

Sarah Parker Reed is seen here in the parlor of her apartment. The apartment was located in the building that was the former cheese factory and, during earlier times, the Methodist church on Coldbrook Road.

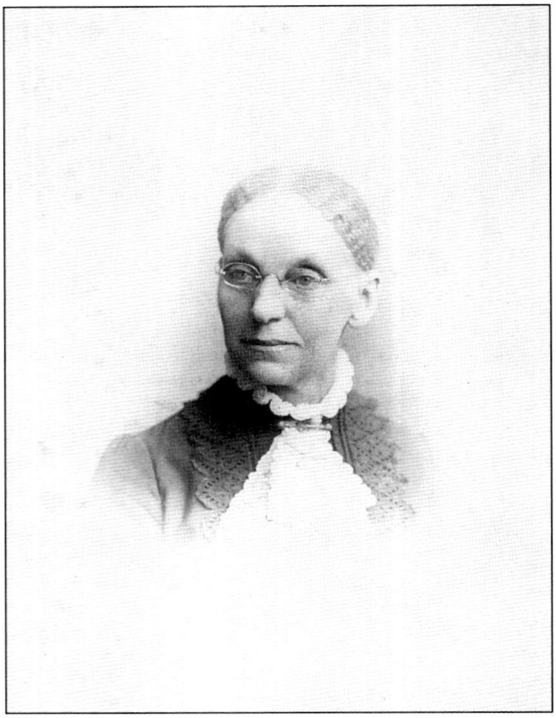

Nancy Wheeler Lincoln, the wife of Abner Lincoln II, is pictured here.

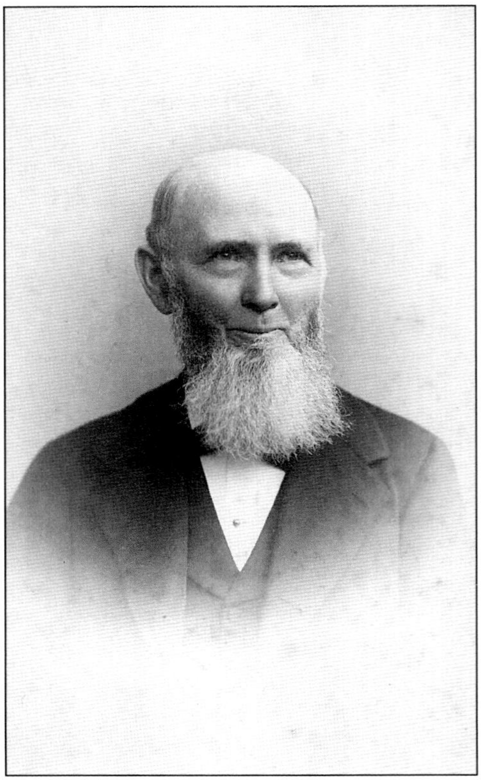

This is Abner Lincoln II, born May 12, 1819.

Rosa Bullard married N. Wendell Packard on December 31, 1878. Rosa was a descendant of Jonathan Bullard, one of Oakham's original settlers.

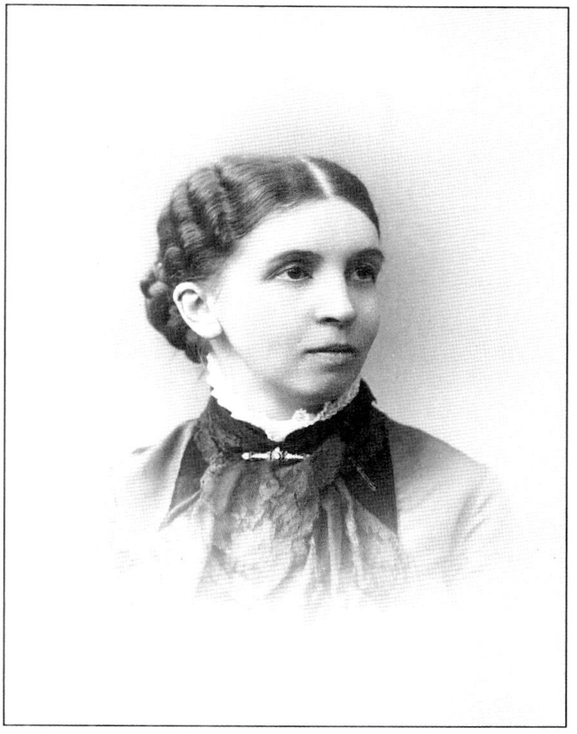

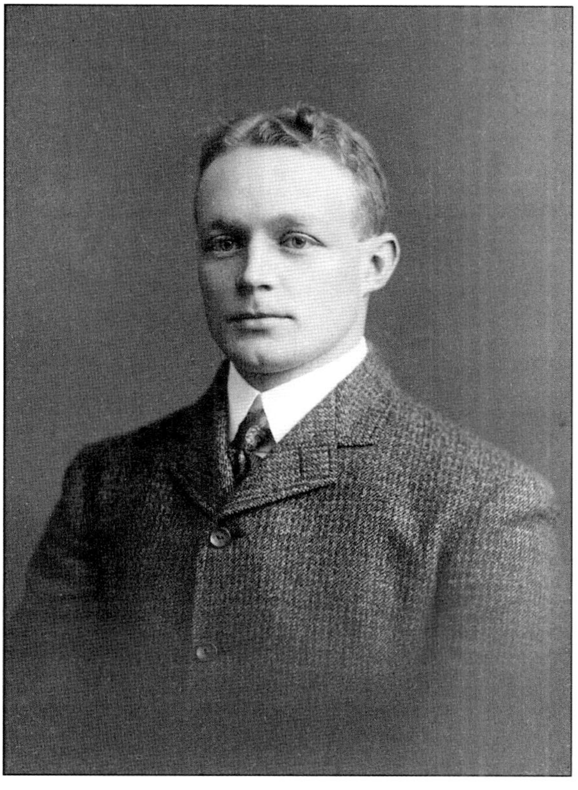

Hiram Nye Fobes, grandson of Perez Fobes, is pictured here. Hiram studied medicine at Harvard and Johns Hopkins. He died four years after his graduation at the age of 29.

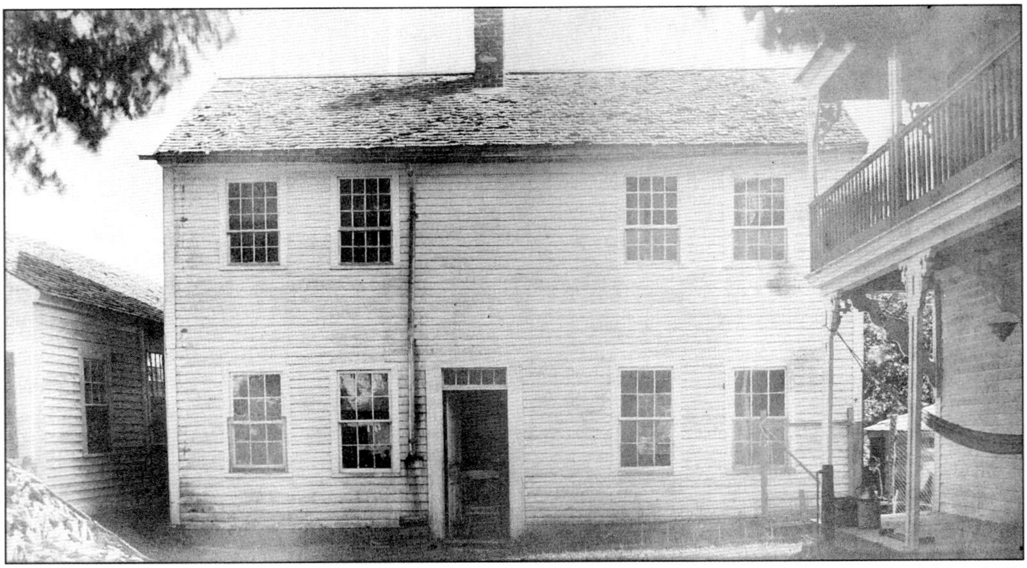

At one time called the "Grandma Wooley" home, this house was located between 50 and 67 Maple Street. Built before 1844, the house was used as a shoemaker's shop, and possibly later on a carriage repair business was located here. Grandma Wooley was the grandmother of Henry P. Wright. The porch of 67 Maple Street is seen on the right.

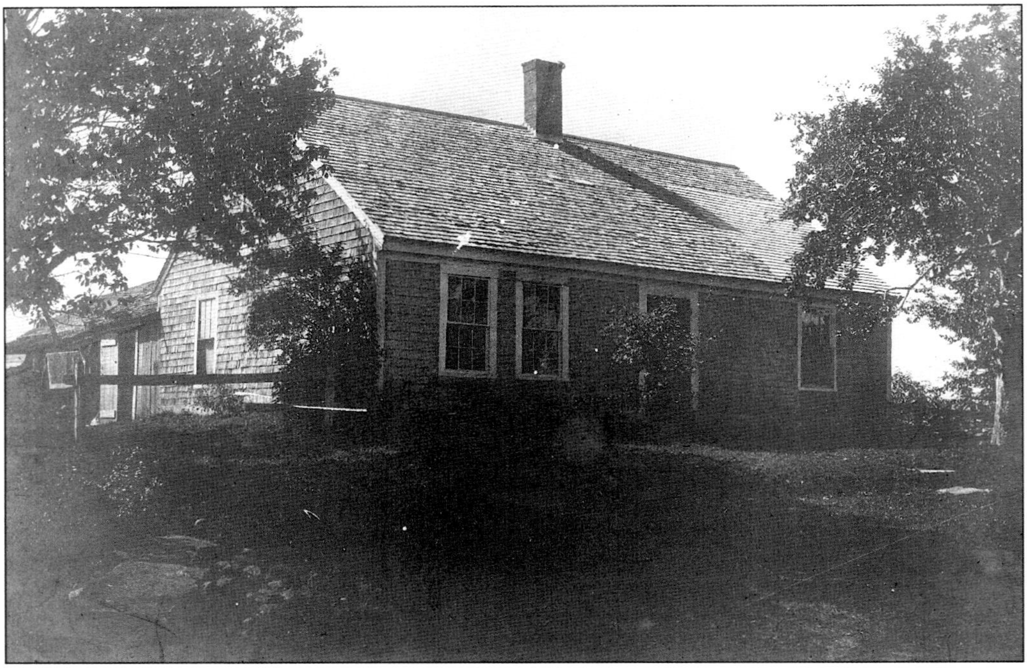

Built prior to 1774 by Issac Stone, this house is located at 409 New Braintree Road. Since its construction, the home has been owned by numerous families, including the Spooners, Haskells, Butlers, Days, and Wilburs.

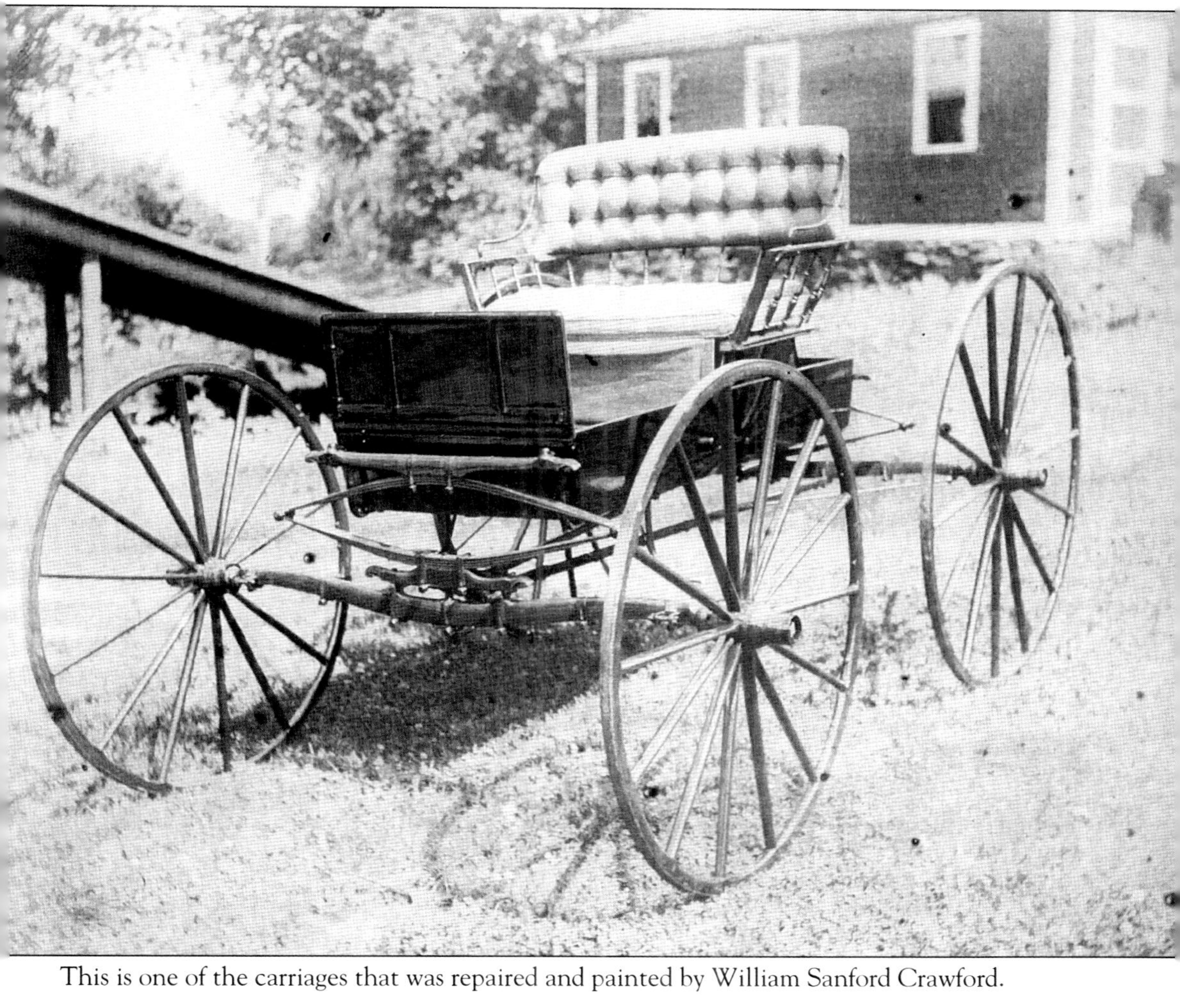

This is one of the carriages that was repaired and painted by William Sanford Crawford.

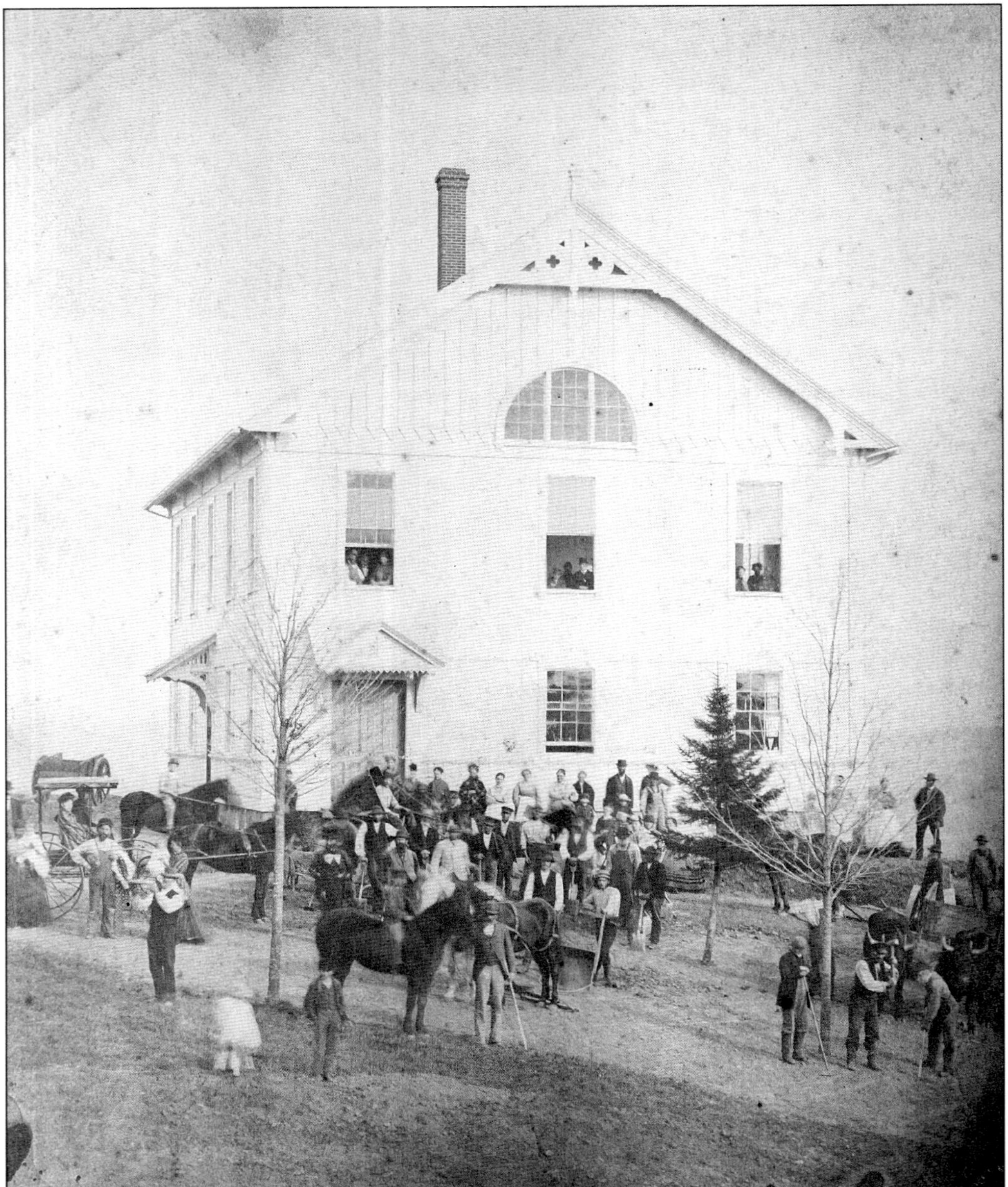

This photograph was taken at the dedication of Memorial Hall in 1874. The elm trees in front of the hall were planted by Reverend Francis Peloubet, who was socially active in town affairs.

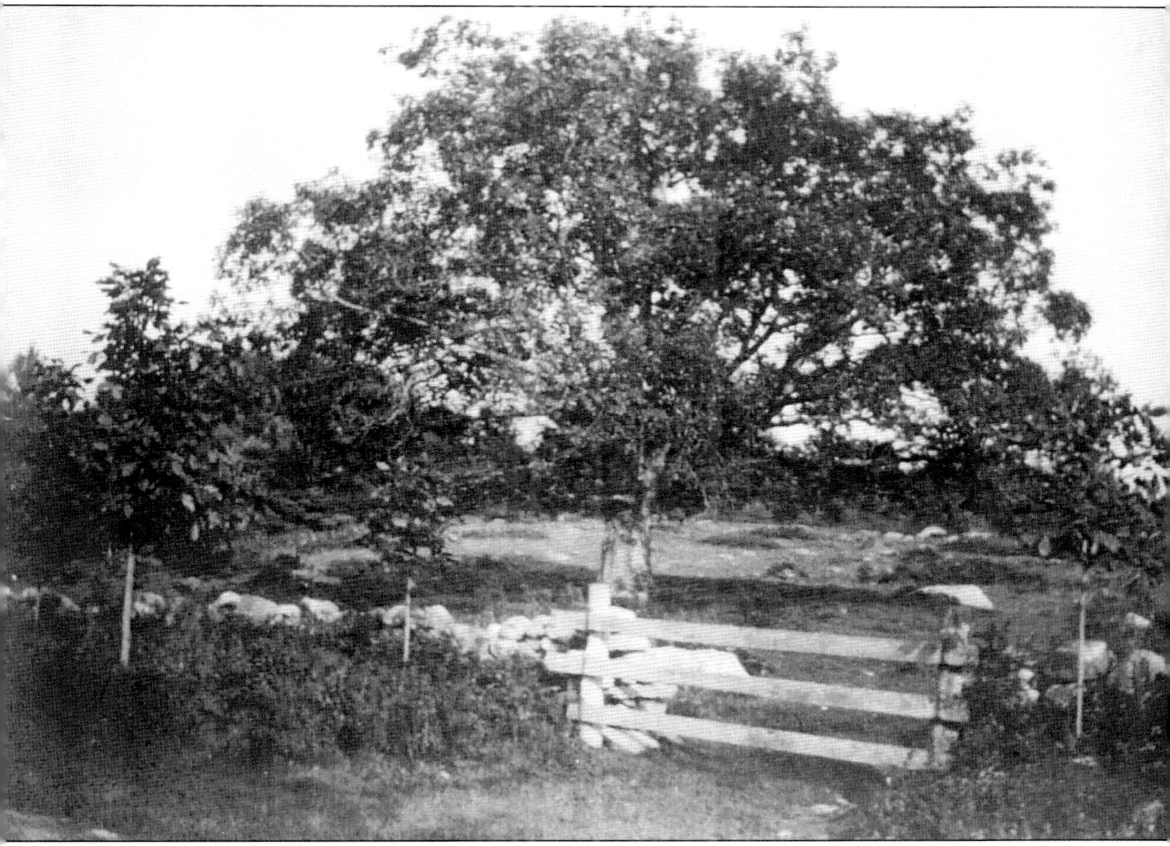

Located in lot one, this oak tree was used as the model for the Oakham town seal.

ACKNOWLEDGMENTS

The Oakham Historical Association wishes to acknowledge the cooperation of the many friends who assisted us in creating this pictorial history of the town of Oakham.

To Marion Charron, Marion Butler, Leone Daniels, Ann Troy, and countless others, who shared their memories and helped us identify people and places many of us never knew, we thank you.

To Mary Lou Berglund and Randall Packard, who shared with us photographs taken by their relatives, Edward J. Crawford and Charles M. Packard, respectively, we thank you.

To the many residents who expressed an interest in this project and provided us with information, enabling us to complete the captions associated with each image, we thank you.

To Megan Young, our typist, thank you for your hard work and interest in the town's history (it appears it's hereditary).

Most importantly, we thank our families. They understood our commitment to this project, and they shared our excitement with each and every discovery.

The diary of Grace Wilbur, written in 1950, says it best,

"We cannot turn to the future with inspiration unless we can remember the past."